An Interweaving Ecclesiology

An Interweaving Ecclesiology

The Church, Mission and Young People

Mark Scanlan

scm press

© Mark Scanlan 2021

Published in 2021 by SCM Press

Editorial office
3rd Floor, Invicta House,
108–114 Golden Lane,
London EC1Y 0TG, UK

www.scmpress.co.uk

SCM Press is an imprint of Hymns Ancient & Modern Ltd
(a registered charity)

Hymns Ancient & Modern® is a registered trademark of
Hymns Ancient & Modern Ltd
13A Hellesdon Park Road, Norwich,
Norfolk NR6 5DR, UK

British Library Cataloguing in Publication data

A catalogue record for this book is available
from the British Library

978 0 334 06076 5

Typeset by Regent Typesetting
Printed and bound by
CPI Group (UK) Ltd

Contents

Acknowledgements

I am deeply grateful to those who have inspired and supported me in this work. First, for the pioneering leaders of Crusaders/ Urban Saints who stepped outside of the Church in mission to young people at the start of the twentieth century. Also, for those who follow in their footsteps and lead groups today – especially those named in the St Joe's and Newtown groups who allowed me to spend time observing the practice in their groups as well as interviewing both leaders and young people. Names of the groups and individuals within them are anonymized throughout this book.

Second, I want to thank Professor Pete Ward of Durham University who supervised the doctoral work from which this book has developed. Pete's wisdom, vision, patience and prompting helped cultivate my thinking more than I can express.

Third, I am so grateful to the staff and students who form the worshipping and learning community of St Mellitus College through which I have been able to try out some of these ideas in teaching and conversation. I am continually formed in my own theological approach through conversation with staff and students alike.

Finally, I need to thank my family – Linda, who has supported me throughout both my doctoral work and in writing this book, and Caleb and Faith who have encouraged me in this work more than I expected for a 14- and 11-year-old!

Especially interpretation
of biblical texts
+ can involve understanding +
communication

Introduction

This is a book about three things: the Church, mission and young people. Except it is really about one thing: the Church, mission and young people. Other than the fact it feels appropriate to begin a work of theology with an interplay of the three and one, these statements set up the contention of this book – that if the Church is to be most effectively the Church in the times in which we live, then it needs to engage with and reflect on the lives of young people in order to be shaped appropriately for the mission of God to which it is called.

Consequently, the contention that runs throughout the chapters that follow is that an ecclesiology, an understanding of the Church, from and with young people will be a gift to the ecclesiology of the whole Church. So, when in this book I talk about the Church, it is for the sake of more faithful work with, and mission among, young people; but when I am discussing work with young people it is for a more faithful Church in the service of the mission of God. Our ecclesiology is all the poorer for not considering the hermeneutical location of young people, and our work with them is all the poorer for not rigorously reflecting on the theology of the Church. Our participation in the mission of God will be the poorer for both. The ecclesiology that emerges from these pages then is one that is flexible and contextual. It will not be possible to simply apply it or use it as a blueprint, but it is an ecclesiology that might free the Church to be the Church in a diverse, complex and changing world.

I will offer here a theological rationale for bringing work with young people into conversations around missional and new forms of the Church by developing a framework for understanding the Church that draws on this practical wisdom from youth ministry. This framework is what I call an *interweaving ecclesiology* in which various groups, congregational activities, relationships and practices make up the Christian community that becomes the Church for young people and their leaders. Unlike most other attempts to talk about the Church in youth ministry, this approach develops an ecclesiology *of* youth ministry, rather than *for* youth ministry. At its heart, this work constructs a vision for ecclesiology, not just the application of it; consequently, it carries within it the potential for offering something to the conversations of the whole Church.

Central to an interweaving ecclesiology are potential ecclesial spaces. These are spaces that hold the possibility of ecclesial life being extended into them as they offer the opportunity of connecting individuals with Christ through engagement in Christian practices and relationships. In this way, church is constructed for and by participants as these potential ecclesial spaces combine to create an experience of church. The research at the heart of this book demonstrated that there is an ecclesial imagination at work within much youth ministry practice that embodies this approach as Christian practices and community are made available for young people, and therefore the groups can be appropriated as part of their ecclesial life. Through potential ecclesial spaces the interweaving of church operates on a personal and institutional level.

Building on this practical ecclesiological wisdom from youth ministry, the book will move to demonstrate how the framework of an interweaving ecclesiology, built through potential ecclesial spaces, offers a distinct approach to the Church in mission that can develop nuance and thinking around Fresh Expressions and pioneer ministry. Resources from within both youth ministry and Fresh Expressions provide the means for regulating this interweaving approach to prevent it becoming an 'anything goes' scenario.

Overview

The book is divided in three parts that form three key aspects in the argument. Part 1 revolves around the importance of the Church in taking account of what is happening with young people through chapters that discuss theological, sociological and practical rationales. The theological rationale of Chapter 1 develops a dialogical theological framework detailing the necessity for effective ecclesiological reflection that takes account of the Church's concrete life in the world; in Chapter 2, the sociological rationale argues that young people are interpreters of culture that, in the light of key socio-economic/cultural pivot points, bring a perspective that is vital to the Church at large; the practical rationale of Chapter 3 takes the form of both historical and literature reviews. The historical review charts the development of an ecclesial imagination within youth ministry through the lens of the work of Crusaders/Urban Saints, whereas the literature review argues that work with young people has largely been absent from reflections on the Church and that theological accounts of the Church are largely absent from youth ministry thinking and practice. Both the historical and literature review demonstrate that there is a gap in our thinking in this vital area.

Part 2 presents the vision for an interweaving ecclesiology through a focus on the description and analysis of ethnographic case studies of two Christian youth groups. As with Part 1, there are three chapters. Chapters 4 and 5 present these case studies at the heart of my research and demonstrate the way that the youth groups studied embody an ecclesial imagination, meaning that the groups carry the potential of ecclesial life for the participants. Furthermore, they will begin to offer a theological analysis of the groups' life and, through this, develop the concept of the groups as potential ecclesial spaces. Chapter 6 argues that potential ecclesial spaces can lead to a reversal of ecclesiological thinking for the Church in mission, in which the opportunity to experience life 'in Christ' through relationships and practices precedes formal ecclesiological structures. This, then, suggests that an interweaving ecclesiology can offer something distinct and bring nuance to current debates about the place and role of young people in the Church, and in so doing cut across some unhelpful paradoxes and contradictions in how we practise and talk about church with young people. In particular, Chapter 6 discusses moves towards intergenerational church, youth church and the tension between local church and parachurch work with young people to highlight the usefulness of an interweaving approach.

Part 3 presents how this vision for the Church develops ecclesiological conversations around Fresh Expressions, pioneer ministry and the Church in mission more generally. Chapter 7 offers a critique of the trajectory within Fresh Expressions towards tightly defining what counts as church and a desire for mature, self-supporting fresh expressions of church, rather than a less structured, institutional approach that seems to be suggested in the original vision of Fresh Expressions. The argument will be made that too much definition and structure squeezes the life out of mission and, in the cultural world in which we live, discipleship. Building on this, Chapter 8 answers the vital question of regulating the interweaving approach to prevent an 'anything goes' scenario. This is developed through essential relationships and practices. Chapter 9 then uses the framework of an interweaving ecclesiology to offer a re-envisioning of pioneer ministry. The interweaving framework releases pioneers from having to demonstrate that they are developing mature churches and frees them to focus on creating possibilities of connection with Christ.

The book concludes by making some general observations about how adopting this approach creates flexibility in church and mission as well as centring young people in the life of the Church in a deeper, more theologically astute way than has been previously suggested.

Assumptions

There are a few assumptions regarding the Church, mission and Christian work with young people that underlie the arguments that follow. The first is to acknowledge the insight from

Gerard Mannion and Lewis Mudge that historically, most ecclesiology has developed out of key questions the Church is seeking to answer in its current time and place.[1] This is related to the oft-quoted – but still vital – warning from Nicholas Healy about 'blueprint' ecclesiologies that do not reflect the actual life and practice of the Church in the world.[2] Consequently, it is important that the Church regularly wrestles with the question of what it is to be the Church and what it looks like to faithfully pursue the mission of God in the world, rather than simply seek to apply previously-held ecclesiological structures with no regard for the contemporary situation. Furthermore, I take as a given that intrinsic to the identity of the Church is its pilgrim nature – that the Church is always seeking how to be the Church in obedience to Christ. The Church is always in via and as a consequence we need an ecclesiology of 'careful walking'.[3] These three concepts are fundamental to my understanding of the Church that I draw on throughout.

Turning then to mission, if the Church is pilgrim and required to always be wrestling with the questions from the situation in which it finds itself, it follows that mission is inherent in the nature of the Church, not simply an activity of the Church. The Church is at its heart a witnessing body with local churches, 'outposts of the Kingdom of God', to quote a phrase from Dallas Willard.[4] As has become the accepted understanding in recent years, this centrality of mission to the nature, not just the activity, of the Church flows out of the life of God – in other words, mission originates in God's life. Moreover, if these foundational assumptions about the Church and mission are accepted, then Stephen Bevans's claim that there is 'no such thing as theology, only contextual theology' is significant.[5] When read missionally, Bevans's models for theology can operate as frameworks for mission in which the Church in dialogue with its context is able to discern how to communicate, when to challenge, what to affirm, and ultimately in what ways and into which spaces the Spirit is leading the Church forward.

Finally, assumptions about young people – and Christian work with them – are important to articulate. First, I have spent my whole adult life invested in youth ministry – on the staff teams of local churches, for Crusaders/Urban Saints as an Area Development Worker, and latterly as a tutor in Theology and Youth Ministry at St Mellitus College in London. I am heavily invested in young people and the Church, believing wholeheartedly that not only are they vital to the health of the Church (universal and local) but, importantly, young people have something unique to bring to the life and understanding of the Church. My rationale for this will hopefully become clear as this book unfolds, but it is important to state this upfront.

In addition, I want to make a key point about youth ministry and in particular the way youth ministry has developed. The practice and understanding of such ministry that is common-place in the UK, especially within the broad evangelical tradition, has become formalized in literature and theology after being handed down in accepted practice. David Bailey has demonstrated this, and the way that this risks the practice of youth ministry becoming 'untethered' from the wider theo-logical tradition.[6] I recognize this history and inherent risk but also believe that this inherited praxis contains theological riches that have yet to be mined for the good of the Church – one such richness being an inherent ecclesial imagination, a way of life that fosters faith. Furthermore, such an ecclesial imagination is exemplified in the practice of a key, yet under-discussed, youth ministry movement in the UK – the Crusaders' Union of Bible Classes, latterly renamed as Urban Saints.[7]

In Chapter 3 I outline the story of Crusaders/Urban Saints in some detail in order to demonstrate the ecclesial imagination and influence on the Church's work with young people in the UK. The Crusaders' Union of Bible Classes traces its origin to 1 April 1900 when a Sunday afternoon Bible class was launched by the Revd Albert Kestin for some boys in his neighbourhood. By 1906, this initial class had inspired others and the Union was formed to support, equip and expand this work. The work of Crusaders was seen as mission work among young people, was non-denominational and was independent of any local churches. Leaders were drawn from different churches within an area who wanted to commit to the work. Groups – or classes as they were originally known – met on Sunday afternoons and these classes were complemented by a local and national network of events, camps and other forms of gathering.

By the start of World War Two, this model of work among young people had grown to include 256 groups reaching 16,000 young people, with its methods inspiring Covenanters and Pathfinders, two organizations seeking to resource Bible fellowships for young people within the Church. As a result of the expansion, influence and subsequent rise of church-based youth work in the second half of the twentieth century, and partly because of the parallel social changes in the UK in the postwar decades, Crusaders began to lose their sense of identity. The classic Sunday afternoon Bible class began to make way for less formal midweek sessions that were akin to regular youth clubs but with a time for a 'God-slot' or Bible study being a priority.[8] By Crusaders' centenary in 2006 the name 'Crusaders' was dropped and the new name, 'Urban Saints', was adopted.[9] This caused some controversy among long-standing leaders of local groups, those who had grown up within Crusaders, and some young people in the groups at the time. I detail the early part of Crusaders' story much more in Chapter 3 and give a fuller analytical history in my doctoral thesis.[10] Suffice to say here that Crusaders' way of working with young people hovers in the background of the inherited accepted practice that became normative in youth ministry in the UK.

Consequently, it is the work of this organization that provides the lens through which I explore the questions raised in this book, and it was to two groups affiliated to the organization that I turned for my ethnographic case studies to draw out the details of their practice and the inherent ecclesial imagination. For now, I give a brief pen portrait of these groups; they are discussed in greater detail in Part 2, though as will become apparent even in these brief descriptions there is, in many ways, nothing remarkable about the groups themselves – they are not particularly innovative or distinct from Christian youth groups up and down the country. This, however, makes the study of them all the more important since they represent much similar work going on among young people, often volunteer-led, week by week.

The groups in brief

On Saturday evenings during term time, at a high school in the city, the leaders of St Joe's Crusaders meet with young people to study the Bible, build relationships and provide social activities. Amazingly, the group has celebrated its centenary, marking 100 years since it launched as part of the Crusaders' Union of Bible Classes. The team of leaders running the group is made up of men and women drawn from churches across the city, while the young people attending are boys and girls from a mixture of schools and backgrounds. Some are involved in the same churches as the leaders; others have little connection with the Christian faith. In 1915 when the group was launched, it met – as it does now – on what could be termed 'neutral ground'.[11] However, rather than meeting on a Saturday evening, the group gathered on a Sunday afternoon at three o'clock, following what was the standard group 'order of service' – an hour of prayers, choruses, hymns, Scripture readings and a Bible talk. During my time studying the group, I saw that the classrooms in which they meet are set up less formally and there is no time spent singing choruses or hymns; instead, there is significant time set aside for games and crafts, though the study of Scripture is still central.

Some 20 miles away, on a Friday evening, a local church building in the market town of Newtown is transformed into the location for another youth group. This youth group, which has been in existence since 2006, is loud with lots of games and activities, making use of an array of media through screens, a sound system and computers. There is a team of leaders running the group who are members of the church, known as Newtown Christian Centre (NCC). The group is part of the outreach work of the church while also being part of Urban Saints, formerly Crusaders. Alongside the games and activities there is time for discussion-based Bible study. These two groups have some similarities but also many differences, not least the length of time they have been in existence and their relationships with local churches – St Joe's is independent of all local churches whereas Newtown is part of a specific local church's work among young people. Despite the differences, the groups create similar modes of belonging among young people and the leaders.

St Joe's group structure sees four separate ages meeting in adjoining classrooms in the local high school that they hire each Saturday of school term time: there are groups for ages 5–7, 8–10, 11–14 and the 'Seniors' for age 15 and over. My observations revolved around the Seniors group which generally consisted of up to ten young people. Hiring rooms in a school retains the tradition of meeting on neutral ground and not being affiliated with any particular local church. Despite the challenges of needing to bring all the equipment each week, and occasionally being affected by the programme of school events, the leaders value this location and its independence.

The evening at St Joe's is split into two halves, with the different ages being ushered into separate classrooms for an opening session that focuses on Bible engagement for about 45 minutes. It is the cornerstone of the group night and seen by the leaders as the most important aspect of the evening. This is reflected in a commitment to always have this teaching section prior to any social time. Even if the young people are disruptive, simply opening the Bible with them is seen as vital. Once the teaching is finished, those in the group disperse into the various free-time options that are available – sports, games and crafts. As the sessions finish, the corridor becomes abuzz with parents collecting their children, who are often running back into classrooms to collect their craft or simply running along the corridor while their parents chat with the leaders. In among this, the older teenagers from the Seniors are often found in the craft classroom chatting with the younger children before their parents pick them up.

In a similar way to St Joe's, an average evening at Newtown involves a mixture of free time for the young people and structured input based around biblical themes and aspects of the Christian faith, though the style is quite different. The evening begins similarly with 45 minutes of programmed teaching input, followed by free time, but here at Newtown there is an additional 15 minutes for small groups. Before the session, a combination of adult and younger (termed emerging) leaders meet at 7 p.m. to set up and run through the activities for the evening. The main leader, Stuart, is in his early thirties and alongside him on the team are other members of the church, a mix of men and women, each roughly in their late twenties or early thirties. Claire has only been involved for a short period whereas the others have been leading Newtown since its launch.

On a group night, the Newtown church building is transformed with the chairs cleared from the 'sanctuary' and large red curtains draped from the balcony around the auditorium to create a more enclosed, informal space. This area is dimly lit with a small stage at the front. Contemporary, popular music is played through the sound system and the group's logo is projected on to a screen at the front. Upstairs is a lounge area with comfortable chairs as well as a tuck shop, pool table, table tennis and table football ready for the social slot. Around 7.30 p.m., the doors open and there is a short period before the programme begins. At this point the young people are called into the auditorium by the leaders. Each evening is focused on a particular theme – the teaching gradually builds throughout the session and tends to include a game or activity to introduce the theme, videos, group discussions and a short, informal talk based on a biblical passage. On occasion, there is some kind of reflective prayer slot to round off the input. After the teaching there is a period of free time when the young people dissipate around the building to take part in their various activities. There is also a chance to play some group games like dodgeball in the auditorium or, depending on the leaders who are there, an arts and crafts table is placed in the foyer.

These groups will undoubtedly sound familiar to many who have any experience of Christian work with young people, especially that which is broadly evangelical and church based. As I have said, there is not necessarily anything exceptional about the praxis embodied in the life of St Joe's and Newtown.

In this ordinariness, though, they carry within them the inherent ecclesial imagination of youth ministry and demonstrate the contribution that work with young people can make to ecclesiological construction.

What this book is not

It is important to be clear as to what this book is not. It is not a 'how to' book. This is particularly important to stress in terms of the book's relationship to work with young people. It can be very tempting when working with them to try to seek answers as to how to do it well or better. This book won't do that. Even in the case study sections in which my focus will be the practice of Christian youth work within the two case study groups, while I describe what they do, the analysis of this isn't to draw out replicable practice as such but rather to bring to the surface the ecclesial dynamics at play in ordinary examples of Christian work with young people. This book is about constructing a theology that might then underpin an understanding of the Church in mission, drawing on the practical wisdom that is inherent within youth ministry.

Consequently, even related to the Church and young people, this book does not tell you how to do it or provide models from which to choose. You will not find in these pages an argument for or against youth churches or congregations per se, nor will you find me championing all-age or intergenerational congregations for their own sake. You won't find advice here about whether to keep young people in a morning service or to have separate groups, or what to do in such groups if you have them. All of these things, and more, are discussed to a greater or lesser extent but not in order to provide an answer to the question 'how do we do it?' My hope is that the way in which I go about the task of thinking about the Church and youth ministry will inspire and release you in mission, so that you are equipped in your thinking and might construct your own faithful practice.

Correspondingly, though this book discusses at length the Church in mission, it will not tell you how to plant churches, lead missional communities or provide a clear model to follow. What I hope the book *will* do, however, is provide a catalyst for your ecclesiological imagination and offer a means by which we might be able to wrestle more faithfully with the challenges of being the Church today.

Notes

1 Gerard Mannion and Lewis S. Mudge, *The Routledge Companion to the Christian Church* (Abingdon: Routledge, 2008), pp. 2–3.

2 Nicholas Healy, *Church, World and the Christian Life: Practical Prophetic Ecclesiology* (Cambridge: Cambridge University Press, 2000), pp. 25–51.

3 Julie Gittoes, 'Where Is the Kingdom?', in *Generous Ecclesiology: Church, World and the Kingdom of God*, ed. Julie Gittoes, Brutus Green and James Heard (London: SCM Press, 2013), p. 113.

4 Dallas Willard, *Renovation of the Heart* (Leicester: IVP, 2002), p. 20.

5 Stephen Bevans, *Models of Contextual Theology* (New York: Orbis Books, 2002), p. 3.

6 David Bailey, *Youth Ministry and Theological Shorthand: Living Amongst the Fragments of a Coherent Theology* (Eugene, OR: Pickwick Publications, 2019), p. 9.

7 See www.urbansaints.org/history (accessed 4.06.2021).

8 Jack Watford, *Yesterday and Today: History of Crusaders* (Crusaders, 1995), pp. 143–4.

9 Throughout this book I tend to refer to the organization as Crusaders/Urban Saints to capture both their current identity and historical significance.

10 Available at http://etheses.dur.ac.uk/12490/.

11 For Crusader classes, 'neutral ground' meant any premises not belonging to a particular local church.

PART I

Foundations

The Dialogical Nature of the Church: Theological Perspectives

Theology is provisional because understanding God is not like other forms of understanding.[1]

This opening chapter presents a case for ecclesiology and youth ministry as essentially dialogical acts of practical theology – disciplines that operate at the interface of theological tradition and the praxis of communities in specific contexts that people inhabit. The interaction between these perspectives is complex since theology is not simply theory to be applied but, rather, theology is performed in practice and expressed in spoken words. As was argued in the Introduction, ecclesiology historically has tended to be shaped by a response to the specific challenges and questions of the time and place in which the Church finds itself. Similarly, youth ministry finds its identity in this interplay and has a tradition of embodied praxis handed down that encapsulates such an approach with an implicit ecclesial imagination.[2]

I locate this dialogical theological perspective in a participatory vision of the Triune life of God in which God is continually inviting humankind and the created order to participate in the relational moves of Father, Son and Spirit. This perspective is enhanced through discussion of Christopraxis in which the role of the Church is seen as seeking to participate in the ongoing ministry of Christ through the Spirit. This theological vision grounds the Church and youth ministry as operating with ontological realism but epistemological relativity – the life of God and the ministry of Christ are ongoing realities, but we only experience and participate in this life in part; or, to use the words of St Paul, we see through a glass darkly.[3]

Consequently, a dialogical approach is necessary in which reflection on the theological tradition and the world around us contribute together to create a theological conversation that can move us closer to a faithful approach to, and understanding of, the Church for our times. This chapter also details the need for observational practices such as taking an ethnographic posture as vital for discerning theological engagement with and in the world.

Theology and the life of God

According to Alister McGrath: 'Christian theology is seen at its best and most authentic when it engages and informs the life of the Christian community on the one hand, and is in turn engaged and informed by that life on the other.'[4] This means that there can be no authentic Christian theology that does not find its place in, and flow back out of, the life of the Church. Theological claims both inform and are informed by the practices of local Christian communities as they wrestle with what it is to be the people of God, and witness to the gospel amid the contingencies of everyday life. The language of 'engaged' and 'informed' alludes to the way that this kind of theological approach requires dialogue between theological ideas and the way communities of believers seek to express their faith together. Dialogue, and engagement to use McGrath's terminology, requires participation – there cannot be a conversation when parties choose not to participate.

Accordingly, a key function of the Church is to participate in theological dialogue, to be part of an ongoing conversation about God and the task of being a Christian community today. Moreover, using McGrath's statement as a point of departure I contend that dialogical participation is not just a function of the Church in this way, but is fundamental to the *theology* of the Church – in other words, ecclesiology should be a dialogical enquiry that is informed by both theology and the ongoing life of the Church. Indeed, the core Christian theological claims about the Triune life of God make this unavoidable.

It is not uncommon for the Church to be described as finding its life flowing out of the life of God. In Scripture the Church is often described in relation to God – the Church is, for example, the body of Christ,[5] a holy priesthood[6] and the people of God.[7] It can, however, be all too easy when thinking about God's life as fundamentally Triune to become caught up in the arguments or paradoxes of God being both three and one. What is important, however, is not the logic of this, but rather the implications. For theologian Paul Fiddes the biggest implication of God's Triune nature is that the relational movements inherent within the Godhead are movements that invite participation.[8] This is, he argues, intrinsic to relational movements within God. In a similar vein Kevin VanHoozer describes the Trinity through the image of 'communicative acts'.[9] Both the ideas of participation and communication invite humanity to join in the flow of movement within the Godhead.

Care needs to be taken, though, in making moves directly from the life of God to the life of the Church. While moving directly from the social Trinity to the life of the Church has become popular in recent times it is inherently problematic. As demonstrated by Pete Ward, it is entirely possible for theologians to begin with the Trinity, assume the social Trinity as the model for church life, and through an applied model of theological construction make quite distinct ecclesiological claims.[10] This is highlighted, says Ward, by the equal and opposite examples of Volf's Free Church ecclesiology and Zizioulas's Orthodox ecclesiological claims. Pushing into this discovery Ward postulates that there is something of an 'affective gravitational pull of the church',[11] or, rather, a pull towards our prior ecclesiological convictions and preferences – 'the way that ecclesial traditions shape and condition reasoning'.[12]

Ward goes on to argue that the limitations of this form of theological reasoning, what I am calling theological construction, demonstrate not the value of theologizing in this way but rather a 'symbiotic relationship between theology and the lived'.[13] Ironically, this form of deductive reasoning can be to try and guard against a slide to liberalism so that the doctrine of the Church is seen to be on solid theological foundations, whereas the affective gravitational pull suggests that prior traditional and cultural shaping is directing the reasoning. Or to use the image of construction – different builders are constructing different buildings from the same set of drawings! This does not mean that there is anything inherently wrong with drawing on Trinitarian theology when thinking about the Church, it is just rather more complex than simple application or deduction. And the task requires the theologian to navigate this relationship between the theological and the lived when making ecclesiological claims. This task is important in ensuring that the forms the Church takes and the ecclesiological frameworks underpinning these forms remain open to new possibilities as the Church pursues its life in the world.

Despite the inherent limitations of the various images to try and demonstrate how God can be both three and one, they can occasionally be of some use. My personal favourite is that of David Cunningham who draws on the musical concept of polyphony.[14] This refers to the way that a musical chord is made up of individual notes that together create a distinct sound. The individual notes each contribute to the overall sound of the chord while the chord does not mean each note loses its identity. The notes, if you like, participate in the overall sound of the chord. It is this sense of participation that draws me to Cunningham's use of the image of polyphony. Extending the metaphor further, without hopefully stretching it too far, participation is of course inherent within music as a whole. A piece of music or a song is written to be played, to be sung, to be participated in. Consequently, the polyphony of the chord is open to the participation of those who hear it and in response wish to join in with the music. This idea of participation is I think central to how the life of the Church flows out of the life of God in a complex and contingent way.[15]

Participation opens up a more complex means by which the life of the Church can flow out of the life of God. Paul Fiddes discusses a wonderful vision of the participative life of God. Reflecting on the life of God in creation, there can be, Fiddes says, nothing outside the life of God, therefore God makes space in Godself for the created order to exist. Consequently, all of creation participates in the life of God, though the Church participates in a particular way.[16] A result of this, Fiddes argues, is that there is an ontological reality about God, but because we know God through participation in his Triune life we can only claim epistemological relativity. Part of the task of the Church, then, is to discern the life of God through pursuing ongoing participation. The Church is therefore a response to God's action, revealed in history but also ongoing in our present time. In turn this means part of the task of the Church is to be constantly discerning and discussing what it means to be the Church.

This participative vision of God's Triune life should come as no surprise, however, since through Scripture God is known as he reveals himself in the world. Specifically, as Brueggemann has detailed, God is revealed through place and history as the God of Israel, the God revealed in particular ways to Abraham, Isaac and Jacob – the God who is known as revealed through particular acts in particular places and moments in history.[17] Furthermore, we see who God is most clearly as revealed in Jesus, a particular human living, breathing and walking the land in a particular place and time in history; the Message paraphrase renders Colossians 1.15 with the words, 'We look at this Son and see the God who cannot be seen.' Central to Jesus' life and ministry is an invitation to participation[18] and Paul's epistles reflect on life in Christ in such a participatory manner. See, for example, Philippians 3.10–11: 'I want to know Christ – yes, to know the power of his resurrection and participation in his sufferings, becoming like him in his death.' Flowing from the life of Christ, the Spirit is revealed, empowering the disciples in the post-Easter events that lead to the spread of the Church in Acts. And as the Church responds to the Spirit's prompting, we see it taking shape in ways that are distinct and draw on interaction with particularities of context. As God is revealed as three in one in the New Testament we therefore find ourselves wrestling with what it means for God's self-revelation to invite participation.

By arguing for the life of the Church to flow from the life of God in line with the image of participation, rather than as a piece of deductive reasoning, the possibility is open for there being new ways of participating that can expand and extend the life of the Church into the world in response to the ongoing moves of the Holy Spirit. This is in essence what Mannion and Mudge have highlighted in acknowledging how many ecclesiological moves come as direct responses to questions and challenges of a particular place and historical moment. This is crucial to the overall argument of this book – that there are new spaces for the Church to grow into, revealed in the way that young people and leaders form youth groups and use these groups as part of their expression of ecclesial life.

To use the language of practical theologians Andrew Root and Ray Anderson, this is about discerning Christopraxis. Christopraxis can be defined as the ongoing ministry of Christ through the power of the Holy Spirit. The participatory vision for how the life of the Church flows from the life of God suggests that this idea of Christ's ministry continuing by his Spirit, with the Church's role to discern and take part, is helpful. There is at least a two-way movement required within this form of participation, requiring attention to both the ministry of Christ in the Gospels and the particularities of the places where we find ourselves. Indeed, as Ward notes:

> The picture of Jesus that comes over in the gospels is of a person who deals with people on an individual basis. By this I mean Jesus took account of the social situation, religious background, and relative position in life of everyone he came into contact with.[19]

Thus, the study of Jesus' ministry in Scripture leads naturally to attention being paid by the Church to the specifics of social situations, backgrounds and positions in life of those to whom it seeks to minister and reach in mission. This is in turn suggestive of the concept of 'double listening' popularized in the *Mission-shaped Church* report.[20]

The notion of Christopraxis helps to make explicit a further important aspect of the participatory vision of the Triune God for which I have been arguing and that Paul Fiddes explicates in his Trinitarian theology outlined earlier – namely, that it is an approach that values both the unchanging and the contingent. As mentioned in the Introduction, Stephen Bevans claims that there is no such thing as theology, only contextual theology. This is a helpful reminder and warning that we only ever do theology from a particular perspective or viewpoint. This of course echoes the claim from Mannion and Mudge regarding the majority of ecclesiologies being developed contextually and suggests something of the task at the heart of the notion of Christopraxis – if all theology is contextual, the pursuit of Christopraxis becomes the task of discerning how the Spirit is revealing who God is and where he is at work in our place and time in history. Consequently, the task of theological construction for the Church is a task that operates in the space created by the eternal Triune God working within the contingencies of specific contexts. A participative understanding of God's Triune nature makes this a quite natural conclusion.

The eternal God within our contingent contexts

The direction of this argument so far naturally leads to the question as to how the eternal and contingent can be held together in this way without one collapsing into the other, either making our participation in God in the present of lesser value, or resulting in some form of relativism in which nothing can be known and therefore all perspectives are valid or equal. Alister McGrath, with his notion of theological attentiveness, is of help here. Building on the idea that if all theology is contextual theology this means that we should take our perspective or viewpoint into account in the task of theological construction. McGrath helpfully takes the metaphor of a window. There are, he explains, two modes of engagement with a window – a looking on or a passing through. You can look at the window for its own sake and admire the architecture and qualities inherent within it or you can allow your gaze to pass through it and use it as a conduit to the world outside. This is, according to McGrath's argument, a deeper form of engagement.[21] Our theological claims and the Christian tradition should operate therefore as a window, a lens or frame of reference that we do not look at for its own sake but through which we observe and 'see' the world around us. Thus, the eternal and the contingent operate together to develop understanding and insight.

Developing these ideas by returning to the central idea in the quotation at the beginning of this chapter, McGrath claims that the authenticity of theological claims is at stake in the way that they make sense and interact with the specificities of the local 'terroir' – a concept defined through a contextual theology of place that 'urges us to value the particular, identifying and appreciating its distinct characteristics, rather than rushing headlong to reduce it to another instance of a more general phenomenon or principle'.[22] What McGrath is suggesting here, to put some philosophical terminology on it, is that a critical realist approach is taken to theology in the life of the Church. Such a critical realist frame holds together three key aspects of the task at hand: 'Ontological realism, epistemic relativism, and judgmental rationality.'[23] In other words, while it is indeed possible to make claims about ultimate reality and to hold that there is such a reality, it needs to be acknowledged how our knowledge of reality is limited and consequently relative and contingent. However, we are able to exercise 'judgemental rationality', which 'recognises that not all accounts of reality are equal, [but] it is possible to make judgements between differing expressions of knowledge'.[24] This is the act of discernment and dialogue that should be at the heart of the Church's self-understanding.

The question flowing from such a critical realist frame, then, is how we go about exercising judgemental rationality so that our contingent, provisional theological constructions are as consistent with that which we hold to be ultimate and real as possible. In other words, to use the language from above, how we discern Christopraxis as faithfully as possible. Pete Ward refers to the need to abide in the Gospels, which is helpful but really only reinforces the question of how this might be done.[25] Practical theologian Don Browning helpfully frames this question in terms of the pursuit of 'phronesis' or practical wisdom that is developed through interaction with both the theological tradition and our already theory-laden practices in specific contexts and communities.[26] Indeed, it is the discipline of practical theology that has wrestled most with these kinds of questions, and as such it is to this discipline that I turn in order to pursue the question of how a participative approach to theological construction might be carried out.

Practical theology – how to navigate this terrain

The discipline of practical theology holds within it the means to operate theologically within a participative critical realist frame of reference. Theology that uses terminology such as 'participative' and 'dialogical' is often referred to as 'practical' theology. This descriptor for theology has, however, proven to be an elusive and misunderstood piece of terminology. Practical can, for example, mean simply that it is to serve some purpose, or have some use, beyond itself. However, if theology has any connection to the life of faith, let alone be understood through Anselm's oft-quoted axiom that theology is faith seeking understanding, then it cannot be anything other than unashamedly practical. Practical theology, however, has been for some time trying to recover from being side-lined by what became known as the 'clerical paradigm' in which it was seen as only relevant to the skills of church leadership[27] – a sort of priestcraft, if you like. My own use of the term lies somewhere in between these two examples and is offered as an understanding of the theological task that takes seriously the participative nature of the Triune God, and the subsequent dialogical nature of his self-revelation, while also acknowledging our own limited perspectives and cultural situatedness. In this sense, theology is 'practical' as it seeks to draw together theory and practice; systematics and the life of the Church; biblical theology and the lives of believers in ways that allow each to inform the other.

Practical theology, then, is concerned with the theological significance of the practices of Christians and Christian communities. Often it is framed as providing means by which the relationship between the theological meaning of Christian practices and prior theological theory can be negotiated.[28] The outcome of reflections on this relationship is seen to be pragmatic action in the form of revised practice;[29] however, it is also important that theoretical contributions can be made to Christian theological understanding.[30] Consequently, practical theology offers a theological 'construction zone'.[31] In addition, it seeks to reflect on specific Christian communities and their practices in order that the 'found' theologies of specific communities might contribute to developing Christian theological understanding.[32] It is therefore the overarching theological discipline in which this study can be placed.

These initial notions about practical theology clearly suggest how the discipline offers an appropriate framework within which we can engage in ecclesiological work. Pete Ward, in developing this idea, and drawing on the work of Nicholas Healy, has said that the Church cannot 'be dealt with in terms of the history of ideas or beliefs'.[33] Rather, the Church should be defined less in terms of ontology and more through agency (of the Holy Spirit) and activity (of human participants). This allows for something of what the Church actually is to be considered rather than ecclesiology merely dealing with the theoretical consideration of what the Church should be.[34] The Church therefore can be understood as simultaneously theological and social/cultural.[35] It is this intrinsic and dynamic interplay between the theological and social/cultural that led some to suggest that the Church is always to be understood as a dialogical community.[36] In essence, and to use some of the language from the section above, the Church is a community seeking to be faithful in discerning Christopraxis and exercising judgemental rationality about how to faithfully live into the gospel, and witness to it, within the contingencies of context, being open to the ongoing dialogue about what this might look like, recognizing that the heart of the matter is participating in God's ongoing life in and for the world.

In pressing into what this looks like, the approach of practical theologian David Tracy is particularly helpful. Tracy argues that approaches to practical theology have historically tended towards one of two extremes. They either apply pre-existing theological theory to practice or use practice to negate theory.[37] Neither of these approaches appropriately accounts for the theology contained within the practices of the Christian community nor the way in which such a form of theology can interact with formal theological discourse. Since this study involves both uncovering the ecclesial imagination inherent within Christian work among young people and placing this in dynamic relationship with contemporary ecclesiology, neither of these tendencies within practical theology is appropriate.

In contrast to these extremes, Tracy then proposes an approach that he terms 'revised critical correlation'. This allows for open-ended enquiry in which practice can enhance or develop theory. He describes this as practice 'sublating' (or enhancing) theory.[38] The strength of this approach is that it brings nuance to the relationship between theological theory and practice, recognizing that neither provides the final word on the Church. By framing theological enquiry as an open-ended endeavour, Tracy's desire to see practice sublate theory rather than negate it – or simply be a response to theory being applied – reflects a concern to locate the doctrinal in the practices of Christian communities.[39]

The intention for theory to be enhanced through interaction with practice rather than applied or negated results in a dialogical approach in which the image of a conversation is helpful. Stephen Pattison has written of his pastoral vision of practical theology by making use of an image of 'critical creative conversation'.[40] The image of conversation is helpful, says Pattison, as it creates a way in which religious practices, traditions and beliefs can be brought into contact with experience and questions to 'engage in a transforming dialogue that has substantial practical implications'.[41] Although Pattison is focused on individual pastoral care, the concept of transforming dialogue helpfully builds on the basic framework offered by Tracy. In such a dialogue all partners in the conversation are open to transformation through this process and the integrity of both the tradition and 'beliefs, actions and perspectives' of the individual or community are reflected.[42] This 'interpretive dialogue' is one in which all parties to the conversation aim to come to understanding together,[43] consequently developing a framework around which McGrath's claims about the authenticity of theology might be held.

Practical theology framed as open-ended dialogical enquiry, then, provides the 'how-to' for the participative vision for theological construction with which this chapter opened. Broadly moving forward, then, the method for theological construction offers a dynamic conversation between the actual practices of youth groups and moves in contemporary ecclesiology. This means, in practice, a two-step dynamic. First, the practices of youth groups can be interrogated for the ecclesiological meaning that can be attributed to them; and then, second, these meanings can be placed into a dynamic relationship with contemporary ecclesiology in order that they can inform ecclesiological conversation and be informed through this relationship.[44] What is required, then, is further articulation of practical theology as open-ended dialogical enquiry.

The image of conversation in practical theology is developed further, and for use within Christian communities, organizations and church congregations, by Helen Cameron and colleagues' concept of 'theology in four voices'.[45] This has been developed through their method of 'theological action research' (TAR). TAR brings the insights of various strands of theology into conversation in order to 'make practice more theological ... and in that way make theology more practical'.[46] The four voices are outlined thus:

- Formal theology – the theology of the academy and professional theologians.
- Normative theology – expressed in the Scriptures, the creeds, official church teachings and liturgies.
- Espoused theology – the theology embedded within a group's articulation of its beliefs.
- Operant theology – the theology embedded within the actual practice of the group.[47]

The aim of practical theology that inspires the four-voice model developed by Cameron and colleagues is to increase the

faith community's theological capacity by 'expanding its theological "vocabulary" and developing faithful mission'.[48] The
helpfulness of the four-voice model is reinforced by assumptions inherent within it and made explicit by Cameron and her
colleagues. I note that the model developed out of an awareness of the weaknesses within classic pastoral or reflective cycle
methods for bringing practice into the theological conversation. As argued by Pete Ward in *Participation and Mediation*,
however, such cycles can distance practice through analytical
moves. This critique is sharpened if only one reflective stage is
named 'theological'.[49] In contrast, the four-voice model, while
not claiming to have resolved all such critiques, offers a 'theological vision that aims to hold these questions constructively
to the fore',[50] seeking to be theological from the outset and
throughout.[51] In addition, it is a vital understanding that just
as the formal theological voice can inform the espoused and
operant, so too can these more embodied theological voices
inform and challenge the formal and normative voices. There
is a commitment to the 'complex theology disclosed through a
conversational method'.[52] This complex conversational understanding of theology is well suited to the arguments of this
book since it opens up ways in which the inherent ecclesial
imagination of youth ministry as revealed by the extended
case studies of current groups' practice can contribute to a
mutual understanding of the Church alongside more formal
ecclesiological thinking.

Significantly, and in response to the surprising way in
which the four-voice framework was picked up and used,
Clare Watkins, one of the original team that developed and
described the framework in *Talking about God in Practice*,
has urged some caution against the rush to use the voices as
'headings'.[53] In other words, while we can be drawn to models
that help to systematize our thinking, it is important to resist
such an urge with the four-voice framework. Rather, Watkins
helpfully reminds us, the four voices recognize the complex
conversational nature of theological, and in particular ecclesiological, construction (or 'disclosure' to use Watkins's preferred
metaphor). The voices need not be explicitly stated to be

acknowledged within the theological task and the manner in which each 'interpenetrates' the others makes this difficult to say the least.[54] The intrinsic value of the four-voice language for my own work, though, is the theological value of practice, expressed in the operant and espoused voices alongside the explicit way that these voices are given a valid and vital place in the conversation. The complex conversational understanding mitigates the unintentional separation of practice and theology that can occur within correlational methods such as the pastoral cycle.[55] Given that my usage of the four voices is explicitly stated to acknowledge and attend to the theological nature of the practice of youth ministry it is important to say a little more about the theological value of what groups of Christians do and say together.

As has already been argued, central to this complex theological conversation is the way that what we do as Christians together embodies a performed theology as we participate in the life of God. So, whereas pastoral or reflective cycles can see practice given secondary status to more formal theological enquiry the four-voice model explicitly claims that what we do and say contains theological expression. In articulating the value of this theology the insights of ordinary theology and Elaine Graham's vision for transforming practice are helpful. This is akin to what has been termed the praxis model for practical theology.[56] Taking account of this form of theological understanding through the operant and espoused voices underpins the espoused and operant theological voices.

Ordinary theology describes lay theology and is seen as prior to academic theology since it is the theology that 'we all start with'.[57] Since the formal theology of the academy is only ever a minority interest in the Church, ordinary theology can be seen *as* the theology of the Church.[58] It is a working theology that elsewhere has been termed the emergent theology of the Church.[59] Ordinary theology is borne out of the first expression, reflection or judgement that people make about their life of faith; it is important because it is a form of practice that '[lets] the story of Jesus have its way' with people.[60] This importance of a way of understanding faith because of the way it is practised relates well to the way that the ecclesial imagination of youth ministry developed as a form of faith community for many; it points towards the value of seeking to draw out the ordinary ecclesiology carried in the way that Christian gathering is practised by those involved in Christian youth groups today. The four-voice model, though, while embracing something of this ordinary theological understanding, appropriates it into a more complex theological structure.

Ordinary theology is not exactly synonymous with the operant and espoused theologies of the four-voice model since it tends to be understood primarily through the way that people express their faith in speech.[61] The difficulty in accessing practices without the researcher putting an undue interpretation of their own on them is acknowledged, so ordinary theology rests on the participants' own articulated understanding of their faith life and practices. Consequently, this can conflate the espoused and operant voices and lose some of the distinction between that which people do and what they say about what they do. Helpfully, though, ordinary theology welcomes the lack of clarity and consistency that there often is in the faith speech of ordinary believers.[62] This is a vital insight as the neat framework of the four voices can give the impression that espoused theology is one thing in any given community rather than the 'hesitant, inarticulate and unsystematic' journey towards understanding that ordinary theology acknowledges.[63]

Elaine Graham's work suggests that something akin to the lay theology of particular communities should be seen as the normative centre of theological construction. She draws on feminist theologies to challenge claims that disembodied truths can mount normative claims, preferring to locate the normative, and therefore grant epistemological priority, to the praxis of particular communities.[64] Graham sees praxis as 'strategies of normative action' that generate new knowledge. Ethics and politics, and by extension theology, become themselves practices and processes rather than ideals or disembodied truths. By locating theological knowledge in the practical wisdom of communities, Graham's work helps to focus the insights of ordinary theology towards the transformative potential of the theology held within community – both espoused as a first step reflection and operant through the community's practices. Consequently, the value of these lines of thinking contributes to holding in tension the various forms of theology held within the four-voice model.

Elaine Graham's focus on the transforming practice of faith communities alongside the emphasis of ordinary theology offers a reminder that theological enterprise is not restricted to the specialized field of the academy.[65] Consequently, that which is understood as normative is the temporary, provisional theology that is drawn from the praxis of particular communities. This is helpful within an ecclesiological exploration such as this one since most dominant ecclesiological moves throughout history can be recognized as coming out of specific communities reacting to the key questions of their time and place. This focus is useful in providing a rich foundation for the earlier ideas around the participative nature of God's Triune life and the role of the Church in discerning Christopraxis.

I will draw to a close these brief comments discussing how to approach a theology of practice with a helpful clarification and word of warning from Clare Watkins: the presentation of the operant voice is problematic, particularly in written form, because, in Watkins's own words, 'as soon as we have discussed, interpreted and reflected upon these actions they have ceased to be practices as such'.[66] The risk of this for Watkins is that they may lose their theological authority in this way. There is an unresolvable issue here that can be best mitigated by simply being clear throughout that what will come later in this book is representations of practice, distilled through analysis and presented as fairly as possible. This is, though, a critique that can be considered in relation to any form of theological expression; but, given that the nature of theology is to try and express eternal realities in culturally conditioned and contingent human language, it is fair to say that the best any of us can hope for is faithful representation in the formulations and constructions.

The four voices – Church, mission and young people

Adopting this complex dialogical outlook for the present study is immediately helpful: it is not that youth ministry needs to understand ecclesiology and apply it, or that ecclesiology must understand youth ministry and be reshaped accordingly, but rather that Christian work with young people and the wider Church understand each other in order for a mutual contribution to emerge from an open-ended dialogue. Indeed, the four-voices framework provides a helpful tool for navigating the terrain of theological construction in the manner outlined.

It is of particular use in the threefold, overlapping fields of church, mission and young people with which this book is concerned. As already detailed in the Introduction, each of these overlapping fields finds its conception in practical questions arising from contexts and situations, with reflections and moves to construct faithful practice being handed down and formalized in literature and/or practice. Ecclesiology, it has been said, is primarily a response from the Church as to what it is to be the Church in the light of the key questions and challenges of the place and time in history in which the people of God find themselves. Similarly, mission sees the people of God confronted afresh with questions of what the gospel is, or at the very least how it might be communicated, in the interaction with new contexts and questions. Bringing these two fields together as a mission-focused response to the Church's desire to reach young people as 'youth' became a distinct life stage, the praxis of organizations such as Crusaders became handed down in a succession of leaderships before this established practice was formalized in youth ministry literature with added theological depth.

These overlapping fields demonstrate the way that something akin to the four-voices approach to theological construction happens intuitively, but in an unacknowledged manner. Consequently, what can appear to be a process of developing formal theological claims with regard to the Church or mission historically, and more recently with regard to work with young people, has come together through a naturally occurring dialogue between praxis, tradition and theology. There are, of course, similarities here with the classic Wesleyan quadrilateral that draws together Scripture, tradition, reason and experience in the task of theological reflection. Nevertheless, I think that the more helpful touchpoint is Browning's fundamental practical theology that begins with the recognition that all practice is already theory-laden;[67] therefore our practices of formal theological construction, the traditions we inherit, how we speak about what we believe and do, as well as our praxis itself, has already been shaped by prior theological moves and claims. What Browning argues the Church must move towards is the pursuit of critically informed, theory-laden praxis in the form of phronesis, or practical wisdom. I contend that the four voices of theology offer a helpful framework through which this can take place and that the dialogical task and identity of the Church is to develop such wisdom within the contingent and specific contexts in which it dwells.

For this book in particular, as should by now be apparent, I will argue that the operant and espoused theologies of youth ministry have a vital contribution to make to the current and ongoing conversations about the Church in mission in our time. Notwithstanding the claim that ecclesiology and youth ministry might seem like unusual conversation partners at first glance, the shared rationale to communicate the gospel relevantly to sections of society unreached by conventional church means that moves towards developing missional ecclesiologies (and the ecclesiology of Fresh Expressions in particular) and Christian work with young people share a discursive space that allows the possibility of mutual contributions from the dialogue. Indeed, it has been identified that Fresh Expressions are asking the same questions that have been asked by Christians working with young people.[68]

Accordingly, in the chapters that follow, the operant and espoused theologies will be detailed through the discussion and analysis of two in-depth case studies of work with young people. As already alluded to, the normative theology of youth ministry tends to refer to the established praxis that has been handed down and formalized in literature. The manner in which this established praxis has become largely detached from specific ecclesial traditions[69] serves to strengthen the influence of this tradition of praxis. Similarly, the normative ecclesiology of movements such as Fresh Expressions is already quite well established despite the relatively recent moves towards this form of ecclesial life within the Church. I will, however, also call out the normative in terms of classic evangelical ecclesial tendencies that are shown up by the case studies to have inherent contradictions and paradoxes within them. The formal theological voice has been largely established in this chapter through the argument that a fundamental understanding of God's Triune life leads to a theological approach that means consideration of praxis, framed in terms of participation in the life of God within our contingent contexts, must be a crucial part of constructing theological claims.

Observing practice – an ethnographic posture

One of the challenges of explicitly using the complexities of the four-voice framework is the need to draw out the operant and espoused theological voices that are present within the praxis and words of a particular community or context. Alister McGrath, citing Iris Murdoch, reminds us that it is 'a task to see the world as it is'. In the language of the social sciences, this task is that of ethnography. Ethnography has become a difficult term to define as its usage has developed from its root in nineteenth-century anthropology.[70] This root imagines the work of a lone researcher travelling to some far-flung place to spend time observing some 'natives' in order to understand their culture and then, upon return, to write the definitive description of that culture. Indeed, there is still some disagreement about the extent to which the term strictly refers to a particular methodological approach, or now more accurately refers to a posture for qualitative research more generally.[71]

In recent times, however, the term has developed more inclusively and has become pervasive across a wide range of disciplinary boundaries, often being employed under the rubric of qualitative research. Ethnography can be succinctly described as a 'mode of looking'[72] that aims to: '[bring] ways of understanding into awareness, making them explicit and public, and building a credible argument that what one has learned should be believed by others'.[73] Michael Agar is particularly informative on the ways in which ethnography has developed. His updated edition of *The Professional Stranger* begins by describing some of these developments, particularly the ideas that ethnographic research should no longer be seen as mere description but should include 'some news for the "natives" too',[74] while also becoming more of a collaborative exercise in which the researcher works participatively with those being studied.[75] Consequently, ethnography can now be understood to have a dialogical ethos. Pete Ward has described the way that ethnography's usage has broadened in recent years and can be used to refer to a 'way of seeing' that is drawn on in an interdisciplinary manner within a variety of disciplines seeking to utilize qualitative research enquiry to develop understanding in their fields.[76] As a result, it should not seem a peculiar step to consider ethnographic methods within a theological framework. Indeed, ethnographic methods have increasingly been seen to be able to bring theological insight into view and in this way move beyond the thick description of James Hopewell's groundbreaking work in studying congregations,[77] towards something where the goal is more transformative. By way of example, ethnography has been argued to be useful in developing pastoral care,[78] in dogmatics,[79] as ethics,[80] and, most importantly for this book, in relation to ecclesiology.[81] Given that in the lived reality of the Church theology is performed and embodied in praxis, then attending to this life makes sense. Indeed, as Ward contends, when seen in this light, 'observation itself can be theological'.[82] Moreover, whereas theologians can lean towards 'methodological laziness' when writing about the contemporary Church, ethnographic rigour can avoid treating the life of the Church with less care and caution than other aspects of the theological task:

When it comes to history or philosophy, we proceed with considerable caution. We take great care to make sure that we abide by accepted academic convention and we want to demonstrate that we are proceeding with academic rigour. Then when we talk about the contemporary church, completely different rules seem to apply. It becomes acceptable to make assertions where there is no evidence. We assume a common perception of contemporary church life between author and reader. We base whole arguments on anecdote and the selective treatment of experience.[83]

As this quotation from Ward suggests, it is important to proceed with appropriate academic rigour when using ethnography and consequently working in an interdisciplinary manner. It can help in this task to consider the ways in which a particular approach used relates to theoretical positions already at play within that discipline. This is perhaps especially key in discussing ethnography since it is common for the discipline to be used in a way that seems to dispense with any prior theory or ontological framework, both of which are necessary if using ethnography to construct theological claims. Sociologist Michael Burawoy, however, develops an ethnographic approach that 'is concerned with the reciprocal relationship between data and theory'.[84] His extended case method seeks to use data to reconstruct, or extend, existing theory, suggesting that data from case studies can be used to 'examine the macro world through the way [it] shapes and in turn is shaped and conditioned by the micro world'.[85]

There are clear parallels between this view and Tracy's vision for practical theology sublating theory. Burawoy goes on to explain how the foundation for analysis of data generated from cases is dialogue, rather than either immersion or distance. This proposed dialogue is seen to be between theory that is of interest, or the researcher is seeking to improve,[86] our own biases and perspectives,[87] and the data generated from the social situation(s). A key contribution to the conversation provided by the data consists of what Burawoy describes as the 'lay theories' or 'common sense knowledge' of the community being studied, and it is this that can often provide the point of departure for reconstructing or reshaping theory.[88] In theological terms this common sense knowledge is akin to ordinary theology or the practical wisdom of the community favoured in the praxis model of practical theology. It is these lay theories of ecclesial life in the operant and espoused theologies of Urban Saints groups that the following chapters seek to discern.

Burawoy contrasts this extended case method with other techniques for dealing with the relationship between theory and data, with the question of generalizability always hovering in the background of the relationship. He contends that his method avoids two unhelpful types of reduction – the positivist and the humanist – that either take the view of the observer or that of the participant to be sacrosanct.[89] Specifically, Burawoy contrasts the extended case method with three other ways of negotiating this relationship between theory and the data of the social situation – grounded theory, the interpretive case method, and ethnomethodology. The key differences here are that both the interpretive case method of Clifford Geertz and ethnomethodology tend to ignore the challenges of generalizability by focusing specifically on the micro world of the particular. For ethnomethodology, it is only the particular that is of interest, whereas Geertz's interpretive case method contends that the general and macro world can be seen being expressed in the particular and micro. The contrast with the extended case method is that Burawoy suggests that the micro world is shaped by external forces of wider society, without necessarily being a concise expression of it.[90]

Conversely, grounded theory shares with the extended case method an understanding that the micro and macro worlds are both discrete and causally related; however, they differ in that a grounded theory approach seeks to construct theory from the ground up. Consequently, those following a grounded theory approach seek to enter the field without a commitment to prior theory, whereas in using the dialogical approach of the extended case method there is space to lay out what is expected to be found before entry into the field.[91] In relation to the specifics of this book, this allows for the espoused and normative theologies of youth groups to be brought into the conversation from the point that the research begins in order that the conversation between theory and practice may be ongoing throughout the data generation process.

Summary

This chapter has provided the theological perspective and laid the theological foundations for the task of theological construction that will take place as the rest of the argument unfolds. This chapter has argued that theological thinking is essentially a participative and dialogical exercise, locating this perspective in the reality of God's Triune nature and the pursuit of Christopraxis. In exploring this further I have located this work in the broad field of practical theology as a result of a desire to bring together theological theory and the praxis of work with young people to aid the task of theological construction. David Tracy's call for open-ended enquiry has been developed with the insights of Theological Action Research and the four voices of theology to show how these voices are a helpful framework to guide the construction to come. Furthermore, I have argued how the tools of ethnography provide a mode of looking that allows interrogation of the practices of youth ministry in order to draw out the practical ecclesiology within.

The next two chapters in Part 1 offer two further foundations for this study. They argue from different perspectives that attending to young people and the Church's work with them in youth groups should be a vital part of constructing ecclesiology. Chapter 2 details the sociological perspective that young people occupy a hermeneutical location within culture, and that consequently good participative dialogue about the Church should draw on the experiences, lives and 'meaning-making' of young people. Chapter 3 argues that Christian work with young people carries within it an ecclesial imagination that has developed from its particular history but one that is largely ignored within discussions of youth ministry and contemporary ecclesiology, leading to a gap in our thinking.

Notes

1 Pete Ward, *Introducing Practical Theology: Mission, Ministry, and the Life of the Church* (Grand Rapids, MI: Baker Academic, 2017), p. 29.

2 This ecclesial imagination is detailed in Chapter 3.

3 1 Corinthians 13.12 (KJV).

4 Alister McGrath, 'The Cultivation of Theological Vision: Theological Attentiveness and the Practice of Ministry', in *Perspectives on Ecclesiology and Ethnography*, ed. Pete Ward (Grand Rapids, MI: William B. Eerdmans, 2012), p. 107.

5 1 Corinthians 12.27.

6 1 Peter 2.5.

7 1 Peter 2.10.

8 See Paul Fiddes, *Participating in God: A Pastoral Doctrine of the Trinity* (London: Darton, Longman and Todd, 2000). This is far from the only implication but is the most pertinent one for this study. Another key implication, for example, is that personhood is fundamentally relational rather than individual.

9 As discussed in David Bailey, *Youth Ministry and Theological Shorthand: Living Amongst the Fragments of a Coherent Theology* (Eugene, OR: Pickwick Publications, 2019), pp. 173–220.

10 Pete Ward, 'Blueprint Ecclesiology and the Lived: Normativity as Perilous Faithfulness', *Ecclesial Practices* 2(1) (2015).

11 Ward, 'Blueprint Ecclesiology', p. 76.

12 Ward, 'Blueprint Ecclesiology', p. 77.

13 Ward, 'Blueprint Ecclesiology', p. 78.

14 David Cunningham, *These Three Are One: The Practice of Trinitarian Theology* (Oxford: Blackwell, 1998), pp. 127–64.

15 This is similar to the much-discussed perichoretic imagery of a dance. See Pete Ward, *Liquid Church* (Milton Keynes: Paternoster Press, 2002).

16 Paul Fiddes, 'Ecclesiology and Ethnography: Two Disciplines, Two Worlds?', in *Perspectives on Ecclesiology and Ethnography*, ed. Pete Ward (Grand Rapids, MI: William B. Eerdmans, 2012), pp. 26–7.

17 See McGrath, 'Cultivation of Theological Vision', p. 117.

18 For example, the regular invitation to come and follow him.

19 Pete Ward, *Youth Culture and the Gospel* (Basingstoke: Marshall Pickering, 1992), p. 117.

20 Archbishops' Council, *Mission-shaped Church: Church Planting and Fresh Expressions of Church in a Changing Context* (London: Church House Publishing, 2004).

21 McGrath, 'Cultivation of Theological Vision', p. 120.

22 McGrath, 'Cultivation of Theological Vision', pp. 119–20.

23 Ward, 'Blueprint Ecclesiology', p. 83.

24 Ward, 'Blueprint Ecclesiology', p. 84.

25 Pete Ward, *Liquid Ecclesiology: The Gospel and the Church* (Leiden: Brill, 2017), pp. 189–92.

26 See Don S. Browning, *A Fundamental Practical Theology: Descriptive and Strategic Proposals* (Minneapolis, MN: Augsburg Fortress, 1996).

27 See discussion of this in Ward, *Introducing Practical Theology*, pp. 2–3.

28 Paul Ballard and John Pritchard, *Practical Theology in Action: Christian Thinking in the Service of Church and Society* (London: SPCK, 1996), p. 43.

29 Richard Osmer, *Practical Theology: An Introduction* (Grand Rapids, MI: William B. Eerdmans, 2008), p. 4.

30 Helen Cameron et al., *Talking about God in Practice: Theological Action Research and Practical Theology* (London: SCM Press, 2010), pp. 59–60.

31 Serene Jones, 'Practical Theology in Two Modes', in *For Life Abundant: Practical Theology, Theological Education and Christian Ministry*, ed. Dorothy C. Bass and Craig Dykstra (Grand Rapids, MI: William B. Eerdmans, 2008), p. 209.

32 Gerardo Marti, 'Found Theologies Versus Imposed Theologies: Remarks on Theology and Ethnography from a Sociological Perspective', *Ecclesial Practices*, 3 (2016).

33 Pete Ward, *Participation and Mediation: A Practical Theology for the Liquid Church* (London: SCM Press, 2008), p. 41.

34 Ward, *Participation*, p. 42.

35 Ward, *Perspectives on Ecclesiology and Ethnography*, p. 2.

36 For example, Merold Westphal, *Whose Community? Which Interpretation? Philosophical Hermeneutics and the Church* (Grand Rapids, MI: Baker Academic, 2009).

37 David Tracy, 'Foundations of Practical Theology', in *Practical Theology: The Emerging Field in Theology, Church and World*, ed. Don Browning (New York: Harper and Row, 1983), p. 61.

38 Tracy, 'Foundations of Practical Theology', p. 61.

39 Ward, *Participation*, p. 47.

40 Stephen Pattison, *A Critique of Pastoral Care* (London: SCM Press, 2000), p. 230.

41 Pattison, *Critique*, p. 217.

42 Patricia O'Connell Killen and John De Beer, *The Art of Theological Reflection* (Chestnut Ridge, NY: Crossroad, 2004), p. viii.

43 Terry Veling, *Practical Theology: On Earth as It Is in Heaven* (New York: Orbis Books, 2005), p. 61.

44 See James Nieman and Roger Haight, 'On the Dynamic Relationship Between Ecclesiology and Congregational Studies', in *Explorations*

in Ecclesiology and Ethnography, ed. Christian B. Scharen (Grand Rapids, MI: William B. Eerdmans, 2012).

45 Cameron et al., *Talking about God*, p. 51.

46 Cameron et al., *Talking about God*, p. 17. In a similar way Don Browning's fundamental practical theology looks to draw on systematics, biblical studies, historical theology and practical theology.

47 Cameron et al., *Talking about God*, p. 54.

48 Cameron et al., *Talking about God*, p. 14.

49 As in John Swinton and Hilary Mowat, *Practical Theology and Qualitative Research* (London: SCM Press, 2016).

50 Cameron et al., *Talking about God*, p. 32.

51 Cameron et al., *Talking about God*, p. 29.

52 Cameron et al., *Talking about God*, p. 56. Indeed, the process of Theological Action Research from which the four-voice method developed is based on actual conversations between insider and outsider researcher teams.

53 Clare Watkins, *Disclosing Church: An Ecclesiology Learned from Conversations in Practice* (Abingdon: Routledge, 2020), p. 41.

54 Watkins, *Disclosing Church*, pp. 45–6.

55 Watkins, *Disclosing Church*, pp. 42–6.

56 Ballard and Pritchard, *Practical Theology in Action*, pp. 66–8.

57 Jeff Astley and Ann Christie, *Taking Ordinary Theology Seriously* (Cambridge: Grove Books, 2007), p. 5.

58 Astley and Christie, *Taking Ordinary Theology Seriously*.

59 Martyn Percy, *Shaping the Church: The Promise of Implicit Theology* (Farnham: Ashgate, 2010), p. 159.

60 Astley and Christie, *Taking Ordinary Theology Seriously*, p. 26.

61 Jeff Astley, 'The Analysis, Investigation and Application of Ordinary Theology', in *Exploring Ordinary Theology: Everyday Believing and the Church*, ed. Jeff Astley and Leslie Francis (Abingdon: Routledge, 2016), pp. 5–6.

62 Astley and Christie, *Taking Ordinary Theology Seriously*.

63 Astley, 'Analysis, Investigation and Application of Ordinary Theology', p. 5.

64 Elaine Graham, *Transforming Practice: Pastoral Theology in an Age of Uncertainty* (Eugene, OR: Wipf and Stock, 2002), pp. 140–1.

65 See also Kathryn Tanner, *Theories of Culture: A New Agenda for Theology* (Minneapolis, MN: Fortress Press, 1997), pp. 69–71.

66 Watkins, *Disclosing Church*, p. 47.

67 Browning, *Fundamental Practical Theology*, p. 6.

68 Sylvia Collins-Mayo, Bob Mayo and Sally Nash, *The Faith of Generation Y* (London: Church House Publishing, 2010), p. 100.

69 Bailey, *Theological Shorthand*, p. 148. See Chapter 3 for more detail.

70 Paul Atkinson et al., *Handbook of Ethnography* (London: Sage,

2007), p. 9; Martyn Hammersley and Paul Atkinson, *Ethnography: Principles in Practice* (Abingdon: Routledge, 2007), p. 1.

71 James Spickard, 'The Porcupine Tango: What Ethnography Can and Cannot Do for Theologians', *Ecclesial Practices*, 3(2) (2016).

72 Hammersley and Atkinson, *Ethnography*, p. 230.

73 Michael H. Agar, *The Professional Stranger: An Informal Introduction to Ethnography* (Bingley: Emerald Group, 1996), p. 1.

74 Agar, *Professional Stranger*, p. 13. This can also be referred to as ethnography providing the basis for action to transform the world; see Hammersley and Atkinson, *Ethnography*, p. 14.

75 Agar, *Professional Stranger*, p. 16.

76 Ward, *Perspectives in Ecclesiology and Ethnography*, p. 6.

77 Hopewell describes a threefold rationale for his studies: developing a greater appreciation of a congregation's value, reflecting on the way the gospel is heard and proclaimed, and gaining a perception of how congregations draw on 'cultural forms of other human communities'. See James Hopewell, *Congregation: Stories and Structures* (Philadelphia, PA: Fortress Press, 1987), pp. 9–12.

78 Mary Clark Moschella, *Ethnography as a Pastoral Practice: An Introduction* (Cleveland, OH: Pilgrim Press, 2008).

79 Nicholas Adams and Charles Elliott, 'Ethnography Is Dogmatics: Making Description Central to Systematic Theology', *Scottish Journal of Theology*, 53(3) (2000).

80 Aana Marie Vigen and Christian Scharen, *Ethnography as Christian Theology and Ethics* (London: Continuum, 2011).

81 For example, Nicholas Healy, *Church, World and the Christian Life: Practical-Prophetic Ecclesiology* (Cambridge: Cambridge University Press, 2000); Ward, *Perspectives on Ecclesiology and Ethnography*.

82 Ward, *Perspectives on Ecclesiology and Ethnography*, p. 2.

83 Ward, *Perspectives on Ecclesiology and Ethnography*, p. 4.

84 Michael Burawoy, *Ethnography Unbound: Power and Resistance in the Modern Metropolis* (Los Angeles, CA: University of California Press, 1991), p. 271.

85 Burawoy, *Ethnography Unbound*, p. 6.

86 Burawoy, *Ethnography Unbound*, p. 10.

87 Burawoy, *Ethnography Unbound*, p. 4.

88 Burawoy, *Ethnography Unbound*, p. 26.

89 Burawoy, *Ethnography Unbound*, p. 4.

90 Burawoy, *Ethnography Unbound*, p. 272.

91 Burawoy, *Ethnography Unbound*, p. 9.

2

The Changing World:
Sociological Perspectives

[Young people] are persons who cannot be dismissed as mad, but are those nascently, but powerfully, interpreting the structures of culture we all share.[1]

This chapter focuses on the role of young people as interpreters of culture in general, and then examines this specifically through three key pivot points in the cultural milieu that demonstrate the need to include the exploration of work with young people as an essential ecclesiological move, for the good of the Church as a whole. These pivot points are a move to a secular social imaginary, political upheaval and hyperconnectivity. The significance of these pivot points here is not so much to do with keeping teenagers in the Church (though that is important), but rather that by understanding the pivot points' impact on the worldview of young people we develop a lens through which to make sense of the world in which the Church is operating and will be in the coming years. This chapter, then, details the broader cultural world in which the research underpinning the argument is situated. This attention to the broader cultural context, before Part 2 details the specific contexts of the case study groups, focuses in particular on the experience of young people as cultural interpreters before honing in on the three pivot points that have shaped, and are shaping, the missional context for the Church.

Young people as cultural interpreters

If, as Pete Ward has argued, the Church is simultaneously theological and social/cultural,[2] then the theological perspective is only one foundational perspective to take in this study of the Church, mission and young people. It clearly follows from Ward's observation that the social/cultural context is also significant. This idea alone makes sense of the way that ecclesiology has tended to develop out of the questions and situations the Church is facing in any given place and time in history. The approach that I take in this chapter, however, specifically directs this observation about the social/cultural nature of the Church by understanding young people as cultural interpreters. This requires consideration of what can be described as both the ultimate and proximate contexts of the young.[3] The ultimate context of young people suggests that there are some aspects of their lives that we should attend to, for young people bring something to our understanding of what it is to be human in the various stages of life.[4] This is slightly precarious territory given that the notion of adolescence as a definitive life stage is contested, with some claiming that significant aspects of what we understand to be 'adolescence' are a social construction.[5] Indeed, Allan Clynne has argued that Christian work with young people tends to unnecessarily overemphasize adolescent development in a way that risks objectifying young people.[6] None the less, Amy Jacober helpfully notes that although adolescence is a 'relatively new construct' the concept is evident much further back in Western history.[7]

In navigating this, Andrew Root offers the helpful perspective that the experience of adolescence is largely constructed but with some 'biological determinism'.[8] This biological aspect is important as it refers to relatively recent insights from the field of neuroscience. From this perspective, the study of adolescent brain development demonstrates that a teenager's brain changes at a greater rate than at any other period of life. The significance of this, according to leading researcher in the field Sarah-Jayne Blakemore, is that many of the characteristics that are typically thought of as 'teenage' can be directly traced to changes in the brain that are going on at the time. Specifically, because of these protracted changes in brain chemistry through the teenage years, Blakemore refers to this period of life as a time of 'inventing ourselves'.[9] Furthermore, in exploring brain development through late childhood and the teenage years, Blakemore demonstrates the way in which adolescence can provide 'an insight into how natural changes in the physiology of our brains are reflected in the things we do and determine who we become as adults'.[10] Essentially, adolescence is a key time of meaning-making in which young people are making sense of themselves and the world around them. The changes that spark this process of making sense that is fundamental to the experience of being young are not a sign of dysfunction, but rather can 'offer us a lens through which we can begin to see ourselves anew'.[11] This ultimate context of young people, as those making meaning in the midst of cultural dynamics as they grow up, therefore leads to a need to take account of proximate context – the specific circumstances in which young people are experiencing the world around them.

There are connections here with the way that ideas around understanding the slippery term 'youth culture' have developed. Central to my argument through this chapter, and therefore the rationale behind exploring work with young adults for its ecclesiological significance, is an understanding that young people do not live, move and have their being in a separate, discrete youth culture – or even youth *cultures* – but that they are, as they make sense of themselves, primarily living out an interpretation of wider culture. Root argues that what is often seen to be 'youth culture' is better understood as the 'hermeneutical location' of young people as they seek to make meaning of what they see in the world around them, in dialogue with who they are and the way in which they have been brought up.[12]

It can be argued therefore that what tends to be termed youth culture is a result of developments, moves and pivots in wider culture. Or, as Graham Cray has put it, young people are at the sharp end of cultural moves.[13] In this way, the worlds and lives of young people, as they make meaning and create symbols in their ongoing interpretation of culture, hold up a mirror to

society as a whole. Consequently, if provided with the opportunity, they can address key questions of our time. Conversely,
labelling youth culture as something 'other' by making claims
of a cultural or generation gap provides a safety net whereby
we can avoid such difficult questions.[14] The contention in this
book is that examining the pivot points that have the biggest
impact on the meaning-making of young people allows the
Church as a whole to wrestle appropriately with questions of
its own shape, identity and participation in the life of God for
this time. It follows, then, that in considering the social/cul-
tural dimension of the Church the experiences and thoughts
of young people and Christian work among them, the operant
and espoused theologies, are vital conversation partners.

Alongside this nuanced understanding of young people
and culture, suggesting that the term 'youth culture' might
be misleading, it is important also to say a few words about
generational theory in relation to the argument that follows.
Generational theory can be connected to the idea of a discrete
youth culture. The concept refers to the idea that a generation
'is defined by the key social, political and economic events
experienced during its youth and which come to shape its
collective approach to public and private life in adulthood'.[15]
Therefore, generational theory can be both helpful and unhelpful when talking about young people and their relationship to
popular culture.

At the risk of oversimplifying a complex debate, I want to
say simply that talking in terms of generations can be helpful
when trying to comment on this, and discerning the overall
trends that shape the way outlooks and approaches to public
and private life have changed over the years. Conversely,
all too often generational theory can be used to make bold
claims that assume all young people (or adult members of a
particular generation) have the same views and characteristics;
often these claims are made in a derogatory manner by those
of an older generation(s) who wish to demonize those younger
than themselves.[16] Equally, too much can be made of supposed
boundaries between generations, with set birth years defining
particular generations' beginnings and endings. Generations in

reality blur between the hard boundaries often used to delineate where one ends and the next begins; in among general trends there are of course vast differences between those within a supposed generation, as well as factors that lead to contexts where there is more in common between generations within specific communities than between those of the same generation in different contexts. In addition, Clynne argues convincingly that uncritical use of 'generationalism', as he calls it, can lead to negative attitudes from adults towards young people as a result of the way that youth culture can then be framed in contrast to adult culture.[17]

That said, in this chapter I use the language of generations, specifically that of Generations Y and Z.[18] I do this despite recognizing the inherent problems with generational theory and am aware that my usage might serve to reinforce unhelpful stereotypes. I do, however, think these terms can provide a helpful (albeit somewhat artificial) framework within which to discuss overarching trends that shape the approach to life within popular culture. I am well aware that such trends are shaping people of all ages and popular culture in general; but my usage of generational terms, and talking about the trends in this way, is to recognize that these are trends that are at their most potent among the young and that, in light of young people being cultural interpreters, we see the way that meaning is being made in among these trends most acutely among the young. It is this understanding of the hermeneutical location of young people that guards me against the dangers observed by Clynne of objectifying or applying negative connotations to supposed youth culture. On the contrary, my reading of these issues demands that positive attention is paid to the lives of young adults so we might better understand the world in which we live.

Additionally, I am encouraged in my use of these potentially controversial generational terms by the research of Ruth Perrin whose findings indicate that many of the emerging trends and values apparent among 'Generation Y' as teenagers are still held as important by those of that generation when they reach adulthood.[19] This consistency is important in demonstrating at least some value in discussing generations in these terms. Moreover, Chloe Combi's work in interviewing many hundreds of young people from diverse backgrounds, communities and cultures in *Generation Z: Their Voices, Their Lives*[20] demonstrates that there are commonalities of experience and points of view among young people known as Generation Z; and while there are also themes in common with previous generations growing up, these themes are expressed and being worked out in particular ways within Generation Z as they seek to make meaning within popular culture.

Consequently, as stated at the beginning of this chapter, I contend that there are three key sociological pivot points shaping the prevailing cultural climate; I call them pivot points because they are things that have shifted the direction of cultural travel in some way, and therefore have become dominant themes in the meaning-making of younger generations in a way that they weren't so much for older generations. These pivot points, then, form the 'proximate' context of young people – the specific experience of the world that is particular to the current generation. This is not though to suggest that there is a generation gap or, as argued above, a 'youth culture' separate from the wider cultural landscape. The pivot points impact all generations, but they do specifically represent shifts in the native world for younger generations – in other words, that which is normal. But because the pivot points operate as signals for society as a whole, they represent at least some of the key questions that the Church should wrestle with in order to faithfully minister and reach out in mission to the communities around us. As stated in the first paragraph of this chapter, these pivot points are the move to a secular social imaginary, political upheaval, and the hyperconnectivity resulting from the digitalization of society.

The previous chapter finished with a call to take an ethnographic stance in the task of theological construction. Such a posture takes seriously listening to and learning from the individuals, communities and world around us. Given that, as stated previously, ecclesiological reflections have always tended to be developed out of the challenges and questions of the cultures in which communities of Christians have found themselves, and that our knowledge and understanding of God flows from a participatory epistemology, such an ethnographic posture is essential to faithful ministry as the people of God. Consequently, this consideration of the broad cultural landscape in which young people are making meaning is a vital – perhaps urgent – task.

A secular social imaginary

In his magisterial work *A Secular Age*, philosopher Charles Taylor discusses changes in what he calls the prevailing social imaginary.[21] This idea of a social imaginary refers to the way in which the world is perceived. In brief, for Taylor, the fundamental shift in this imaginary is from a world in which it was almost impossible not to believe in God to one in which it is almost impossible to maintain or contemplate such a belief:

> The change which takes us from a society in which it is almost impossible not to believe in God, to one in which faith, even for the staunchest believer, is one human possibility among others ... Belief in God is no longer axiomatic. There are alternatives. And this will also likely mean that at least in certain milieux, it may be harder to sustain one's faith ... There will be many others to whom faith never even seems an eligible possibility.[22]

In unpacking this claim, it is clear from Taylor that this imaginary does not consider 'belief' to be simply a cognitive assent to a claim, but rather it refers to the way in which individuals understand and approach the overall structuring of society. In the prevailing social imaginary of a few hundred years ago the world was seen to be ordered around the controlling presence of the transcendent. This was a way, therefore, of structuring society in which the centre of meaning-making is external, and the lives of individual humans and communities are ordered by an overarching transcendent or divine force. Consequently, all human life was seen through this lens and, for better or for worse, the way in which society operated, including the position of individuals within society, was deemed to result from the workings of such a transcendent or divine force.

Religious questions therefore revolved around the specific manner in which the transcendent power, or spiritual forces, might be at work in the world. The shift Taylor traces is one in which belief in transcendence or faith in the divine becomes difficult, even for the most faithful religious adherent. Behind the scenes and under the surface of this shift there is a deconstruction of the order and centring of society from an external transcendence to the internal in which 'authenticity' of the self becomes the guiding light. As Andrew Root has put it in discussing the significance of Taylor's thought, 'Five hundred years ago ... The measure of what was true, real and authentic was never assumed to be *my* own subjective experience. I was always being encountered by other (spiritual) forces.'[23] This has become quite well-worn territory for anyone familiar with Andrew Root's work. He has become one of the most prolific theologians writing with a youth ministry background and argues persuasively for the significance of Taylor's thought in understanding the challenges of working with young people and for the Church as a whole. Central to Root's interpretation of Charles Taylor is the way that the structuring of society no longer awakens the imagination to the transcendent, but instead reflects what Taylor terms the 'age of authenticity'.[24] Root has explained that the mark of the secular age is that what it is to be human is that each of us gets to decide what it is to be human.[25]

In other words, the reference point in making sense of life has shifted from an understanding that there is an external, controlling transcendent reality to something internal. It is not that individuals *cannot* become open to the transcendent, but, rather, experiences that might involve transcendence have little or no frame of reference through which to make sense of them. The default position does not require, let alone acknowledge, that there might be an external sense-making reality. This move to the internal, away from an overarching external framework, as the locus of sense-making helps to explain a key finding from research into Christian relational outreach to 'Generation Y' teenagers in the early 2000s.

This research coined the phrase 'happy midi-narrative' to capture the way that the young people interviewed made sense of their lives by seeking happiness and equilibrium through a reliance on their close knit circle of friends and family alongside their 'own reflexive self'.[26] Interesting, in relation to what has been explored above, is the way that purely relational outreach work by Christians at the time, with no explicit telling of the Christian story, served only to reinforce this narrative – in other words, relationships built with Christian leaders, even when the young people were aware of the Christian faith of these leaders, actually led to the young people themselves gaining confidence in their own already held beliefs about themselves and the world, rather than leading to an interest in faith and gospel-sharing opportunities.[27] This is the 'age of authenticity' in action. More recent research into Generation Y as adults has found that this happy midi-narrative still holds true.[28]

In reflecting on these findings, when the research was first analysed the researchers suggested the lack of Christian narrative was problematic in the purely relational work, and consequently the young people didn't have the means through which to make connections between the care and interest shown by the youth workers and their Christian faith. This tallies with the observations of Root: that key to individuals becoming open to the possibility of transcendence is telling stories with invitations into these stories.[29] The thinking of Charles Taylor himself suggests that such has been the emptying of the transcendent from the structures of public life that there is a fundamental need to be awakened to the possibility of the divine. The earlier quotation from Taylor suggests that this is crucial for those with belief in a transcendent reality to be able to maintain such faith, as well as for those without to become alert to the possibilities.

None of this is to imply that openness or awareness of the transcendent is impossible in the secular age, but instead it is something that needs to be awakened – and possibly awakened again and again. Intriguingly, something of this sense of opening up to the transcendent comes through in the description and analysis of the case studies that form Part 2 of this book. There is something in the approach of the youth groups studied that engages in the task of opening the young people (and at times the leaders) to the ongoing possibility of faith in a transcendent God.

This taps into Taylor's concept of there being three different shifts that characterize the pivot towards the secular age. He traces the shift in the social imaginary through three different understandings of secular that have defined the relationship between the transcendent and the secular. He labels these as secular one, secular two and secular three. It is secular three, he claims, that is the most pervasive, yet conversely least considered by religious institutions in their cultural analyses.[30] As described above, encapsulated within these changes is the shift from an external sense-making schema shaping the internal world of individual human beings. The first of these shifts (secular one) is in terms of the state and public life. The institutions and the way in which institutions form the structures around which society is ordered no longer have an automatic connection to the sacred or transcendent. The classic expression of this in recent generations is the oft-quoted comment from the then Communications Director for the Labour Party, Alastair Campbell, who interrupted, when an interview with the then new Prime Minister Tony Blair was beginning to veer into matters of personal faith, to say, 'We don't do God.' What this encapsulated in a moment was the move of the sacred from the overarching institutional sense-making schema to the realm of the private. Consequently, what we see in this shift is the separating of the secular from the divine, in a way that changes our relationship with the divine or transcendent as it is no longer required for the order and structuring of society. Once this shift has taken place, and transcendence is no longer interwoven with the structures that order society, then faith – engagement with the divine – becomes a matter of personal, private choice. Once the role of God has been safely confined to the private then the possibility grows of choosing life without reference to the transcendent. Ultimately, this calls into question not just the possibility of faith but the whole necessity of its existence. Furthermore, this move into the realm of choice creates the environment in which Taylor's second form of the move to the secular becomes apparent.

The second shift (secular two) exists within the space of personal choice. It is seen in the dropping-off of religious practice and affiliation. This is not news to most of us in the West and the UK specifically. We are not strangers to the statistics about the decline in church attendance and the way that this is seen in the younger generations in particular.[31] It is often these statistics that are used to motivate church planting and new forms of the Church. The risk, however, is that the Church becomes stuck in thinking that the key cultural battleground is therefore its relevance. Root encapsulates this challenge, and the combined impact of secular one and secular two, when reflecting on it in terms of the role of the church leader:

> Our day-to-day order is detached from the divine. The institutions and structures we live in, whether private or public, make no presumptions that they reflect God's act – the chain of being has been broken. Because this has occurred, the pastor has been left with *only* the hope of building a vital institution and therefore winning the right to speak into people's private lives ... In our time, the pastor has to spend time and energy winning a cultural place for his congregation.[32]

Building on this, however, in secular three the place of the sacred is moved from personal choice to one in which the conditions of belief, what Taylor calls the social imaginary, do not allow space for the sacred or transcendent. This is secular, the cultural sea in which we all swim. It is unacknowledged and yet seen instinctively as the neutral position from which any expression of faith in the sacred is difficult. Transcendence is at best a contested notion, at worst rarely discussed. It is in this third form of the secular that the notion of the age of authenticity discussed above becomes pervasive.

For Taylor, a consequence of this shift in the social imaginary is one that ultimately has made belief in God and active

acknowledgement of the sacred realm almos
These are the conditions of belief that provide
for the mission of the Church today. However, a
the Church can find itself fighting the wrong ba
that the key challenge is over affiliation or churc
Turning again to Root's articulation of the problem: 'for us
to help people in our churches experience faith is not to battle
for space or commitment'.[33] Rather, the key question is how
to awaken the imagination to the possibility of faith. In the
light of this analysis of the move to the secular what is at stake
in our missional activities is not affiliation to the Church or
church attendance, but the need to awaken afresh an imagination in which the sacred is plausible and possible.

Given that the primary missional response within the Church
in recent years, especially within the Church of England, has
been to look towards church planting and fresh expressions
of church to reach people and to win back those who have
stopped going to church, the battle that is being fought can
implicitly be understood as the battle for affiliation and attendance. The language used – that those to be reached are the
'unchurched' or 'dechurched' – is highly suggestive of church
engagement being seen as the critical issue. Indeed, John Hull's
helpful and gentle critique of the Fresh Expressions founding
document, *Mission-shaped Church* – that there is a risk of the
focus simply being on creating more café churches in order to
win people back to the Church – seems to back this up.[34] This
centralizing of the Church is problematic as it can play into
the secular two context of personal choice rather than secular
three where there is little or no concept of the sacred through
which interest in the communal expression of an institution
such as the Church might become an appealing option. The
shift that is needed within the Church is to realize that declining church affiliation and attendance is a symptom of a greater
malaise that needs to be considered, rather than the problem
itself.

The contention throughout this book is that there is practical
wisdom in work with young people that provides some tools
for the task of mission amid a secular social imaginary that

.alues ecclesial life without centralizing the Church; the case studies demonstrate something of the way that this works. But before turning to that task in Part 2, there are two more key shifts that need to be taken into account: the political upheaval of the second decade of the twenty-first century, and the hyper-connectivity of the digital age.

Political upheaval

The second pivot point that provides the sociological perspective for an interweaving ecclesiology is the political upheaval of the second decade of this twenty-first century. This upheaval is seen on the surface in the events surrounding the UK's referendum vote to leave the EU and the election of Donald Trump as President of the USA. Both these events of 2016 were disruptions of political power as well as the trajectory of political will towards the globalization of recent decades. These two seismic events and the implications of them must, however, be understood in light of wider trends visible in the worldview of younger and emerging generations – Generations Y and Z. These trends must be seen in the context of the argument outlined earlier in this chapter that younger generations should not be seen as embodying distinct cultures, but instead are primary interpreters of society's values. Consequently, we need to look at these trends within younger generations to understand the times in which we live.

After spending time interviewing many teenagers in 2015 for her book *Generation Z: Their Voices, Their Lives*, author and researcher Chloe Combi described the teenagers of Generation Z as those 'growing up in a world shadowed by economic uncertainty, shrinking job prospects, widening social inequality and political apathy'.[35] It is easy therefore from statements such as this to jump to the conclusion that young people are disengaged from politics; however, this could not be further from the reality of many in this age group. This is the era of Greta Thunberg and Emma Gonzalez – individuals who have respectively made headlines concerning the climate crisis across the globe, and gun control protests in the USA; they are young people who have stepped into the debates surrounding key political issues because they don't see the adults in power using political influence to good effect. Further, these individuals didn't stand alone in their causes, but inspired and rallied many hundreds and thousands of others to protest, walk out of school, and go on strike to raise awareness of these issues that are close to their heart. Nearer to home, and on a smaller though no less important scale, research by Tearfund and Youthscape has shown that a high proportion of young people are deeply concerned by issues of poverty, discrimination and climate change. On the issue of climate change (the key focus of the research), over 90 per cent are concerned but only 1 in 10 think the Church is doing enough to address the problem.[36] This speaks of political engagement, not apathy.

So, what might be going on here? There are two possibilities – one is that Combi's words, being written in 2015 before the political events on both sides of the Atlantic took place the following year, simply became out of date very quickly and subsequent events shook younger people out of their political apathy. More likely, though, is that the apathy noted is directed towards political structures and institutions, not political issues themselves. A report from the think tank Demos provides some evidence to reinforce this claim, stating:

> One of the dominant narratives about younger generations is that they are disillusioned with politicians and forms of traditional political engagement. This has led some commentators to conclude that younger generations are lazy, apathetic and self-centred. Our research suggests that this is not the case but there is instead a growing gap between young people's interest in social issues (which is increasing) and their engagement via politics (which is decreasing).[37]

This would certainly tally with some of the institutional suspicion suggested by Taylor's account of secularization and the move to internal means of authority in the age of authenticity. Moreover, it makes sense when looking at events that have shaped the two most recent generations – Y and Z.[38]

Generations Y and Z are generally reckoned to be those born approximately between 1982 and 1999 (Generation Y) and those from 1999 onwards (Generation Z). As discussed above, generational theory needs to be read with a degree of trepidation as there are no clear, hard and fast boundaries between generations and it operates in broad generalizations. However, taken in the light of the understanding of culture above, it can be helpful in highlighting trends and key events that have shaped outlooks and approaches. It is in this light that I proceed with a brief overview of both Generations Y and Z.

Generation Y is a generation shaped by a world at first seeming to open up for those within it before shrinking around them, resulting in expected hopes and opportunities being dashed. This can be seen broadly in the understanding that Generation Y are a generation whose living memory growing up from childhood, through adolescence to adulthood, is bookended by the falling of the Berlin Wall and the global financial crisis, leading to the years of economic austerity.[39] These two bookends function as icons of the Generation Y social imagination – a world in which walls were falling and new hopes for a peaceful, connected world were opening up, before the economic prospects that were connected to this all came crashing down. In digging a little deeper, Generation Y can be said to have grown up with the three key coordinates of globalization, electronic media and consumerism as the shaping factors of their life and outlook.[40] The use by New Labour of the song 'Things Can Only Get Better' as the theme tune for their successful general election campaign in 1997 seems to sum up the outlook provided by these three coordinates. Each in their own way speaks of a world opening up in a manner that means life can and should get better. New opportunities for travel, for communication, for shopping. New products, new friendships, new politics.

However, gradually it became clear that the world that was becoming mapped out as a result of these three coordinates was not quite the world of opportunity that it seemed at first to be. The tragic and world-shaking events of the 9/11 terrorist attacks, viewed in real time across the world as a result of 24-hour media, demonstrate the fragility of international relations. The focus of Western fear shifted from communism to the oxymoronic 'war on terror', focused initially on the Iraq War. Similarly, the pace at which the world was being consumed, and the growing awareness of the impact of the rampant consumerism of the West on the developing world, fuelled concerns around sustainability that became focused on climate change. Ultimately, the fears that emerged from the years when things were supposed to be getting better became encapsulated in the financial crash and subsequent wage stagnation, political moves towards economic austerity, and the shrinking of public services in the UK and elsewhere.

As already discussed, analysis of Generation Y as they began to move into their late teens, the traditional age-marker of adult life, suggested strongly that their outlook and approach to life could be described in the phrase 'happy midi-narrative'. The happy midi-narrative is a phrase used to describe the way in which, in the midst of the opening up and then closing in of the opportunities that Generation Y have experienced, they have coped by focusing on that which is manageable within the future they can foresee – who are the people who will help them move towards happiness for the foreseeable, only mid-term, future? The answer being: those who help to sustain this happy midi-narrative are friends, family and an individual's own reflexive self.

There is a paradox at work in this response to contemporary culture – on the one hand, Generation Y are a globally aware generation and yet they tend towards relying on a fairly small, safe group or community to support them and see them through for the foreseeable future. In this manner they can be described as 'altruistic individualists'[41] who are acutely aware of issues of injustice but perhaps need a personal connection to motivate engagement with the issues at hand. Interestingly, the overlapping of the secular social imaginary, denying as it does an overarching sense-making structure resulting in the age of individual authenticity, alongside the disruptions of hyperconnectivity, make trust an earned commodity. This means that the role of personal experience is heightened markedly in the way that these younger adults approach life. There is a clear sense in which they must 'taste and see' that something is good and trustworthy before they will commit. This plays out in personal relationships (hence the importance of the happy midi-narrative), in engaging with society and in matters of faith. This should come as no surprise for a generation who have had the rug of expectations and hopes pulled from under them. There is, however, a hopefulness in this, since the value placed on personal experience creates the context in which these younger adults will connect with relationships, faith and institutions – they are a generation longing for something in which to invest.

In turning to the younger generation, known most commonly as Generation Z, the key pivot point in understanding their political[42] outlook remains the same – the global credit crunch and subsequent austerity. Generation Z are those who can be described as growing up at a time when their only experience is one of austerity.[43] In sharp contrast to the outlook associated with Generation Y, those born from the early 2000s onwards have not been brought up in the hope that things can only get better. Their financial prospects are worse than that of their parents. The society and outlook they have inherited is one in which, for many, life is seen as tough and that they are the ones who are paying for it: rising tuition fees for higher education, housing shortages, growing experiences of loneliness – to name but a few specifics – mean that adolescence is challenging to navigate with little certainty as to what the future holds as this generation enters adult life.[44] Indeed, the traditional markers of adult life and the end of adolescence are increasingly hard to reach as autonomy is financially near impossible for many until their late twenties at the earliest.[45]

At the time of writing, however, research suggests that this youngest generation are responding to the limited outlook they have inherited with a realization that they are the ones who need to do something about it. This is a generation who care about the world and their future because they know it is not being handed to them. Further than that, there is a growing sentiment that the older generations have failed in the task of leading the world and addressing societal challenges so they cannot be trusted. Generation Z are the generation who will have to do things for themselves. This is facilitated, for example, by their position as digital natives – in the hyperconnected world they are the ones who have known no different; they are the experts, the natives with knowledge at their fingertips and growing clarity about how to operate in the world. It is normal and natural to them; they do not need the older generation to guide them and pass on knowledge.

In this context the younger generation are responding to the climate into which they have been born and are being raised by challenging and throwing off the institutional structures that have traditionally been the foundations that shape approaches to society and civic engagement. The first of these can be noticed in relation to religious affiliation. In previous generations, even when church attendance was clearly declining, the rate of identification with religious or denominational markers declined more slowly – people might still tick the box related to what they saw as their inherited religious identity. Such nominal connections and identifications are no longer needed as the younger generation have grown in confidence in identifying as having no religious affiliation.[46]

This is a form of passive challenge to the status quo; however, in other areas the challenge has not been so passive with young people challenging the institutional responses to issues they see as growing threats to the prosperity of their futures – climate change, gun and knife violence and intolerance. As we noted, the headlines have been made by the likes of Emma Gonzalez and Greta Thunberg, but these two young women are merely the figureheads for much more widespread dissatisfaction – leading to school climate change strikes across the globe, walk-outs to protest against gun violence in the USA, and student protests against what they see as increasingly heavy-handed legislation against Hong Kong by the mainland Chinese government. This is a generation who do not want their views to be ignored and who will challenge a church that is quiet on the issues they see as vital.[47] Or, as Chloe Combi writes, 'Generation Z all around the globe seem to be waking up to the fact they need to get boots on the ground and out

in order to really make change happen ... gov-
ignore what's loud and in their faces, and no
ernments more than large bodies of angry and
ng people.'[48]

        uences of these things for those of us who are
older is that we must engage and include the voices of the young,
we must allow ourselves to be challenged and led by them.
The structures within which we operate must be less institutional, more flexible and relational to welcome their voice and
expertise. There is also the challenge to our assumptions – this
is not necessarily a generation who have turned down the gospel story because they have heard it and chosen to ignore it;
rather, they choose not to affiliate or identify with the institution of the Church but know little of the gospel story itself.[49]
The call for the Church must be to allow the gospel to become
afresh the empowering narrative of the in-breaking kingdom
of God once again, dialoguing with younger people about the
message of hope and challenge to the empire. Although the
following sections of this book don't discuss these and other
political issues specifically, the comments around the impact of
political upheaval and young people serve to highlight their role
as cultural interpreters, and emphasize the need therefore of an
ecclesiological approach that dialogues with young people and
refuses to assume that they are apathetic and unwilling to be
involved in the social, cultural and global challenges of these
times. This need is further demonstrated in the exploration of
the final sociological pivot point – hyperconnectivity.

Hyperconnectivity

It is undeniable that perhaps the key defining feature of life
for Generations Y and Z is the rise of electronic media and the
digital age. Generation Y grew up in parallel with this development, as its association with the key coordinate of electronic
media suggests, whereas Generation Z are the first generation
to be termed 'digital natives'.[50] Together they have become
the generations that embody the notion of being 'always on' –
more commonly known as 'hyperconnectivity'.[51]

Hyperconnectivity relates to the notion that the digital world of electronic media and devices pervades each and every aspect of life – indeed, the internet is increasingly shifting the world of everyday goods and services to the digital. It is almost impossible to live and interact in contemporary society without being connected, without being always on.[52] This is the default, and to turn off is to be disconnected. Research in 2019 highlighted the impact of this by identifying that when unable to access the internet or removed from smartphones, it is common for individuals to display traits similar to withdrawal from addiction.[53] This is not to bemoan the digital – indeed, it has facilitated ongoing work and relationships during the required social restrictions of the global pandemic at the start of the 2020s – but rather to highlight its all-pervasive nature. In a mirroring of Taylor's claim about the secular being a move from its being impossible not to believe in God to a time when it is almost impossible to believe in God, hyperconnectivity moves us from a time when it was impossible to imagine the digital world to one in which it is almost impossible to imagine or navigate life without it. The incredible thing is that this change has happened within the span of two generations.

It is important, however, in discussing hyperconnectivity not to try and over-analyse the details – such as how many devices we have or hours that are spent connected to the online world; it is not to look at the rise and fall of various social media accounts or what technologies might be on the way – such comments will be outdated as quickly as they are written. Instead, what is significant to this chapter and the unfolding argument of this book is the sociological impact of this move to the digital, to being 'always on'. In brief this impact can be seen as a series of disruptions – first, a disruption of normal generational divides; second, a disruption of normal relational divides; and third, a disruption of normal lifestyle divides.[54]

The digital age disrupts the traditional ways in which knowledge is held and passed on from generation to generation as well as where the centre of gravity for collective wisdom is held. Knowledge is no longer a commodity that is accumulated over time; it is now at our fingertips in our devices. In this way knowledge can be said to have been democratized with equal access available to all. The younger generations no longer have the necessity of looking to the older generations for knowledge. Indeed, in some ways it is the older generation who need to look to the younger. Not for knowledge so much, but in terms of skills. The traditional role of older generations to formally and informally mentor younger generations in the life skills needed to thrive and contribute to society is disrupted as the younger generations are growing up as digital natives with the attached core skills developed naturally. In response to this in the business world a number of firms are incorporating reverse mentoring schemes into their regular practice.[55] Of course, it is not just knowledge that is important in developing the skills to thrive and contribute in society, it is the wisdom to use that knowledge well. Here also, the digital world is disrupting the traditional role of a wider community through which wisdom is developed and crafted, as this is perceived as being cultivated in the online space. People are able to curate bespoke online communities that authenticate ways of life, allowing individuals to be affirmed in what they would see as the inherent wisdom of their own instinctive lifestyle choices.[56] There is in this, then, a reshaped version of the happy midi-narrative of Generation Y in which a curated online community can play a significant part. This is, of course, connected to the interpretation of secular three, as defined by Charles Taylor, as the age of authenticity in which what it is to be human is for each individual to decide. The ubiquity of hyperconnectivity in the digital age both initiates and perpetuates this.

The second disruption is to relational divides. This is about transparency.[57] Hyperconnectivity and the way in which the digital age has revolutionized communication and human interaction through social media usage results in a greater level of relational transparency that in turn leads to higher levels of suspicion and scrutiny. We each share much more of ourselves than in previous generations and this sharing is not always discriminate, meaning that parents, friends, colleagues, line managers and many others can develop a picture of us from the wealth of online information, much of which is self-published and difficult to escape from.

One only needs to consider the plight of the would-be politicians who find themselves having to defend or apologize for social media posts, or archived articles – often from a number of years earlier – that are all too easy to find but not necessarily recalled by the individual concerned; or the way that employers will consider it quite standard practice when recruiting employees to scour the online world and social media profiles to help develop their picture of the potential team member. Things that previously would have been unknown and therefore not impacted employment prospects can now be carefully scrutinized. There is a paradox in this as the greater transparency and scrutiny can, in turn, create a greater level of suspicion. Is the online profile or the way that life is presented an accurate portrayal of the individual? Or in face-to-face interaction will we be accepted at face value or will we be scrutinized in the light of our online interactions as well? The two worlds overlap and interact with each other. The recent rise of what is termed 'cancel culture' has become a particular expression of this whereby online interactions, often from years earlier, can be brought to light and used to shame individuals.[58]

Ultimately this means that for younger generations trust is an earned rather than assumed currency in relationships. Trust is not bestowed as a result of status or relational role but earned over time.[59] This becomes apparent in relationships with individuals as well as institutions. And in the age of authenticity trust is a precious commodity that is bestowed on those who the individual believes will enhance, protect or support the authentic self. The impact of this in relation to the Church and the Christian faith is immediately apparent – the Church cannot assume to have a right to speak into the lives of young people. Trust will need to be earned in dialogue and the relationships that build through this; and, second, the Church may need to think about the spaces it creates through which individuals can develop such trust. The importance of 'safe space' within the youth group case studies to come exemplifies this.[60]

The third and final disruption of the digital age is to normal lifestyle divides. This refers to the way that hyperconnectivity blurs and, to some extent at least, erases lines that previously would have enabled a clearer sense of separation between distinct aspects of our lives – for example, work, home and social lives. The icon of hyperconnectivity is the smartphone and in these devices the means of communication and organization for all aspects of life are often brought together. No longer is it straightforward to leave work or school at the office door or school gates, allowing home to be a place of separation and perhaps sanctuary.[61] The consequences of this disruption are the essence of what it means to be 'always on' in the age of hyperconnectivity. The use of the smartphone as a single, all-purpose device means that it is by our side at all times of day and night, whether to listen to music or the radio, as an alarm clock, television, computer or even perhaps as a telephone! It is this all-purpose nature of the smartphone that results in our culture being one of individuals who are 'always on'. When the smartphone is our clock and alarm it is all too easy to check in on emails and messages first thing in the morning (even before we get out of bed); when the smartphone is our primary music device it is all too difficult to ignore the notifications coming in; when we are out with friends or having dinner with our families, or when we are relaxing by watching a film (often on our devices) it is easier to respond quickly to the emails and messages that come in rather than waiting for the next day when they will have built up.

While this can become a self-perpetuating (often vicious) circle in which the more we respond to the messages that come in, the more colleagues, friends and others expect our responses and thus the pressure to be always on increases, it is young people who are at the forefront of navigating this and the other disruptions – because for them they are not disruptions, but the way of life that is native, that is normal. Consequently, these three key disruptions, to generational, relational and lifestyle divides, demonstrate the way that life and relationships interconnect for young people, and increasingly for all of us. Hyperconnectivity fundamentally shifts the expectations and dynamics around the way that generations, relationships and aspects of our lives operate and flow in and out of one another. Young people are native in this world, but it is the world in which all live, and hyperconnectivity has fundamentally shifted these dynamics of normal everyday life.

Impact of Covid-19

It is not possible to write about sociological perspectives on young people without reflecting at least briefly on the experiences and impact of the global Covid-19 pandemic in 2020 and 2021. In many ways this has been an experience of collective trauma, one that has caused disruption and one whose effects will continue to be felt for years to come. While the long-term impact of the pandemic cannot be predicted it is not too much of a stretch of the imagination to presume that the ripples will be most felt among the young, those who are in the most intense period of neurological development that will shape their sense of identity for years to come. Already the economic impact is being most felt among the youngest end of the job market, with under-35s being significantly more likely to have lost their job as a result of sectors of the economy being shut down for months on end.[62]

Given the suggestion discussed above that each generation's approach to adult life is shaped by the events experienced in its youth it is not a stretch to suggest that the current generation of children and teenagers will live their adult life forever shaped by the seismic and unprecedented experiences of 2020 and 2021. So, while the precise and long-term ramifications of the pandemic will be impossible to predict in detail, it will be young people who are most required to reimagine and reinterpret life as a result. Consequently, the call in this chapter to take account of the experiences and cultural interpretations of the young is only reinforced by this – it will be the responsibility of the Church to ensure that it listens well and takes account of the experiences and emerging interpretations of young people. The challenge the Church will face in this is to hold these experiences of young people and walk with them through the coming months, years and decades. For me, one way of approaching this will be to heed the warning of Montague Williams in his analysis of how churches in the USA tend to respond to young people's experiences and wonders about race, racism and racial identity. His ethnographic research concluded that churches tend towards at least two of three common responses: underestimating, forgetting or dismissing student experiences in this area.[63] It seems to me that falling into these same traps will be entirely possible for the Church in its dealings with young people in the post-Covid years. How easy it will be as life resumes some sense of normality to underestimate, forget or dismiss young people's experiences, traumas and interpretations of the pandemic's impact. Ironically, what the Church needs to do is the exact opposite – deliberately amplify the experiences and interpretations of young people for all the reasons already discussed in this chapter.

Summary

The thrust of this chapter has been that there has been a profound period of cultural change that creates a new lens through which the Church needs to understand those among and with whom it seeks to minister or reach in mission. The implications of what has been discussed in this chapter represent significant changes to the way that individuals relate to one another, to institutions and to the notion of faith. The established societal rhythms and structures have been rewired through the secular social imaginary, political upheaval and hyperconnectivity that mark the experience of younger generations. These younger generations are those interpreting, and therefore living in, the sharp end of these cultural changes.

The consequence of this is that the Church has a challenge in its self-understanding. In a cultural world that does not recognize the validity of faith or of institutions, in which younger generations feel let down by those who came before them and are increasingly sensing the need to get on and sort things out for themselves, the Church might need some new imagination. This imagination might not, as is often thought, be primarily about the structures of the Church, although these may at times become part of the conversation. Rather, it is about developing an ecclesial imagination that builds flexibility and humility into the Church's self-understanding, into the way that it is positioned towards wider culture and the younger generations in particular. This reimagined posture draws on the dialogical theological positioning for which the previous chapter argued and the sociological perspectives of this chapter.

If it is true, as St Paul writes to the church in Colossae, that all things hold together in Christ,[64] then the whole world, all people, participate in some way in the relational moves of God and thus the Church must acknowledge in a humble posture towards the world that there is still much to learn. Encouragingly, though, by drawing together the theological and sociological thread of these opening two chapters it is possible to contend that such a humble posture towards the world is not mere pandering to cultural changes or societal shifts; it is not watering down the gospel in order to remain relevant, but rather a theological imperative drawn from the nature of the Triune God and how he operates in the world. These sociological changes are able to realign the ecclesial imagination towards the God in whom we live, move and have our being. The following chapter builds on this by detailing further how our ecclesial imagination has been lacking, especially with regard to the potential of work among children and young people to stimulate our thinking and practice. As detailed above, this is especially significant at a time of cultural change in which younger generations are interpreters of the cultural sea in which all of us swim.

Notes

1 Andrew Root, 'Youth Culture: A Theoretical Examination for the Sake of Ministry with Young People', in *Christian Youth Work in Theory and Practice: A Handbook*, ed. Sally Nash and Jo Whitehead (London: SCM Press, 2014), p. 43.

2 Pete Ward, ed., *Perspectives on Ecclesiology and Ethnography* (Grand Rapids, MI: William B. Eerdmans, 2012), p. 2.

3 I am indebted to Christian Noval and work he has presented at

conferences of the International Association for the Study of Youth Ministry (IASYM) for this terminology. I also draw on it in my article 'Interruption and Co-construction: Toward a Theology of Equal Opportunity for Mission and Ministry with Young People', *Anvil: Journal of Theology and Mission*, 34(2) (2018).

4 See, for example, Kenda Creasy Dean's argument that 'passion' is an ultimate characteristic of being young and that young people are specifically placed to bring this to the Church (Kenda Creasy Dean, *Practicing Passion: Youth and the Quest for a Passionate Church* (Grand Rapids, MI: William B. Eerdmans, 2004)).

5 This is seen in the way that adolescence is seen to have a physiological beginning but a sociological ending, with both boundaries shifting in recent years and therefore extending what might be termed 'adolescence' to the extent that it almost becomes meaningless; see, for example, Kenda Creasy Dean, Chap Clark and Dave Rahn, *Starting Right: Thinking Theologically About Youth Ministry* (Grand Rapids, MI: Zondervan, 2010).

6 Allan Clynne, 'Uncovering Youth Ministry's Professional Narrative', *Youth and Policy*, 115 (2015).

7 Amy Jacober, *The Adolescent Journey* (Downers Grove, IL: InterVarsity Press, 2011), p. 51. In my view, Jacober's work is among the very best in bringing theology and adolescent development together.

8 Root, 'Youth Culture', p. 43.

9 Sarah-Jayne Blakemore, *Inventing Ourselves: The Secret Life of the Teenage Brain* (London: Doubleday, 2018).

10 Blakemore, *Inventing Ourselves*, p. 2.

11 Blakemore, *Inventing Ourselves*, p. 7.

12 Root, 'Youth Culture', p. 43.

13 Graham Cray, *Youth Congregations and the Emerging Church* (Cambridge: Grove Books, 2002).

14 Noting Clynne's critique of the use of generational theory and the concept of youth culture.

15 Sylvia Collins-Mayo, Bob Mayo and Sally Nash, *The Faith of Generation Y* (London: Church House Publishing, 2010), p. ix.

16 See, for example, the use of the term 'generation snowflake' to describe Generation Y (also known as millennials).

17 Clynne, 'Uncovering'.

18 I discuss these terms in detail below, but Generation Y tends to refer to those born between approximately 1982 and 1999, with Generation Z being those born after 2000. The key point here is that generations tend to be defined by the events within the conscious memory of their growing up – the experiences of Generation Y therefore have been said to be bookended by the falling of the Berlin Wall in 1989 and the credit crunch/financial crash of 2009.

19 Ruth H. Perrin, *Changing Shape: The Faith Lives of Millennials* (London: SCM Press, 2020).

20 Chloe Combi, *Generation Z: Their Voices, Their Lives* (London: Windmill Books, 2015).

21 Charles Taylor, *A Secular Age* (London: Harvard University Press, 2007).

22 Taylor, *Secular Age*, p. 3.

23 Andrew Root, *Faith Formation in a Secular Age: Responding to the Church's Obsession with Youthfulness* (Grand Rapids, MI: Baker Academic, 2017), p. 4.

24 Taylor, *Secular Age*, pp. 473–504.

25 Andrew Root, conference paper at St Mellitus College 2018.

26 Collins-Mayo, Mayo and Nash, *Faith of Generation Y*, pp. 35–53.

27 Collins-Mayo, Mayo and Nash, *Faith of Generation Y*, p. 65.

28 See Perrin, *Changing Shape*.

29 Listen to the interview with Andrew Root on episode one of the 'Youthology' podcast – https://podcasts.apple.com/gb/podcast/1-01-andrew-root/id1478752528?i=1000448624087 (accessed 9.06.2021).

30 The impact of these shifts is key to Andrew Root's thinking and theology. His 'Secular Age' trilogy of publications – *Faith Formation, The Pastor* and *The Congregation* (Grand Rapids, MI: Baker Academic, 2017, 2019 and 2021) are important reading and hover in the background of the brief comments in this section.

31 See, for example, the following report debated at General Synod in February 2020: www.churchofengland.org/sites/default/files/2020-01/GS%202161%20Children%20and%20Youth%20Ministry%20Full%20with%20Appendix%20-%20Final.pdf (accessed 9.06.2021).

32 Root, *The Pastor*, p. 54.

33 Root, *Faith Formation*, p. 150.

34 See John Hull, *Mission-shaped Church: A Theological Response* (London: SCM Press, 2006).

35 Combi, *Generation Z*, p. 1.

36 Youthscape Centre for Research/Tearfund, *Burning Down the House: How the Church Could Lose Young People Over Climate Inaction* (Luton: Youthscape, 2021).

37 Jonathan Birdwell and Mona Bani, *Introducing Generation Citizen* (London: Demos, 2014).

38 Even allowing for the limitations of generational theory discussed earlier.

39 Collins-Mayo, Mayo and Nash, *Faith of Generation Y*, p. ix.

40 Sara Savage et al., *Making Sense of Generation Y: The World View of 16- to 25-year-olds* (London: Church House Publishing, 2006), pp. 143–50.

41 Ruth Perrin, 'Altruistic Activists: Averting Millennial Breakdown', *Discipleship Research*, September 2018, https://discipleshipresearch.com/2018/09/altruistic-activists-averting-millennial-breakdown/ (accessed 9.06.2021).

42 In the broad sense of the word rather than narrowly relating to party politics.

43 See Combi, *Generation Z.*

44 A sense that will likely only be heightened by the effects of the global pandemic of 2020 and 2021.

45 Chloe Combi, 'The Death of the Teenager', *Chloe Combi*, December 2019, https://chloecombi.net/the-death-of-the-teenager/ (accessed 9.06.2021).

46 This has been termed 'the rise of the nones' due to the increased rates in which younger people will select 'none' when asked for their religion in censuses and surveys. See, for example, James Emery White, *Meet Generation Z: Understanding and Reaching the New Post-Christian World* (Grand Rapids, MI: Baker Books, 2017).

47 For example, Youthscape Centre for Research/Tearfund, *Burning Down the House.*

48 Combi, 'The Death of the Teenager'.

49 They are said to be 'memoryless' of the Christian narrative. See Savage et al., *Making Sense.*

50 Emery White, *Meet Generation Z*, p. 41.

51 Thomas Koulopoulos and Dan Keldsen, *The Gen Z Effect* (New York: Bibliomotion, 2014), pp. 43–76.

52 The experience of life in the global pandemic of 2020 and 2021 highlighted and exacerbated this to the extent that personal, social interaction relied almost entirely on online platforms.

53 See, for example, Sean Coughlan, 'Smartphone "addiction": young people "panicky" when denied mobiles', *BBC News*, 29 November 2019, www.bbc.co.uk/news/education-50593971 (accessed 4.03.2021).

54 Koulopoulos and Keldsen, *The Gen Z Effect*, pp. 51–67.

55 Koulopoulos and Keldsen, *The Gen Z Effect*, pp. 67–70.

56 Chloe Combi discusses this in episodes one and two of her podcast 'You Don't Know Me' in relation to body image and political viewpoints among young people. See Chloe Combi, 'Cancel Culture' and 'Body Image', 'You Don't Know Me' (podcast), 11 and 18 January 2021, https://podcasts.apple.com/gb/podcast/you-dont-know-me/id1545582529 (accessed 13.10.2021).

57 Koulopoulos and Keldsen, *The Gen Z Effect*, p. 54.

58 See Chloe Combi, 'You Don't Know Me' podcast, episode two on Cancel Culture.

59 Koulopoulos and Keldsen, *The Gen Z Effect*, p. 54.

60 See Part 2.

61 This has become even more apparent in the pandemic of 2020–1 with the required increase in working at home for many.

62 See, for example, 'Under 35s Bearing Brunt of Jobs Crisis', *BBC News*, 20 April 2021, www.bbc.co.uk/news/business-56812163 (accessed 9.06.2021).

63 Montague R. Williams, *Church in Color: Youth Ministry, Race, and the Theology of Martin Luther King Jr* (Waco, TX: Baylor University Press, 2020), p. 6.

64 Colossians 1.17.

3

The Current Gap in our Thinking: Practical Perspectives

The role of youth work in shaping and forming the mind, methods and spirituality of the Church has largely been ignored.[1]

This chapter concludes Part 1 and in doing so completes the foundational work that sets up the main work of theological construction to be done in Parts 2 and 3. Chapters 1 and 2 offered theological and sociological perspectives that have argued for the Church to take account of the lives, worlds and wisdom of younger people in its self-understanding, posture and framework. The description of how God is at work in the world that leads to a dialogical theological perspective, alongside the detailed description of the cultural landscape, has set up the approach to ecclesiology that follows. This chapter completes the foundational task of asking why this book is necessary by identifying the gap in current thinking around church and mission, specifically by identifying and articulating an inherent ecclesial imagination running through the history of Christian work with young people that has been handed down in accepted norms of practice.

This ecclesial imagination operates in an unacknowledged manner, in large part as a result of the way that the history of youth ministry has meant that there has rarely been any good, rigorous ecclesiological reflection on work that is done among young people. Accepted norms of practice that have been passed down from generation to generation and become normative were developed in non-church situations as evangelical Christians launched parachurch organizations to reach young people, before these ways of working migrated into the life of the Church. The result of this lack of good ecclesiological reflection within youth ministry is that the possible influence such reflection might have on the wider life of the Church is limited.[2] An overview of the literature can broadly identify three limited approaches to ecclesiology and youth ministry – ecclesiology that is assumed, imposed or alluded to.

An assumed understanding makes the mistake of assuming a shared understanding of the Church between author and reader without detailing what this is or where it has come from. It is disconnected from tradition and denomination, using only thinly explored metaphors of, for example, family, community or body of Christ. An imposed approach takes an established approach to the Church and then describes how youth ministry might look if such an approach was adopted. This is the approach often taken when franchises such as Mission-shaped, Post-Christendom or Purpose Driven are given a specific youth ministry articulation. These provide a particular, often interesting, approach to the Church with and for young people, but they do not do the critical work of asking what an ecclesiology that works the other way around might be – starting with young people and moving to the wider life of the Church. Both these approaches give little if any agency to the young people themselves and revert to a much-criticized blueprint approach to ecclesiology.

Other research does offer a critical approach to working with young people but does so without the question of ecclesiology being at the forefront. The research questions at the heart of these approaches are more to do with faith formation or the way that young people hold faith. Intriguingly, these kinds of work allude to the significance of ecclesiology, but tackling this question is beyond the scope of the research. *Faith Generation* by Nick Shepherd (2016)[3] and *The Faith of Generation Y* by Sylvia Collins-Mayo and colleagues are examples.[4]

Uncovering the ecclesial imagination of youth ministry

The communicative gap between ecclesiology and work with young people comes about in part as a result of youth ministry's historical roots and normative centre of gravity. Youth ministry as we know it is largely a modern and evangelical phenomenon with an inherent ecclesial imagination formed outside the boundaries of denominational and local church life. The history of youth ministry has been told from a US perspective but rarely from a UK point of view, and although there are undoubtedly many similar themes, it is important to chart some of the key characteristics from this side of the Atlantic.[5] These key characteristics can be best viewed through the lens of one important (but often underrepresented) organization in the UK – Urban Saints, formerly the Crusaders' Union of Bible Classes.[6] Central to this story is the development of an ecclesial imagination in work with young people, while highlighting that the missionary focus leading to work outside the usual boundaries of church and denominational life resulted in a gap between such an imagination and more formal ecclesiological thinking, even when the format of the work with young people became incorporated into mainstream church life.

Using the origins and influence of Urban Saints (initially as the Crusaders' Union) as a lens through which to understand this will highlight in particular the paradox of Crusaders being outside of the Church and yet in some ways resembling aspects of ecclesial life for its participants. The roots from which Crusaders grew can be traced to 1867 and the drawing rooms of a Mr Josiah Spiers of Islington and a Mr Tom Bishop of South London. Independently of each other, both Spiers and Bishop had begun special services for children in their drawing rooms. Additionally, in 1868, while on holiday in Llandudno, North Wales, Spiers spontaneously held a Bible meeting for children on the beach. As a result of the similarity in the work they had both begun Spiers and Bishop decided to collaborate and the Children's Special Service Mission (CSSM) was born.[7]

They worked together pioneering this new style of mission to children for over 40 years. A significant aim of their work was to communicate the Christian faith in a way that was accessible for the children themselves. This innovative approach led to the importance of simple songs and choruses and the production of their own CSSM chorus books for use in the meetings. Pete Ward describes how the 'simple words and lively tunes' of the hymns, alongside 'an informal style of preaching', came from the expectation that the children themselves could and should personally respond to Christ.[8] Furthermore, in 1879 they built on this belief that the Christian faith was accessible to children through providing daily Bible passages for children to read and launched the Children's Scripture Union.[9]

Towards the end of the nineteenth century, a gentleman called Albert Kestin was involved in a Bible class in which a younger man, Herbert Bevington, was being nurtured in his Christian faith.[10] Kestin then joined the Church Missionary Society (CMS) and, from 1895, spent some years in Calcutta as a missionary.[11] On his return to London, while on furlough and studying for ordination in 1900, he lodged with a Mr W. P. Saffrey and his wife in Crouch End.[12] While Kestin was staying with them, Mrs Saffrey suggested the idea of a 'Bible Class for some of these boys who do nothing on Sunday afternoons' and, further, in a manner resembling the now established work of CSSM among children, offered their drawing room as a meeting place.[13] As Kestin recalls: 'In her drawing room on Sunday afternoon, April 1st, 1900, four boys met me in the first "Crusaders" class. Next Sunday there were only two boys and for the first few weeks little progress was registered so that I began to ask myself if we really were working out any plan of God.'[14]

From these inauspicious beginnings a youth ministry movement that was to influence the Church in the UK during the twentieth century was born. The class began to grow, and after leading on his own for 12 months Kestin recruited co-leaders in his 'old boy' Herbert Bevington and a missionary student known to Kestin through the CMS, a Mr E. S. Daniell.[15] In the autumn of 1901 the now ordained Revd Kestin returned to Calcutta with CMS.[16] The class now numbered 60 and was left under the leadership of Bevington and, until he left for the overseas mission field, Daniell. The class continued to grow and in October 1902, upon growing too large for the Saffreys' drawing room, moved to meet in the dining room of Oakfield School.[17]

Herbert Bevington's business took him to Brighton for two years and, motivated by his leadership of the original class in Crouch End, he launched a Brighton and Hove class on 21 February 1904, experiencing great growth in this new class almost immediately. With Mr Daniell now readying himself for the mission field, an additional CMS missionary student, Mr Claude D. Ovens, took over leadership of the class in Crouch End.[18] Inspired by this work, in 1906 there were further classes in Richmond, Clapham, Blackheath, Camden, Hull, Stroud Green, Ealing, Chiswick, Wandsworth and Muswell Hill.[19] Among these classes were some, such as Muswell Hill, that were launched and led by senior members of the original Crouch End class.[20] Additionally, a class in Hull came into existence as a result of the boys who launched it meeting and being inspired by members of the Crouch End and Richmond classes at a CSSM beach mission event they attended while on holiday. This new class was launched in September 1905, immediately after the return of the boys from the holiday.[21]

By the time Kestin returned once again from Calcutta in 1906,[22] as well as the original group in Crouch End there were 11 other independent 'Crusader' Bible classes, with others being planned.[23] There was also informal communication between them through the sharing of prayer requests. In late March 1906, inspired by the energy of Herbert Bevington, the leaders of these various classes met together and the Crusaders' Union of Bible Classes was born.[24] The minutes of this first meeting highlight some important aspects of the origins of Crusaders. First, the significance of CSSM is clear. A formal association through membership of the CSSM was proposed alongside a decision to request that Crusaders use the CSSM magazine, *Our Boys' Magazine*, but with a distinctive Crusader cover[25] and some additional pages of specific Crusader news. Further inspired by CSSM, Crusaders also decided there was a need to have a chorus book for the classes that would, as with the songs used in children's services by CSSM, help to communicate the Christian faith in ways accessible to the boys attending the classes.[26] Second, the influence of missionary work is demonstrated in that three of the early Crusader class leaders present were commended as they were shortly leaving for missionary work overseas.[27] Indeed, the early leaders of Crusaders saw the work not as youth ministry, but as a missionary movement reaching out to young people.[28] Third, from the beginning those setting up Crusaders were firmly committed to the ethos of evangelicalism and were insistent that each class elected to the new organization would be equally committed to being evangelical in nature. Specifically, the following would be expected from each class: 'The whole Bible be taught as the Word of God, and a keen evangelical and protestant spirit be maintained, the classes remaining unsectarian and working as far as possible in harmony with all denominations and local churches.'[29]

The significance and impact of the evangelicalism of Crusaders will be discussed in more detail shortly. However, for now, I turn to the fourth and final characteristic of Crusaders that was made explicit at the Union's inception in that first Leaders Conference of 1906 – this being the particular boys who were the target for the mission of the Crusaders' Union. The record of the meeting states: 'It was felt impossible to lay down very hard and fast lines owing to varying local conditions, but the meeting laid down as a guiding principle that the Crusaders' classes aimed at the upper middle-class boys attending public and private schools and do not accept board schoolboys.'[30]

It may seem strange that Crusaders articulated such a specific, narrow focus for this work; however, with some reflection, the reasons behind this become clearer. Mark Senter has written of the way in which specific social conditions, and times of social change in particular, can provide the ideal conditions in which an innovative, grassroots youth movement takes shape under an acknowledged leader.[31] It follows, then, that Crusaders' concise mission focus is likely to have come about as a result of the social situations of the late nineteenth and early twentieth centuries. Among these changing social situations was the Industrial Revolution in which the move from child to adulthood was slowed, thus creating space for a new category of adolescence to appear as a recognized life stage[32] and, alongside this, the rise of evangelicalism as a 'much louder and more intrusive' form of Christianity.[33]

More specific social conditions can also be seen to lead directly to the particular and narrow focus of Crusaders' work with boys from public and private schools. In order to expand on these specific social conditions I will briefly highlight the rise of the Sunday school movement through the nineteenth century. It was evangelicals who launched the first Sunday schools in the late eighteenth century to provide a place of education for the children who, as a result of the requirements of the era to work other days, didn't have the opportunity for this elsewhere in the week.[34] Sunday schools were able to attract the children of the working classes by offering an education that, because of work commitments, they would otherwise have been unable to have. The opportunity was then used to ensure that the education provided was Christian and involved the reading and reciting of hymns and Scriptures. The Sunday schools tended to meet on both a Sunday morning and afternoon.[35] It follows, then, that with the main reach of Sunday schools being among the working classes, those from the middle and upper classes who, significantly, would have been attending public or private schools during the week, were less likely to be attached to a Sunday school on a Sunday afternoon. It was precisely one of these unattached groups of boys with free time on a Sunday afternoon that came to the attention of Albert Kestin and formed the group from which his initial Bible class began.[36] Additionally, CSSM co-founder Tom Bishop identified a trend among 13- and 14-year-old boys who, often as a result of starting work, felt they were too old for Sunday school and thus were beginning to be lost to the churches.[37]

As described above, those setting up Crusaders were firmly committed to the ethos of evangelicalism and were insistent that each class elected to the new organization would also be committed to being evangelical. Evangelical religion had been in existence in Britain for at least 150 years by the beginning of the twentieth century.[38] Evangelicalism cannot be seen as a coherent, narrow movement but rather is diverse and known for its complexity.[39] However, amid this diversity one of the traits generally acknowledged as being key within evangelicalism is activism typified in innovation.[40] The origins of Crusaders demonstrate the way in which this inherent evangelical tendency towards innovation leads to evangelical organizations.[41]

However, as demonstrated, evangelicalism is only one of the influences that led to Crusaders taking shape in the way it did. Of equal significance is the specific work of the CSSM in providing both the inspiration for the methods and important relational connections, the missionary outlook of Kestin and other early leaders trained for and experienced in overseas missionary work through the CMS, and the clearly articulated and narrow focus on mission to boys from public or private schools. These four influences find expression in a vital characteristic that was embodied in the work of Crusaders – the independence from formal church or denominational structures and affiliation, articulated as the classes being 'unsectarian' in the minutes of the first Leaders Conference.[42] This independence, however, did not mean a complete separation from church; rather, through the leaders and core practices of the groups, a consistent connection to the Church was maintained within the independence. As a result of this, a characteristic ambiguity in relation to the Church developed within the work.

By arranging themselves in the manner that they did, as a union of classes outside the normal channels of ecclesial life, the pioneers of Crusaders were following the moves made by others in this early evangelicalism. This is unsurprising in the light of a claim by McGrath that in the pre-war era evangelicalism was a 'despised minority' in the English Church.[43] As this despised minority, the influence of evangelicalism would have been limited. Churches or parishes sympathetic to evangelicalism were few and far between. It is from this place on the margins of ecclesiastical life that innovative moves of evangelicalism were made and that helped to shape the extra-ecclesial stance of many of these innovations.[44] The situation was such that Bebbington describes a 'displacement [of evangelicals] within the Church of England by men of higher churchmanship'.[45] It is likely that in the light of this situation for evangelicals within church life in the UK, especially when placed alongside the natural activism inherent in the evangelical outlook, evangelicals sought belonging, connection and community outside of formal ecclesial boundaries and often through the organizations they were quick to launch. Stanley Grenz describes this as the 'parachurch ethos' of evangelicalism.[46] Consequently, it has been noted that historically evangelicals were not committed to any particular theory of the Church or denomination, living with a minimalist ecclesiology. Moreover, the rise of evangelical Christianity has not been confined to any one denomination, neither is it a denomination in itself.[47]

Despite this minimalist ecclesiology, and a lack of formal ecclesial understanding, the way in which Crusaders gathered, and their core practices when they did so, displayed a resemblance to ecclesial life that was an outworking of their evangelical drive to innovate. Bruce Hindmarsh observes what he describes as the 'ecclesial consciousness' of evangelicalism characterized by subordinating church order in favour of personal evangelical piety.[48] He highlights three ecclesial experiments that anticipated the evangelical movement, naming these as: first, radical congregationalism, which emphasized the importance of an experience of personal conversion; second, Pietism, in which committed believers do not form a new church but meet in smaller groups across or outside of ecclesial boundaries; and third, Moravianism, which encouraged the growth of the 'interconfessional and international brotherhood'.[49] Traces of these, Hindmarsh claims, would be taken up within the modern evangelical movement and, in his words, be turned into 'something unprecedented'.[50]

My suggestion is that one of these unprecedented moves of evangelicalism was the rise of the parachurch youth ministry organizations, and that Crusaders exemplify this. There are certainly distinct signs of these traits in the work of

Crusaders and, influenced by Crusaders, modern youth ministry in general. The Bible classes that were the heart of the work of Crusaders have echoes of radical congregationalism, while the emphasis on the personal faith of the young people mirrors in some ways the emphasis of Pietism. The influence of Moravianism, encouraging fellowship in the extra-ecclesial way described by Hindmarsh, can be identified in some moves from the earliest days as Crusaders became formalized into an organization, and ways of providing fellowship for the leaders and boys from across the different classes were sought. These included an annual 're-Union Gathering' to bring leaders and senior boys together in London and a programme of summer camps.[51]

Furthermore, the underlying evangelical ecclesial consciousness helps to develop what can be termed an inherent ecclesial imagination among participants within this early form of youth ministry. Craig Dykstra uses the phrase 'ecclesial imagination' to describe what happens when a Christian community develops a way of life that fosters faith.[52] He notes in particular how this 'emerges among the people themselves' and operates in the 'many contexts where [people] live their lives'.[53] Drawing on this, Ward describes the ecclesial imagination as a practical form of 'wisdom that shapes the lives of disciples'.[54] Similarly MacDougall refers to an ecclesial imagination that 'runs deeper and broader' than academic ecclesiologies. It is an imagination that 'takes shape as it is lived' and operates in a place of intersection between ideas and practices.[55] It is this notion of an instinctive form of corporate Christian life, one that fosters faith and a Christian way of seeing life, that I want to invoke to argue for the place of work with young people in ecclesiological conversations; the idea of an inherent ecclesial imagination helps to articulate what it is that is embedded in the practices that became normative within Crusaders as leadership passed from generation to generation, and significantly as the practices became influential in youth ministry as a whole.

Though outwardly independent of the Church, Crusaders displayed such an ecclesial imagination, fostered by passing on leadership, values and organizational norms. Consequently, a strong practical normative approach to the Christian faith and the Church was developed within Crusaders and became part of the underlying identity of Christian work with young people more broadly. This ecclesial imagination of Crusaders, and the forms of gathering and practice that it involves, are examples of evangelical spirituality being formed outside the flow of mainstream church life.[56] For those growing up in Crusaders, however, the parachurch became the mainstream. Intriguingly, though, what Crusaders did exceptionally well for the first 50 years of the movement was to ensure a clear connection between their classes and the wider life of the Church, as testified by the numbers of boys converted to Christianity through Crusaders who were recorded as going on into church leadership roles.

The influence of Crusaders on the life and shape of the wider Church, however, is seen in the way in which the Bible class model became the blueprint for church-based youth groups to develop, thus taking the parachurch model, and this inherent but unacknowledged ecclesial imagination, into the life of the Church. In the period between the two world wars this Bible class model of working with young people developed by Crusaders under the influence of CSSM was taken up within churches. The development of movements such as Covenanters and Pathfinders recognized the benefits of providing Bible study alongside other Christian practices and activities for young people separate from the wider congregation, while seeking to place the work directly within the ministry of local churches and parishes. Covenanters developed as an association of Bible classes linked to the youth work of mostly non-conformist churches after the success of an initial class launched by businessman John Laing in 1928 at Woodcroft Evangelical Church. Laing was heavily involved in Crusaders and naturally considered whether the Crusader format would help with work among older boys within the church. Consequently, he decided to be released from his Crusader leadership role with Mill Hill Crusaders in order to focus on this new work.[57] Similarly, in 1935, the Revd Herbert Taylor began a work called Pathfinders to cater for the young people from his parish who were too old for Sunday school. This work spread beyond the parish and became a significant form of youth work catering for young people within Anglican parish churches.[58] From these beginnings the 'youth fellowship' model became the primary, almost universally accepted, manner of working with young people in the life of a local church.

This demonstrates the way, from the early days of what became known as youth ministry in the UK, that which is normative for work with young people is practice that was established outside of the Church and then handed down. David Bailey has written about the way this accepted practice then became enshrined in various writings so that youth ministry practice became established outside of church tradition and without regard for ecclesiological specifics.[59] This is not to say that youth ministry has developed with no ecclesial regard, rather, as described above in relation to Crusaders, it has developed a distinct ecclesial imagination – a way of life that fosters faith. It is the task of this book to identify this and then close the gap in our thinking by drawing on the practical wisdom encapsulated within that imagination.

Encouragingly, there are hints already as to what this might look like that can be detected in anecdotal fragments in writing about youth ministry and young adult faith. What is missing to this point is developing the ecclesiological significance of these as a framework or posture for the Church in mission. By way of example, Jonny Baker, currently Director of Mission Education for the Church Mission Society, reflected on his time leading Oxygen, a town-wide youth ministry, in which he describes a 'dynamic network of young Christians spread out as an expression of church'. There was, he says, a 'fluid nature of loyalties and alliances across the churches',[60] but that this did not seem to matter to the young people themselves. In a similar way, Sally Nash reflects on her own time as a young Christian:

Thinking back to my adolescence I was involved with a church youth group, an independent Crusader group (now

Urban Saints) and the Young Sowers League, as well as the school Christian Union. Looking back now I think I learnt about mission from church, worship and the Bible from Crusaders, the Bible from the Young Sowers League and the importance of peer support from the Christian Union. Young people today may have a similar experience.[61]

These anecdotal memories are reflected in Ruth Perrin's research among the young adults known as Generation Y, in which they have a more fluid way of affiliating with the Church than has traditionally been the case.[62] This fluidity tallies with the cultural discussions of the previous chapter in which relational connection with individuals and issues carries more weight than institutional affiliation and loyalty. These hints that articulate the reality of the underlying ecclesial imagination of youth ministry point towards the need for an ecclesiological framework that takes account of how young people develop, create and maintain Christian community with less regard to the usual boundaries of parish and denomination. They also begin to shine a light on the lack of good ecclesiological reflection about, or coming from, Christian work with young people. It is to this that the next section turns its focus.

The gap in youth ministry thinking and practice

Underlying questions that revolve around youth ministry and the Church find some articulation in youth ministry literature, though fall short of the kind of ecclesiology that takes account of the inherent ecclesial imagination of youth ministry explored above. Kenda Creasy Dean, for example, bemoans the way that youth groups often leave young people having only marginal contact with the rest of the church:

> The congregation worshipped in the sanctuary; youth met in the basement. The congregation gathered on Sunday mornings; youth gathered on Sunday nights. The congregation listened to sermons; youth heard 'youth talks'. The congregation had Bible study; youth had devotions. The congregation

has a budget; youth had a bake sale. Nothing that happened in the life of the congregation as a whole looked even vaguely familiar to youth ghettoized in youth groups.[63]

Dean goes on to conclude that this lack of interaction between youth groups and the Church results in a 'chasm between youth ministry and the theology of the church as a whole'.[64] It is certainly the case that ecclesiology is generally an underrepresented – or only superficially discussed – subject within popular youth ministry literature. In my experience, and backed by my reading of such literature, discussion of the Church in youth ministry seems to fall into one of three types. First, an agreed understanding of the Church is assumed; second, a particular ecclesiological approach is imposed; or, third, the Church is alluded to but not central to the discussion. I will illustrate each of these, with examples, to highlight the gap that there is for concerted ecclesiological reflection on youth ministry. The problem at the heart of each of these approaches is that they fail to take account of the participative, dialogical theology and the sociological perspective that utilizes young people's role as cultural interpreters that the previous chapters have detailed, as well as failing to recognize the ecclesial imagination described.

An assumed understanding of the Church is one that either uncritically presents a particular ecclesiological position, or where the focus is on drawing young people into a pre-existing church structure without questioning the appropriateness of such a focus. In *Christian Youth Work*, Ashton and Moon provide a clear example of when an agreed understanding of the Church is assumed. Though the authors raise the need for a 'thoroughly biblical doctrine of the church as a basis for youth work'[65] this amounts primarily, however, to the Sunday congregation family church model favoured by evangelicals in the late twentieth century.[66] This is clear in their statement of the need for young people to be part of a mixed church community in which all ages gather together.[67] Despite also asserting that there is no biblical blueprint for what church should look like,[68] some things are clearly ruled out – they describe youth churches, for example, as 'faintly ridiculous' and an 'unbiblical contradiction in terms'.[69] However, they also assert that the Church is seen as boring by young people[70] and advocate an approach that focuses on those from church families being integrated into church life.[71]

Similarly, the 'Inside-Out' model of Christian youth work seeks to socialize young people into a particular church through the witness of those already involved, meaning the 'home' church ecclesiology is a given.[72] Doug Fields details this approach at length in his *Purpose Driven Youth Ministry*.[73] This fleshing out of an inside-out approach proposes activities and events that are designed to draw young people through a system and into the life of the Church. The assumed nature of this approach is extenuated since this is a youth ministry version of a popular book that promotes the specific values and style of Saddleback Church in the USA.[74] When youth ministry operates from an assumed ecclesiology in this way it tends to be an approach to the theology of the Church that is biased towards those already within the Church. It also doesn't acknowledge the way that work with young people can shape ecclesiological discussion.[75]

Where the assumed understanding of church in youth ministry literature fails to adequately detail its ecclesiological foundations, the imposed approach takes a more detailed consideration of the Church before describing what youth ministry might look like if such ecclesiological considerations were placed upon it. This approach is seen, for example, in *Mission-shaped Youth*.[76] By being part of the burgeoning Mission-shaped series this book essentially takes as given the ecclesiological assumptions detailed in *Mission-shaped Church* and discusses what a youth ministry that takes them seriously would look like. This approach claims the influence of para-church organizations is diminishing as a result of a growing understanding that mission is integral to the identity of the Church.[77] Similarly, *Youth Work After Christendom*[78] imposes the view of the Church from the post-Christendom series on to work with young people.[79] Of particular interest in these examples is a fundamental disagreement about the role of parachurch work in contemporary UK church life – whereas *Mission-shaped Youth* dismisses it, the post-Christendom series sees it as a potential model for the wider Church to mirror moving forward.[80]

A further example of how views of the Church can be imposed on youth ministry is found in the call for intergenerational or family-based church as the primary model.[81] This is a view of church that focuses on the congregation as the centre of gravity of church life and operates from the assumption that the whole church family should be present together in one place at the same time. There are echoes of this approach in Ashton and Moon's assumptions about young people and the Church highlighted above. The problem at the heart of these approaches is that, despite calls for inclusivity,[82] they can inevitably result in young people adapting to fit in with the requirements of the congregation.

There are occasional moments in the youth ministry literature, however, that try to break out of the assumed or imposed categories. *Four Views of Youth Ministry and the Church*,[83] for example, presents four different approaches and visions of the Church and creates space for conversation between proponents of each. This undoubtedly offers a more nuanced way of dealing with the issue; however, each individual view can be seen to make either assumptions or impositions on youth ministry in relation to the Church. Both of these approaches, to assume and to impose, fall into the trap within broader ecclesiological work identified by Ward and discussed in Chapter 1, that: 'It becomes acceptable to make assertions where there is no evidence. We assume a common perception of contemporary church life between author and reader. We base whole arguments on anecdote and the selective treatment of experience.'[84]

Here, I focus on the Church within youth ministry without either assuming an understanding of the Church is agreed or by imposing a view on the youth ministry of Urban Saints. Rather, I heed Ward's warning to only make assertions and claims where the evidence of the research data leads, and then humbly point towards possibilities. This is not to say there is a total absence of rigorous empirical qualitative research on youth ministry practice; however, these studies tend to allude to the ecclesiological at the edge of their central research questions. Studies employing qualitative approaches have tended to be focused in one of three ways. First, by adding a qualitative element to a quantitative study to try and understand why young people are leaving the Church;[85] second, by exploring how young people understand the role of faith in their life and in what things they tend to put their faith;[86] and third, by looking at a particular aspect of Christian work with young people, such as identity formation or the role of worship.[87]

These approaches, which each allude to ecclesiological significance within youth ministry, provide an interesting picture of the relationship between young people and the Church as it exists with actual young people involved in youth work settings and churches. Further, Emery-Wright's work suggests that where young people are engaged in communities of authentic Christian practice, they are willing to engage with the claims of the Christian faith.[88] This corresponds with the findings of the *Faith of Generation Y* research that the 'deceptively simple' solution to young people's indifference to the Christian faith is involvement in authentic Christian community.[89]

Developing this, Shepherd suggests that it is important not only that youth groups function as a genuine Christian community for the faith development of young people, but also that the group should be embedded within a larger 'ecology of faith'.[90] Consequently, he raises questions about the wider life of the Church for youth ministry, including ones concerning the relationship of a youth group to this ecology of faith. These questions were beyond the scope of Shepherd's thesis but, taken together, these studies point strongly to the importance of Christian community in young people's Christian identity, and that a faithful transmission of faith to them best takes place where they feel this authentic community exists. In addition, the presence of certain practices seems to identify a community as Christian.

Building on this critique of youth ministry that assumes, imposes or alludes to ecclesiological reflections, David Bailey has recently made a helpful contribution to the pursuit of good theological thinking for youth ministry that helps to frame and understand what is going on in these various limited approaches to ecclesiological thinking within and for youth ministry. Bailey has coined the phrase 'theological shorthand' to describe the phenomenon of ministry practice being informed by mere fragments of theology, disconnected from a wider or deeper theological tradition. These fragments represent a 'thin' theology. The strength of Bailey's work is that it is drawn from attending patiently to the contours, rhythms and stories of youth ministry practice itself rather than being an imposed or assumed theological approach.[91]

Bailey's contention is that there are two ways in which this theological shorthand can operate – one is that it becomes the theological expression that sustains youth ministry practice. This, he argues, is risky as it is relying on thin, fragmented theology to sustain the challenging practice of ministry among young people; the second approach, however, is that these fragments operate as 'icons of epistemology' that can draw our gaze along and into the riches of the Christian tradition in order that our understanding, and therefore underpinning, of ministry practice might be enhanced. Bailey then uses the interpretive lens of theological shorthand to analyse youth ministry practice further through looking at the content of worship songs and ready-to-use meeting guides. In this analysis of meeting guides, Bailey acknowledges the way that 'church' can be used as a form of theological shorthand without further reflection – in particular, he notes the way that there is no reference to specific ecclesial tradition within the resources looking at the doctrine of the Church. Church, Bailey's analysis suggests, is taken to be a single homogenous thing when explored within youth ministry (and conversely, it follows, that youth ministry is taken to be a single homogenous thing regardless of the ecclesial tradition within which it is located).

This is clearly problematic and Bailey's solution is to ensure that youth ministry becomes reconnected with the riches of the Christian tradition. There is much within Bailey's analysis and framing of the fragmentation of theology within youth ministry that is immensely helpful to the task of this book – by calling out thin theology and a reliance on shorthand expressions, or understandings, to inform ministry, Bailey's work offers a timely reminder of the need for rigour in the way that theology and ministry interact. This is precisely the task of this book – to think rigorously about the Church and young people in a way that moves beyond the imposed, assumed or implied. There is, however, an inherent risk in Bailey's work of thinking about the Church and young people. By calling for a move through the expression of youth ministry to the riches of Christian tradition, Bailey's intended thickening of theology in work with young people might result in a short-circuited process in which an understanding of church is drawn in its entirety from the tradition, and becomes an imposed or assumed ecclesiological foundation – thus ignoring the potential contribution of young people themselves and work with them. An example of this is *Looking Good Naked*[92] – in pursuing the important task of seeking to relocate an ecclesiology for youth ministry in the biblical tradition through the lens of the Pauline image of the body of Christ, Andy Du Feu wrestles with what this might look like but does not seek to tackle the constructive question of what work with young people has to offer *to* an understanding of what it is to be the body of Christ. This is all the more frustrating given the metaphor of the body specifically suggests that all parts are considered to develop a faithful understanding of the whole.

As argued in Chapter 1 it is precisely this conversational contribution that this book is looking to address. If God is at work by his Spirit within and outside the Church today, and if this means that all of creation is in some way participating in these movements of God, then this needs to be brought into the task of theological reflection and construction. An ecclesiology for working with young people needs to also be an ecclesiology from and with them. And as this move is made the ecclesiology from and with young people will become a gift to the whole Church, and lead to a richer understanding of what it is to be church for all. The idea of theological shorthand and the critique it brings is helpful to the task of this book as it is a call to move beyond thin theology – to move beyond the imposed, assumed or implied – in our thinking about church and young people. What is required, though, to make this move beyond is not only to look beyond the shorthand theological statements to the riches of our Christian tradition, but also then to draw that tradition into dialogue with practice in order that both might be enriched. This is crucial in ensuring accountability in an interweaving ecclesiology and is explored further in the relational moves that regulate the interweaving in Chapter 8.

The gap in recent ecclesiological moves

Having detailed the limited way in which the youth ministry literature, building on inherited practice, reflects on the theology of the Church, this section now examines the gap in our thinking from the other direction: the way that recent ecclesiological moves do not bring the ecclesial imagination of youth ministry to bear on their reflections.

Rowan Williams has said that 'church is what happens when people encounter the Risen Jesus and commit themselves to deepening and sustaining that encounter in their encounter with each other'.[93] He acknowledges that this definitional point of departure for ecclesiology allows room for 'theological diversity, rhythm and style'[94] in how church is expressed. Consequently, it is possible for the community of a youth group in which participants encounter Jesus, and sustain their faith in him through the encounters and practices of the group, to have some ecclesiological value. This might be especially true as the youth group also considers its place in the wider ecology of faith.[95] The implication here is that ecclesiological reflection is a previously unacknowledged component to faith transmission with young people, yet a vital one.

While there is this gap in much ecclesiological thinking, recent moves in missional ecclesiology, with a particular focus on the Fresh Expressions movement in the UK, grew out of a desire to close the gap between the Church and contemporary society.[96] This gap is often framed in terms of perceived shifts in cultural climate, usually termed as the move from modernity to postmodernity and from Christendom to a post-Christendom context.[97] The language of the secular social imaginary is largely missing as is any acknowledgement of the key claim from Chapter 2 that young people operate as cultural interpreters. Fresh Expressions, however, seek to respond to the perceived gap by planting new forms of church that are envisioned to be primarily for those who are not already Christians or churchgoers.[98] The movement is about a 'reforming re-imagination of the Church'.[99] Each individual fresh expression is intended to look different, shaped by its local context, rather than beginning with a prior model of church.[100] In this way they are to be churches born out of mission, or are mission-shaped. The intention is that these newly planted fresh expressions of church have as much legitimacy as traditional parish churches within the Anglican Communion.[101] A 'mixed economy' in church life has been proposed and much discussed to allow inherited and new forms of church to exist with equal standing and legitimacy.[102] Fresh Expressions of church were initially anticipated to demonstrate maturity by becoming self-propagating, self-governing and self-financing, though the language has developed somewhat to suggest that 'ecclesial communities' with potential to become churches is more appropriate language to use.[103] Essentially though, they are seen as 'new ways of living out and communicating the Gospel'; this, however, raises a number of questions about what it means to be the Church.[104] These are vital questions that I return to in Part 3 of this book.

Fresh Expressions are just one aspect of wider moves within the UK and USA that have sought to reshape the Church to better connect with contemporary life.[105] These moves to reshape church are predicated on perceived changes to the way in which people live and connect within contemporary life. With a focus on networks rather than geography it is argued that an individual's relationships and time no longer centre on a local community but on an array of interest groups, activities, friends and colleagues, none of which need be within the locality of their home. Proponents of Fresh Expressions extend this thinking into church life and consequently render the parish model as outdated, no longer adequate to attend to the way that individuals live their lives.[106] While these moves in church life are seen as relational and incarnational,[107] they are also strongly challenged as a misreading of contemporary society with the counterclaim that the parish model itself is intrinsically incarnational as a result of its local emphasis.[108]

There is some connection between these ecclesiological movements and work among young people. The influence, for example, of youth congregations in shaping their missiological emphasis is documented.[109] Similarly, there are influential voices within the Fresh Expressions movement who developed their understanding of the Church and mission, at least in part, through work with and reflection on young people.[110] There are also examples of established Fresh Expression churches that are predominantly aimed at young people. However, an ecclesial imagination drawn from reflection on the way Christian youth groups run is largely absent from these conversations. This fundamental gap in our thinking, on both sides – youth ministry and ecclesiology – is all the more peculiar given the shared rationale to communicate the gospel relevantly to sections of society unreached by conventional church. This means they share a discursive space that allows the possibility of mutual contributions from the dialogue. Indeed, it has been identified that Fresh Expressions are asking the same questions that have been asked by Christians working with young people.[111]

Consequently, I hope this book will make a contribution to both Christian work with young people and the debate around appropriate ecclesiology for contemporary contexts. This contribution will be made in two steps: first, by revealing the underlying interweaving ecclesiology that describes the ecclesial imagination inherent within youth ministry; and second, by demonstrating the way that this interweaving ecclesiology constructively develops conversations about the Church.

Summary

This chapter concludes Part 1 by arguing that there is a gap in our thinking around the Church, mission and young people. This gap is best articulated by reflecting on the lack of writing on these three – the Church, mission, young people – together. The writing that there is on young people and the Church tends towards one of three typical approaches: an assumed approach in which there is a shared ecclesiological understanding between author and reader; an imposed approach in which an ecclesiological approach is applied for work with young people; and an alluded approach in which ecclesiological reflection is hinted at but not directly part of the discussion. None of these approaches acknowledges the ecclesial imagination inherent within the development and praxis of youth ministry, as exemplified through the story of Crusaders/ Urban Saints. In particular, it outlines the way that a form of Christian life fostering faith was established outside the boundaries of churches and denominations before being drawn into the life of the churches and becoming normative for much of the Church's work with young people. These are key things missing from the conversation about the Church, mission and young people.

The constructive work in Parts 2 and 3 of this book seeks a different approach by developing a theological approach to the Church and young people that draws on the practical wisdom of work with them in conversation with contemporary missional ecclesiology. This will allow a flexible ecclesial posture that also takes account of the theological and sociological foundations discussed in Chapters 1 and 2. These foundations argue that from both perspectives a dialogical approach is needed that takes into account reflection on the participative nature of God and the hermeneutical location of young people. These perspectives together with the review of literature above suggest that the lack of ecclesiological reflection that draws on the actual practice of work among young people is a gap that needs addressing – and addressing in a particular way. This will begin in Part 2 with an ethnographic account of the practice of two youth groups to draw out the operant and espoused theological approach to the Church.

Notes

1 Pete Ward, *Growing Up Evangelical* (London: SPCK, 1996), p. 8.

2 An exception to this is John Hall, 'The Rise of the Youth Congregation and its Missiological Significance', PhD thesis, Birmingham, 2003.

3 Nick Shepherd, *Faith Generation: Retaining Young People and Growing the Church* (London: SPCK, 2016).

4 Sylvia Collins-Mayo, Bob Mayo and Sally Nash, *The Faith of Generation Y* (London: Church House Publishing, 2010), p. ix.

5 See, for example, Andrew Root, *Revisiting Relational Youth Ministry* (Downers Grove, IL: InterVarsity Press, 2007) for the US perspective. A helpful – though now quite old – UK angle can be found in Ward, *Growing Up*.

6 See www.urbansaints.org/history.

7 Ward, *Growing Up*, pp. 27–30.

8 Ward, *Growing Up*, p. 27.

9 Nigel Sylvester, *God's Word in a Young World: The Story of Scripture Union* (London: Scripture Union, 2017), pp. 13–17.

10 Crusaders, 'Notes on the History of Crusader Classes (Pt1)', *The Crusader*, 1906. I am extremely grateful to Urban Saints for granting me unlimited access to their archive. The documents cited in this section were accessible due to this kindness.

11 Albert Kestin, in *Extracts from Annual Letters 1895* (CMS, 1895).

12 Crusaders, 'Leaders Conference Minutes, 20th March 1907' (1907).

13 Albert Kestin, 'Looking Back', *The Crusader*, 1919.

14 Kestin, 'Looking Back'.

15 The archive records of the Church Missionary Society show that Mr E. S. Daniell served in Uganda in 1903–4: CMS, 'Church Missionary Society Archive: Index to Printed Volumes of *Extracts from the Annual Letters of the Missionaries* (1886–1912), Part I: 1886–1904', ed. Birmingham University Cadbury Research Library (1886–1904).

16 Albert Kestin in *Extracts from Annual Letters 1902* (CMS, 1902).

17 Crusaders, 'Notes on the History of Crusader Classes (Pt1)'.

18 Crusaders, 'Notes on the History of Crusader Classes (Pt1)'.

19 Crusaders, 'Notes on the History of Crusader Classes (Pt2)', *The Crusader*, November 1906; Kestin, 'Looking Back'.

20 Crusaders, 'Notes on the History of Crusader Classes (Pt1)'.

21 Crusaders, 'Notes on the History of Crusader Classes (Pt2)'.

22 Kestin's return at this time was not planned but instead, according to the gentleman who took over his CMS work in Calcutta, was due to ill health. See the Revd B. Grundy in *Extracts from Annual Letters 1906* (CMS, 1906).

23 The name 'Crusaders' came about quite by chance. According to two official histories of the movement, Kestin came across a picture in a book of a medieval Crusader with the motto 'Be Strong' and, finding the image appealing for an invitation card he was preparing for his Bible class, acquired the printing block for the picture. Thus the Bible class became the Crouch End Crusaders and the name spread as further classes were launched (see Jason Watford, *Yesterday and Today: A History of Crusaders* (Crusaders, 1995), pp. 2–4).

24 Watford, *Yesterday and Today*, p. 5. By the end of 1906 there were 19 classes in existence.

25 Featuring the illustration first used by Kestin in his invitation cards for the Crouch End class.

26 Crusaders, 'Leaders Conference Minutes, 29th March 1906'.

27 Crusaders, 'Leaders Conference Minutes, 29th March 1906'. These men were the now Revd Ovens (mentioned above in connection with the Crouch End class), a Mr S. F. Ford and a Mr F. E. Keay. Both Ovens and Ford were linked with CMS in particular (see CMS, 'Church Missionary Society Archive: Index to Printed Volumes of Extracts from the Annual Letters of the Missionaries (1886–1912), Part II: 1905–1912', ed. Birmingham University Cadbury Research Library).

28 See the reflections of Watford, *Yesterday and Today*, p. 12.

29 Crusaders, 'Leaders Conference Minutes, 29th March 1906'.

30 Crusaders, 'Leaders Conference Minutes, 29th March 1906'.

31 Mark H. Senter, III, *The Coming Revolution in Youth Ministry* (Wheaton, IL: Victor Books, 1992), pp. 62–6.

32 Root, *Revisiting Relational Youth Ministry*, p. 28.

33 Callum Brown, *Religion and Society in Twentieth Century Britain* (Abingdon: Routledge, 2014), p. 49.

34 Ward, *Growing Up*, p. 24; and Naomi Thompson, *Young People and Church since 1900: Engagement and Exclusion* (Abingdon: Routledge, 2018), pp. 27–62. Core among the aims of the Sunday school movement was Christian education and bringing the children to Christ. The pattern set by the Sunday schools of gathering children separately for Christian education and religious instruction was influential in the development of what Pete Ward calls 'youth fellowship work' where young people gather separately from the rest of the Christian fellowship.

35 David W. Bebbington, *Evangelicalism in Modern Britain: A History from the 1730s to the 1980s* (Abingdon: Routledge, 1988), p. 123.

36 Crusaders, 'Leaders Conference Minutes, 29th March 1906'; Watford, *Yesterday and Today*, p. 1.

37 Ward, *Growing Up*, p. 29.

38 Its origins as a movement have been dated to the 1730s (see Bebbington, *Evangelicalism*, p. 1). Use of the term to describe a strand

of the Christian faith, however, goes further back to the sixteenth century (Alister McGrath, *Evangelicalism & the Future of Christianity* (London: Hodder and Stoughton, 1996)).

39 Ward, *Growing Up*, p. 6; also Leanne Van Dyk, 'The Church in Evangelical Theology and Practice', in *The Cambridge Companion to Evangelical Theology*, ed. Timothy Larsen and Daniel J. Treier (Cambridge: Cambridge University Press, 2007), p. 128.

40 Bebbington, *Evangelicalism*, p. 3.

41 Ward, *Growing Up*, p. 23; Senter, *The Coming Revolution*, pp. 42–6.

42 Crusaders, 'Leaders Conference Minutes, 29th March 1906'.

43 McGrath, *Evangelicalism & the Future of Christianity*, p. 35.

44 Bebbington tells a story of the rising influence of evangelicalism in church life in Britain until the mid-nineteenth century, but highlights a 'contraction of evangelical influence' from the 1870s (see Bebbington, *Evangelicalism*, p. 141).

45 Bebbington, *Evangelicalism*, p. 146.

46 Stanley Grenz, *Renewing the Center: Evangelical Theology in a Post-Theological Era* (Grand Rapids, MI: Baker Books, 2006), p. 288.

47 Richard T. France and Alister McGrath, *Evangelical Anglicans* (London: SPCK, 1993), pp. 3–4.

48 Bruce Hindmarsh, 'Is Evangelical Ecclesiology an Oxymoron? A Historical Perspective', in *Evangelical Ecclesiology: Reality or Illusion?*, ed. John G. Stackhouse Jnr (Grand Rapids, MI: Baker Academic, 2003), p. 15.

49 Hindmarsh, 'Evangelical Ecclesiology', pp. 23–5.

50 Hindmarsh, 'Evangelical Ecclesiology', p. 25.

51 Crusaders, 'Leaders Conference Minutes, 20th March 1907'. Pete Ward discusses the significance of camps in the development of evangelical youth ministry more broadly in *Growing Up*, pp. 36–41.

52 Craig Dykstra, 'Pastoral and Ecclesial Imagination', in *For Life Abundant: Practical Theology, Theological Education, and Christian Ministry*, ed. Dorothy C. Bass and Craig Dykstra (Grand Rapids, MI: William B. Eerdmans, 2008), p. 57.

53 Dykstra, 'Pastoral and Ecclesial Imagination', p. 57.

54 Pete Ward, *Introducing Practical Theology: Mission, Ministry and the Life of the Church* (Grand Rapids, MI: Baker Academic, 2017), p. 110.

55 Scott MacDougall, *More Than Communion: Imagining an Eschatological Ecclesiology* (London: Bloomsbury T&T Clark, 2015), pp. 1–2.

56 Ward, *Growing Up*, p. 42.

57 Watford, *Yesterday and Today*, p. 88.

58 Ward, *Growing Up*, p. 49; Watford, *Yesterday and Today*, p. 89.

59 David Bailey, *Youth Ministry and Theological Shorthand: Living Amongst the Fragments of a Coherent Theology* (Eugene, OR: Pickwick Publications, 2019), p. 148.

60 Jonny Baker, 'Youth Ministry Changes More Than You Know', in *Global Youth Ministry: Reaching Adolescents Around the World*, ed. Terry Linhart and David Livermore (Grand Rapids, MI: Zondervan, 2011), p. 51.

61 Sally Nash, *Youth Ministry: A Multi-Faceted Approach* (London: SPCK, 2011), p. xvii.

62 Ruth Perrin, *Changing Shape: The Faith Life of Millennials* (London: SCM Press, 2020).

63 Kenda Creasy Dean and Ron Foster, *The Godbearing Life: The Art of Soul Tending for Youth Ministry* (Nashville, TN: Upper Room Books, 1998), p. 30.

64 Dean and Foster, *Godbearing*, p. 30.

65 Mark Ashton and Phil Moon, *Christian Youth Work* (Chorley: Authentic Media, 2007), p. 117.

66 Ward, *Growing Up*, p. 143.

67 Ashton and Moon, *Christian Youth Work*, p. 114.

68 Ashton and Moon, *Christian Youth Work*, p. 114.

69 Ashton and Moon, *Christian Youth Work*, p. 115.

70 Ashton and Moon, *Christian Youth Work*, p. 115.

71 Ashton and Moon, *Christian Youth Work*, p. 115.

72 Pete Ward, *Youthwork and the Mission of God: Frameworks for Relational Outreach* (London: SPCK, 1997), pp. 7–11.

73 Doug Fields, *Purpose Driven Youth Ministry* (Grand Rapids, MI: Zondervan, 1998).

74 Rick Warren, *Purpose Driven Church* (Grand Rapids, MI: Zondervan, 1995).

75 See, for example, the role of youth congregations in shaping the missiological approach of the wider church in Hall, 'The Rise of the Youth Congregation'.

76 Tim Sudworth, Graham Cray and Chris Russell, *Mission-shaped Youth: Rethinking Young People and Church* (London: Church House Publishing, 2007).

77 Sudworth, Cray and Russell, *Mission-shaped Youth*, p. 8 and pp. 96–7.

78 Jo Pimlott and Nigel Pimlott, *Youth Work After Christendom* (Milton Keynes: Paternoster Press, 2008).

79 Stuart Murray, *Church After Christendom* (Milton Keynes: Paternoster Press, 2004).

80 Murray, *Church After Christendom*, pp. 141–2.

81 See Mark DeVries, *Family-Based Youth Ministry* (Downers Grove, IL: InterVarsity Press, 1994); Jason Gardner, *Mend the Gap: Can the Church Reconnect the Generations?* (Nottingham: IVP, 2008).

82 For example, Malan Nel, *Youth Ministry: An Inclusive Congregational Approach* (Pretoria: Design Books, 2000).

83 Mark H. Senter, III et al., *Four Views of Youth Ministry and the Church* (Grand Rapids, MI: Zondervan, 2001).

84 Pete Ward, *Perspectives on Ecclesiology and Ethnography* (Grand Rapids, MI: William B. Eerdmans, 2012), p. 4.

85 For example, Peter Brierley, *Reaching and Keeping Tweenagers* (London: Christian Research, 2003).

86 For example, Collins-Mayo, Mayo and Nash, *Faith of Generation Y*.

87 For example, Steven Emery-Wright, 'A Qualitative Study Construction of How 14–16 Year Olds Understand Worship', *Journal of Youth and Theology*, 2(2) (2003); Shepherd, *Faith Generation*.

88 Emery-Wright, 'A Qualitative Study Construction', p. 76.

89 Collins-Mayo, Mayo and Nash, *Faith of Generation Y*, p. 98.

90 Nick Shepherd, *Faith Generation: Retaining Young People and Growing the Church*, p. 85 (ebook version).

91 Bailey, *Youth Ministry and Theological Shorthand*, pp. 87–120.

92 Andy Du Feu, *Looking Good Naked: Youth Work and the Body of Christ* (Eugene, OR: Resource Publications, 2020).

93 In Archbishops' Council, *Mission-shaped Church: Church Planting and Fresh Expressions of Church in a Changing Context* (London: Church House Publishing, 2004), p. vii.

94 Archbishops' Council, *Mission-shaped Church*, p. vii.

95 In the foreword to *Mission-shaped Church*, Williams also acknowledges the need for churches to learn from one another in the proposed diversity, thus endorsing consideration of the wider ecology of faith.

96 In large part the motivation behind Fresh Expressions is a decline in church attendance that has been taking place within the Church of England for nearly a century (Bob Jackson, *Hope for the Church* (London: Church House Publishing, 2002), p. 1). Often this has been reported with dramatic headlines and provocative language. It is a 'time bomb' (Archbishops' Council, *Mission-shaped Church*, p. 40) in which various denominations are at risk of 'meltdown', leading to their predicted non-existence within a generation (Brierley, *Reaching and Keeping Tweenagers*, p. 1). The talk of a time bomb refers specifically to the drop in the number of children and young people involved in church life.

97 A significant amount of the literature discussing contemporary ecclesiology in the UK devotes time to discussing postmodernity, post-Christendom or both. For a focus on postmodernity see, for example, Pete Ward, *Liquid Church* (Milton Keynes: Paternoster Press, 2002); Graeme Fancourt, *Brand New Church? The Church and the Postmodern Condition* (London: SPCK, 2013); John Drane, *After*

McDonaldization: Mission, Ministry and Christian Discipleship in an Age of Uncertainty (London: Darton, Longman and Todd, 2008). For more of a post-Christendom focus, see, for example, *Fresh! An Introduction to Fresh Expressions of Church and Pioneer Ministry*, ed. David Goodhew, Andrew Roberts and Michael Volland (London: SCM Press, 2012); Murray, *Church After Christendom*.

98 Michael Moynagh, *Church for Every Context* (London: SCM Press, 2012), p. xiv.

99 With 'faithfulness to the past and contextual faithfulness to the present held together', George Lings, 'The Day of Small Things: An Analysis of Fresh Expressions of Church in 21 Dioceses of the Church of England' (Church Army, 2016), p. 9.

100 Archbishops' Council, *Mission-shaped Church*, p. 105.

101 Known as 'inherited church' within *Mission-shaped Church* and more widely.

102 I look at the mixed economy in detail in Part 3. The benefits and challenges of this concept are much discussed. See, for example, Moynagh, *Church for Every Context*, pp. 431–47; Andrew Davison and Alison Milbank, *For the Parish: A Critique of Fresh Expressions* (London: SCM Press, 2010), pp. 73–5; Stephen Conway, 'Generous Episcopacy', in *Generous Ecclesiology: Church, World and the Kingdom of God*, ed. Julie Gittoes, Brutus Green and James Heard (London: SCM Press, 2013), p. 25.

103 Michael Moynagh, *Church in Life: Innovation, Mission and Ecclesiology* (London: SCM Press, 2017).

104 Archbishops' Council and the Trustees for Methodist Church Purposes, *Fresh Expressions in the Mission of the Church* (London: Church House Publishing, 2012), p. vii.

105 See, for example, the vast literature discussing the emerging church movement and other forms of missional church.

106 Archbishops' Council, *Mission-shaped Church*, pp. 1–15.

107 Cathy Ross and David Dadswell, 'Church Growth Research Project: Church Planting' (Ripon College, Cuddesdon: Oxford Centre for Ecclesiology and Practical Theology, 2013), p. 29.

108 Davison and Milbank, *For the Parish*, pp. 52–6.

109 Hall, 'Rise of the Youth Congregation'.

110 For example, Graham Cray and Jonny Baker.

111 Collins-Mayo, Mayo and Nash, *Faith of Generation Y*, p. 100.

PART 2

The Case Studies

4

An Interweaving Ecclesiology in Practice: Presenting the Case Studies

It's an interweaving thing.[1]

The first two chapters of Part 2 detail the thick description and initial analysis of two in-depth case studies that begin to draw out the espoused and operant theological voices of this project while also beginning to articulate the inherent ecclesial imagination contained within youth ministry praxis. It is here that the concept of an interweaving ecclesiology will begin to become apparent. Consequently, these chapters begin the task of theological construction that builds on the theological, sociological and practical foundations of Part 1. This task of construction starts with the praxis of youth ministry as explored through two case studies in order that these voices, which are more often obscured as a result of the dominance of formal and normative theology, speak first into the conversation. This positioning is of course a deliberate choice on my part and makes explicit that which was unpacked in the theological rationale – the way that discerning participation in the life of God in the present is a vital part of the theological task, and that this is the case for good theological reasons.

The case for foregrounding praxis in theological construction is perhaps even more significant in the specific discipline of ecclesiology, given what was discussed in Chapter 1 about the way ecclesiology has often developed by way of wrestling with key questions of its era. The focus on amplifying the voice of praxis is vital to ensure that the affective gravitational pull of the Church is not felt too strongly as practice becomes distilled and unpacked through various analytical moves.[2] It is also significant that these espoused and operant voices contain, at least in part, the voices of young people. These are voices that are not often invited to the table of theological construction – they are non-elites who construct meaning in practice but can be overlooked.[3] They are also, as argued in Chapter 2, those on the forefront of meaning-making within contemporary culture and consequently need to be considered. As already highlighted, while writing on race, racial identity and racism in the USA, Montague R. Williams identified the way that churches tend towards underestimating, dismissing or forgetting the experiences of young people in their midst.[4] My intention in foregrounding praxis in the task of theological construction is that this tendency is then avoided.

The two in-depth case studies highlight the role of youth groups as potential ecclesial spaces within which participants (young people and leaders) are able to engage in Christian practices, become awakened afresh to the possibility of transcendence and, through this, connect with Christ in community. In addition, the case studies signpost how these potential ecclesial spaces can form part of the life of church as they weave together, in and out, with other forms of ecclesial life – this is the interweaving ecclesiology. This combined voice of young people and youth leaders brings a practical wisdom, an ecclesial imagination developed through praxis, that provides the building blocks for this chapter and the subsequent chapters in Part 2.

Specifically, the research demonstrates the way that youth groups offer various modes of belonging – social space, safe space, multi-generational relationships and engagement with a broader tradition – that draw young people in, allowing them to access the group easily. They are also places within which participants can engage in simple Christian practices. The interplay of these modes of belonging and Christian practices creates an ambiguous space that can be both church and not church. Regular practices of youth ministry – creating fun, welcome and encouraging questions – operate as interruptions that open participants to the possibility of connection with Christ and therefore engagement with the Church. This experience is not uniform, though, because for some participants the groups are not aspects of church at all and remain youth groups. However, as youth groups they still play a role in identity formation and friendship development for the young people – the modes of belonging still operate.

By offering the possibility of providing an experience of Christian community, but only as the young people choose to utilize the groups in this way, the groups offer the possibility of an experience of church, but in and of themselves are not aiming to be churches – this is the heart of what it means to describe the groups as 'potential ecclesial spaces'. Intriguingly, the research uncovers the way that the groups provide vital expressions of Christian community for the leaders as well as the young people themselves. In addition, this experience of Christian community is multi-faceted, as it is within the group itself but also, where the groups are part of an organization or network, the sense of Christian community expands out into the network in the present and through connection to the past, thus providing something of a tradition to which participants belong. This discovery is crucial in moving the conversation on from being solely about youth ministry and towards a vision for church with an interweaving framework. The groups in and of themselves are quite normal and much of what is presented as their usual practice will be of no surprise – what is important is the task of teasing out the underlying theological themes and ecclesial imagination at work.

Having provided an overview of the two case study groups in the Introduction, this chapter begins with the modes of belonging and develops a description of the groups' practice from there. In many ways there is little about the groups that is unique or distinct from many young people's groups being led by Christians and churches up and down the country; what this chapter is, though, is a work of ethnography that, through the particular mode of looking described in Chapter 1, brings things to light in a new way.

Modes of belonging

On my first observation at St Joe's I sat and chatted with Linda, one of the regular attendees among the young people, as she watched the sports going on during free time. During the conversation, I asked her why she started going to Crusaders and she simply replied that she 'wanted something to belong to'.[5] This idea of the groups providing a place to belong stuck with me through the case study research. Out of this conversation, the term 'modes of belonging' developed to provide a framework for describing the reasons why young people stayed connected to the groups. Such a framework is important as it became apparent that the groups articulated multiple purposes and identities, some more dominant than others. Upon analysis it is clear that the groups are capable of offering different things to different people at different times. Central to this variety, however, are the ways in which different people, young people and leaders, develop a sense of attachment to the groups; these modes of belonging are categorized into four main headings:

1 Social space
2 Safe space
3 Intergenerational significance / leadership development
4 Connection with a broader tradition

Social space

The two groups in the case studies share the quality, not uncommon when creating groups for young people, of the space in the groups being seen by them as 'their' space. This is the essence of the groups as 'social spaces' – that not everything that happens through a group evening is dictated for the young people; instead, the praxis of the groups intentionally enables those in them to have some ownership. This is experienced by the young people as the groups' social space allows both fun and friendships to be cultivated. Further, the ethnographic approach brings to light the way that the leaders value these things as well. In addition, basic as these things might seem, they are crucial in enabling the more complex and obviously ecclesial practices in the groups.

According to Stuart, main leader at Newtown, groups need to be places where the young people are 'just relaxed and they know they are going to have fun'. This is essential, Stuart says, because '[with] youth work, if you're not thinking fun then you're not going to have any youth work, are you – I hope we have lots of fun and laughter.' The importance of fun is high on the agenda on an average Friday night. By way of example, at the end of one pre-session run-through, an emerging leader, Lucy, prayed specifically that the evening would be fun for those coming along. In a similar way at St Joe's, Richard and Peter discuss how the games are one of the main reasons the young people come and that one way of measuring the success of the group is whether those in it are enjoying themselves. Indeed, the significance of fun and games is that it provides a reason for them to be there. The opportunity to meet people, and through that make friends, is also important, and it is the social space of the group that allows this to happen. For Alison this is in contrast to her experience of church:

> [At church] we go out to the back and then go into our separate groups so you don't really see the others. With [St Joe's] you do the games afterwards and, like, socialize with them.

Similarly, making friends is given as one of the most important aspects at Newtown. Stuart, the main leader at the time, expresses simply the desire for Newtown to be somewhere 'where friendship grows and develops'. It is clear in talking to the young people that this happens and they regard the friendships they build through the group as particularly significant. They expect them to be 'friends for life' and 'friends that will last forever'.[6] Even when not talking of the friendships formed at the group in such terms, they still recognize something different about these friendships compared to those formed elsewhere. Christian expresses this well:

> The people here are quite friendly ... and it's completely different than if you've had a day at school or college or in 6th form and it's been all rough, then you've come here and the people that are here are genuinely nice people.

The social space of the group provides a place in which this building of friendship occurs not just between young people, but also between leaders. This is something I was initially sceptical about; however, during one observation at Newtown when I entered the lounge during free time I saw three leaders and one young person sitting on the sofas together. The young person, Michael, was not engaged in conversation with the leaders and was comfortably spending the time on his phone while the leaders chatted and laughed together. I sat down with them and my initial scepticism subsided somewhat as I sensed that this was clearly an important social space for them, just as it is with the young people.

Importantly, the significance of the groups as social spaces is seen as more than an end in itself – the fun and friendships serve a larger purpose. Stuart hopes that the group is fun and may act as an introduction to church and help change young people's perceptions of church:

> It's supposed to be fun and an introduction to the fact that church isn't necessarily the stereotyped image of somewhere dark and stone walls and cold and all that kind of thing ... it is running around inside the building and throwing gunge at each other and things like that, that's church.

Implicit within this thinking is a critique of church – specifically that church tends not to be fun and the groups need to demonstrate something different in order to connect young people, not just with one another but with the Christian faith. This was communicated more starkly by young people at St Joe's.[7] Alison and Helen, for example, express similar viewpoints:

> Alison: It is getting more people involved I think because it's a funner [sic] way to do it with, like, the crafts afterwards

and the activities in the gym. I think it's better than going to church on a Sunday.

Helen: [St Joe's] has got the game aspect of it so it's a bit more fun learning I find. There's a lot more interaction – maybe like a few more games. At church it's definitely a bit more serious.

For others, the contrast is not communicated so sharply, but the opportunity for fun and games alongside the Bible study is a significant part of the experience. In relation to the inter-weaving ecclesiology that emerges from analysis of the case study data, the social space of the groups, exhibited through fun and friendship, allows the groups to be places that the young people recognize as being theirs. Further analysis of the thick description from the groups in the next chapter goes on to reveal the way that creating fun specifically operates as one of the practices of interruption, opening young people to the possibility of transcendence and the groups as Christian community through interaction with the more ecclesial practices. In this way the experience of the group as 'theirs' facilitates an experience of Christian community that communicates something vital to the young people participating in it – that there is space for them, there is room for them. This leads to the second mode of belonging.

Safe place

As implied in the way the social space of the groups creates ownership, the groups in turn provide what could be termed a safe place for the young people. This is demonstrated in three ways. First, as a place where those coming along feel comfortable being themselves; second, through creating space for them to ask questions without judgement; and third, for those with church backgrounds the groups provide a place to explore and cultivate the Christian faith away from negative experiences in congregational church life.

Within Newtown, the concept of safe place is shown by the group providing a place that allows young people to be themselves. The idea of creating a safe place for them to express themselves away from criticism and judgement is a recurring theme. Stuart describes Newtown as a 'safe place for young people who only know Jesus as a swear word'; Judy contends that it is both 'a safe place to hang out and a safe place to find out about God if they want to open up'; and David thinks of the group as a place that is 'first and foremost a safe place ... that you know you're not going to feel any way threatened or made to feel insecure'.

The safety of the group is communicated through the use of words such as 'community' and 'family'. Beth told me about what she sees as the 'community' of the group. When asked what she means by this she explains that there is no 'hierarchy ... everyone is equal [and] it's not like you see leaders as leaders, they're more people you can get along with'. The group was also described as being like a family in terms of the way people relate to one another – this is true for young people and leaders alike. For Andrew, the group is akin to 'a big family' in which the boundaries that might normally be expected in a youth group are blurred because the people 'are not like leader and young person [rather] you are all part of a family'. Reinforcing this, one of the young people told me that 'what [Newtown] mostly means is family; it's like a second family'.

In both groups, young people feel valued and welcomed regardless of circumstances. This can be through something as simple as not being made to feel that it is a problem when they arrive late. In fact, contrary to it being made a negative, Victoria is perfectly happy to stop the teaching to welcome a latecomer and to ask how they are before summing up the session so far and getting back to the teaching from where she had left off. It never failed to amaze me just how much Victoria knows about each of the young people. She knows their family situation, their interests, the details of their school life, as well as their hopes and plans for the future. The consistency of Victoria being the leader for the older ones in the group week after week ensures that this welcome and value is consistent.

These young people know that at St Joe's they will find someone who is interested in them and happy to see them.[8] In this
way, they experience the group as a safe place.

Both groups seek to express the safety of the groups for
young people by cultivating an environment in which asking
questions is encouraged and valued – at Newtown, the group
night was sometimes introduced in this way, as a place where
the young people can 'genuinely ask questions', this being
expressed at the start of one group night. Beth's story serves
to illustrate the success of this ethos. Having been drawn to
Newtown through the invitation of a friend she describes one
of the leaders as the only Christian she knew who was willing
to explain to her why they believed what they did. Initially, she
felt on the outside before feeling part of the group, and critical
among the factors that helped her make this transition was the
way that Newtown allowed her to 'be an atheist in the middle
of a Christian church'. During small-group discussion time one
evening, she expressed this same thing succinctly by describing
Newtown as a place where she can be herself and knows she is
accepted even when she speaks her mind.

At St Joe's, the teaching session always ends with the young
people being asked if they have any questions. The leaders are
pleased if they do as this fits in with the desire for them to
discover and develop their own understanding of the Christian
faith. Sometimes there are no questions but on many occasions
there are – this is always encouraged by ensuring time is available to answer, though if it is past the time when the Bible
study is due to finish they do offer the others in the group the
chance to leave. They tend not to take up this option, seem-
ingly realizing the importance of this time in the group's ethos.

Significantly, the belonging provided by the groups as safe
places can create an environment in which the Christian
faith can be explored away from a context where it had
been tarnished by difficult experiences. This is demonstrated
by the experiences of some at St Joe's who joined the group
after experiencing difficult situations in churches they had
attended with their families. Sally spoke eloquently about this,
describing the way in which her parents both held positions

of responsibility in their local church and, from Sally's perspective, put up a front when at church in order to give people a better impression of the family than the reality. She also describes her frustration at being known as the churchwarden's daughter rather than a person in her own right.

Both Newtown and St Joe's provide a place of safety. This is expressed predominantly in their members' feeling comfortable to be themselves and not under pressure from others, a sense often exemplified in the freedom felt to ask questions and not to be pushed into viewpoints they don't hold. Whereas at St Joe's, the safety of the group was expressed through their being able to explore the Christian faith away from these, perhaps negative, experiences of church, within Newtown the safety was more in terms of the group being perceived as a place to explore faith while also being accepted for who they are.

Intergenerational significance / leadership development

In contrast to the vast majority of Christian youth groups, St Joe's encourages the 'intermingling' of different ages. This intermingling is important, says Victoria, and when entering the school sports hall during free time, seeing this mix of ages clearly having fun with the leaders, then experiencing it by joining in, I was struck by the sense that this is something quite unusual. The experiences of older teenager Timothy seem to reinforce this sense. He contrasts this aspect of St Joe's with his experiences of local church-based youth groups:

> In other youth groups they kind of split the ages up and don't allow the different ages to mingle and just be with everyone … Churches try to divide the ages up into like you're Year 10 and you can only be with those up to Year 13 and stuff, and you're Year 9 and you go with the younger kids and stuff. But it's not like that, there should be a time when you get to hang out with everyone, and everyone gets a chance to play and be involved with everyone.

This demonstrates the intriguing, yet vital, mode of belonging that can be described as intergenerational significance. This emerges differently in each group but with similar themes underlying the way it is expressed. The importance of this intermingling of ages at St Joe's goes beyond spending the social time together – when interviewed, Timothy went on to describe how the intergenerational intermingling has the effect of encouraging him to try and set an example for the younger ones, seeing himself as 'a bit of a role model'. It seems an informal sense of leadership development is happening. Sally experiences something similar in the context of the craft activities, saying, 'the older ones will help the younger ones do it and I don't know what it is, it is just kind of the way that it's not really a question'. The implication here is that this interaction is a natural and valued part of the group's culture, encouraging and deepening the belonging of the older teenagers – they talk positively about this in contrast to the way that conventional churches tend to segregate age groups more strictly. Those who have been in the group since they were younger value the way in which they got to learn from the seniors so the idea that the younger groups look up to them comes naturally.

There is a more formal process of leadership development in Newtown – as those in the group move through it to their older teenage years they can become emerging leaders. This involves them taking on some responsibility within the group and adds to the way these young people experience belonging. Becoming an emerging leader is seen as a way of 'growing more' if the young people want to and creates a means of deepening the relationships between these older young people and the adult leaders. There are a few aspects of being an emerging leader that create a particular sense of belonging for the attendees: responsibility, opportunity to grow and preparation for adulthood. Steve outlines the responsibility involved with the role, explaining that for him to be an emerging leader 'means quite a lot':

> It means you have to come here early and stay late; it means you have to do all the chairs and set the games room up but

it also means that you have to do some of the games, which lead up to the main talk, and I think last week some of us led small-group time as well.

Robin concurs with this but describes it in terms of having more to worry about:

When you just come to enjoy it you don't have to worry about the ins and outs and what's happening and running games and the numbers of people coming, but once you become a leader you worry if there's going to be enough people to do this game and is there going to be enough people coming full stop.

Often a leader and emerging leader will work together to lead an aspect of the group (but with no pressure for the emerging leaders to lead 'up front'). The safe place of the group, though, encourages emerging leaders to have a go, and at times developing the confidence to do something new is seen as a significant step in their 'journey' and is widely celebrated. Intriguingly, growth experienced is also in terms of the Christian faith with self-professed atheist Freddie recognizing that the extra responsibility and involvement that goes with being an emerging leader has helped to develop his thinking about the Christian faith and grow in this way.

Furthermore, intergenerational significance expresses the way that the belonging created by the groups extends to adult leaders and, in St Joe's especially, parents of the children and young people. At the end of the evening at St Joe's, as parents are collecting children and the clear-up has begun, there is a clear distinction between leaders who take on what could be called a pastoral role and those who stick to more practical tasks. These are not formal distinctions but seem to be how different leaders naturally engage – the most long-standing leaders such as Victoria, Richard and Dorothy are engaged in conversation with the many parents that are there. For these leaders, this time with parents, though informal and outside of the normal group time, is a significant part of the ministry and outreach of the group. I use the word 'ministry' deliberately as it is more than simply friendly conversation that occurs with these parents, who are mostly not from churched backgrounds but who are increasingly 'hanging around'.

This connection and ministry with parents is not an articulated, formal aim of St Joe's but is how the group has developed. There is a recognition among the leaders that this developing focus on adults, and thus on some of the whole families, is not the norm among youth and children's groups but, in their view, this doesn't make them a church – 'even though we're not a church, we do care for parents,' says Victoria at a leaders' meeting. There is a feeling as well that this 'not church' status that the group holds dearly actually makes it easier for some parents to be involved than if they were formally a church or a group that is part of the Church. Peter spoke up in one of the leaders' meetings to comment on how a new family involved 'might not associate [St Joe's] with the church' and that this had made it easier for them to feel comfortable.

For Newtown, intergenerational significance is shown in the role the group plays in the lives of the leaders. When interviewed, each of the core Newtown leaders spoke eloquently of the way in which being part of the team was a significant part of the experience of church relationships for them. In keeping with the experiences described above, Judy likens the relationships on the team to feeling like being 'part of a family'. Similar phrases, describing being part of the team as 'like a small group' and a place where 'we support each other', were commonplace. Additionally, some of the leaders talked of the way in which becoming involved in the group was a precursor to joining the wider life of the Church and provided a place of greater connection with God. For example:

> I didn't really come to church ... [the group] was almost my way in and it's been a bit of a journey. I never planned it this way, you know, as my involvement with [the youth group] has grown so I found myself drawn into the church, come regularly on Sundays ... What [Newtown] gave me the opportunity to do was to feel involved and it was through feeling involved and through doing something I suddenly felt

connected to God again in a way that I don't think I'd ever done up to that point and that sort of brought me in and as a result of that involvement I think I've enjoyed church a lot more in general.

This experience of a leader experiencing a connection with God through the group points to the role that Newtown, despite being a youth group, plays in helping to develop and sustain faith in the lives of the leaders as well as the young people. Andrew continues this theme, describing the role Newtown plays in developing faith as being a 'two-way thing': as the leaders try to coax the young people on, they find that they themselves are being pushed on. The leaders value this opportunity to grow and find support through the group, whether through the relationship with one another or, as Andrew describes above, with the young people themselves. Also noteworthy is how involvement as leaders spills over into wider experiences of church as a whole. Alongside the experience of David described above, Stuart found that his leadership in Newtown had the effect of drawing him into the wider life of the Church. For Claire, choosing to become a leader when new to Newtown Christian Centre (NCC) was key in her developing friendships in the church that helped her settle, and the leaders became the people that she 'hangs out with'.

Despite Newtown being quite a new group and linked directly to a specific local church, it provides a place through which the faith and communal Christian life of the leaders is enhanced. This significance for leaders is not confined to Newtown; for many of the leaders at St Joe's, leadership of the group is likewise a vital part of the ongoing expression of their Christian faith, though here the significance is in the connection to the broader tradition of Crusaders and this is detailed in the next section. What is clear, though, is that the groups, though presenting as youth groups, develop belonging connected to cultivating Christian faith that isn't confined to a limited age range but has an intergenerational significance. Consequently, these youth groups raise fascinating and vital questions about the ecclesial value of what they do.

Connection with a broader tradition

As with each interview, I finished my interview with Robert by asking him if there was anything else he wanted to say to me about St Joe's. His response, without hesitation, was to say, 'Well, what is significant is next year is the centenary.' Anniversaries such as the centenary are important in the life of St Joe's. Those leaders that have long histories in the group refer back to the ninetieth and earlier anniversary services and celebrations. These times seem to play a role of reinforcing the identity of the group, especially with its independent nature. The historical connections and community that were formed through being part of Crusaders are valued and, indeed, missed when no longer present. In addition, the members of the Seniors group expressed their pride in being part of such a long-standing group when Urban Saints organized a weekend event called 'Spree'. Given the longevity of the group, and the way in which the majority of main leaders are those who have been in St Joe's since they were children themselves, the sense of identity with Urban Saints/Crusaders is strong in the group. For these leaders, the belonging is not simply to the local group but to the organization, the history and the original vision of Albert Kestin and others from the early days of the movement. Given the changes in the organization as a whole as it has moved from being Crusaders to Urban Saints, the sense I got is very much that the ongoing involvement in St Joe's is a way that these leaders can keep a legacy of Crusader tradition going. This keeps them connected with their past and that which was significant in coming to faith as children or teenagers.

For the young people and leaders of Newtown the connection to the broader organizational tradition of Crusaders/Urban Saints is not historical, but current in the way that the group taps into the opportunities offered by the wider Urban Saints Network, especially through two residential events. These are an annual summer holiday to an Urban Saints-owned centre called Westbrook on the Isle of Wight, and ReBuild, a short-term mission trip that allows those in the group to spend ten days helping build a house for a family in South Africa or Mexico. I wasn't able to join either of these trips but both in my interviews with young people and on group nights their significance is talked up. For Robin, the Westbrook holiday introduced him to the bigger picture of Urban Saints through meeting people from other Urban Saints groups and churches. He describes two effects of this: first, that it helped him feel part of the wider organization; and second, that through conversation with a Westbrook leader from a different church he came to realize that the Christian faith was plausible. He put it in this way:

> I was speaking at Westbrook to loads of different leaders from different churches and eventually one of them, like, made sense to me and it actually opened my eyes to what the beliefs and views actually meant. It sort of put the points that other people had made into perspective and it made me understand them.

The ReBuild trip to South Africa has a similar impact, though it was interesting that the group of young people who chose to go was made up entirely of emerging leaders. Stuart, the main leader of the Newtown group at the time, who also led the ReBuild team, explains this:

> I'm not going to say we only invited emerging leaders but actually in a sense that's kind of how it played out. They are the guys we're on a journey with, they're the guys we're trying to encourage and that sort of thing so of course they're the ones we're going to be looking at, you know, an opportunity to grow and move on.

For the young people at St Joe's whose parents retain a historical Crusader legacy the connection to the broader tradition is something to which the whole family relates. Both Alison and Helen have been part of Crusaders since they were very young, because their parents Richard and Julia are among the core leaders who themselves in part grew up through the group.

Both Helen and Alison feel this very acutely but, unlike those for whom St Joe's provides a kind of oasis of Christian community away from the more negative family-linked experiences of church, this is communicated as a positive thing. They enjoy the fact that St Joe's is part of what they do as a family and, although they also attend church together, where the parents are equally involved in the children's and youth work, the sense of belonging to St Joe's is greater. I would go as far as to say that Crusaders/Urban Saints is part of the identity of this family, whereas church is something they attend together.

Similarly, the connection with the wider tradition of Urban Saints experienced through residentials at Newtown is understood to add extra layers to the depth of belonging and experience among the young people. The residentials provide experiences that the leaders believe would be much harder to come by without them being run and organized by Urban Saints centrally. This is in part because the pressure of the time and effort to organize them is taken off the local leaders, but the leaders also credit the connection with a wider community of Christian leaders and young people. Leaders and young people alike value the extra time and focus that being away can provide:

> Being down in Westbrook you spend time with a bunch of Christian leaders and [there are] times every day when there's a specific kind of meeting where Christianity is being explored and people are going to offer to pray for you and they are going to offer to open the Bible and read some passages to you during the week. Those bigger experiences [offer] opportunities to respond and so typically that's where more responses occur.

> I guess taking us out of the secluded environment ... there's not much you can do on a Friday evening but you can do quite a lot in ten days.

Despite these experiences on the residentials taking place away from the local church, they seem to have an impact on the way in which young people connect with the wider Church. Sometimes it might be a young person's experiences on one of these trips that leads to them being baptized in the local church, or simply provides the catalyst to start going to Sunday services following their experiences at Westbrook.

These four modes of belonging – social space, safe place, intergenerational significance and connection with a broader tradition – helpfully categorize the ways in which both the young people and leaders articulate and express their belonging to the groups. Each unveils something of the complexity at work in the groups and begins to bring to light how the manner of belonging in the groups is at times faith related and at times not – for both young people and leaders, and for those who are Christians already and those who are not. This hints at the ambiguous identity of the groups that is analysed in more detail in the next chapter. For now, this chapter concludes by building on these modes of belonging through discussion of the groups' connections with the local church, both operant and espoused.

Connections with church

In the case studies relating to both groups, mission and outreach is the primary way of defining the relationship with the wider life of the Church. The idea of church is rarely discussed directly at Newtown, though the building is known as 'the church', with particular emphasis on the auditorium as the 'sanctuary'. The young people themselves can joke about the distinction between the different areas of the building as being the church and also about the fact that the building itself isn't the church – the people are. At different times, though, the leaders describe Newtown as being both part of the Church and able to do what church is meant to do. However, as if to highlight the ambiguities in how church is understood, there are deliberate ways in which the young people are encouraged to connect more with the local church itself. An Alpha Youth course was advertised to those in the Newtown group on Friday night, before it was launched on the following Sunday evening. By running it on a Sunday evening it was being run as part of – or alongside – the Newtown Christian Centre (NCC) adult Alpha course and consequently was an NCC event. The course was presented as an opportunity to take faith more seriously, with the further rationale that it would connect them with something of the wider life of NCC.

The Newtown group is considered to be an introduction to the Church. It is a place that is 'not as intense' while the Sunday morning worship service includes groups for young people that are 'more church'. Andrew describes 'the flow we really want to see' as being individuals moving from the Friday night Urban Saints group through other activities to fully participating on a Sunday morning. Judy alludes to this as well, 'Once you get them thinking you can kind of point them in the right direction.' The consistency of this desire among the leaders is shown in David using very similar language, saying that, 'Obviously we want to bring more of the young people into the church; quite simply, we want to see more of them there on a Sunday.' There is some evidence of this happening in a limited way. On visits to the Sunday morning service, I was able to observe a good proportion of the young people from the Newtown group there and engaged in the service, about half of whom were from unchurched backgrounds. Others who were not there when I was observing spoke warmly of having been on occasions and enjoying it.

So, the idea is that the Newtown youth group is very much a beginning, an introduction, and is only able to operate as church in some way while it is connected to the Church and is able to point people onwards in the flow. In this flow, it is the events and activities of Sunday mornings that are most often considered the destination and most fully church. This is the case even though the young people up until the age of 17 spend most of the Sunday morning in their own group in a different building. The fact that it is on a Sunday morning while the adult worship service is going on seems to validate it mostly as being where and when the church can be found. Interestingly, though, for the Senior Pastor, while Sundays are a vital part of the expression of NCC, it is not 'bums on seats' that is essential but rather the young people feeling like they're 'part of this family'. The paradoxes and contradictions contained within these words and practices are analysed and explored in the next chapter.

For St Joe's, the group's independence from any particular local church frames the way the leaders use the language of outreach to describe how the group fits into the broader picture of Christian activity in the city. Indeed, it is the detachment from conventional church that helps to give them this focus. Dorothy shares her understanding that churches tend to cater more for their own young people whereas being independent allows St Joe's to 'do something totally different'. Peter also recognizes that the distance from local churches creates the space to be more focused on outreach. The distinction from church and the fact that the group is not seen as church makes mission easier. However, Peter is also vague about his own church commitment and at one time left me with the impression that St Joe's was the only Christian community he operated in at that time. I was regularly told that parents are more likely to be comfortable bringing their children to a school building on a Saturday night than to a church. The young people already there, Richard says, are more likely to invite friends to the group than to church.

Within the framing of St Joe's as mission is a sense of frustration at times that the role they play is not recognized. Victoria, for example, feels that it would be very easy for the large local Anglican church she attends to acknowledge or utilize St Joe's as part of its own outreach to children and young people since it meets within the parish. However, she also expresses exasperation at the limited vision within the church that seems restricted to work and ministries that it has launched itself. Dorothy also alludes to this. With a sense of frustration, she talks of how she sees churches only really interested in their own work. In addition, St Joe's self-understanding as one of mission is enhanced by the sense that they are able to meet a need that the churches aren't meeting. This is seen as being in part a result of the social status of some of the families that are bringing their children along to Crusaders. There is believed to be a 'niche' of young people who wouldn't go to a church, but are happy to come to a youth group, and – despite experiencing criticism that the group isn't church-based – the leaders remain convinced that there are those who come and therefore are introduced to the Christian faith who wouldn't otherwise have the opportunity.

Despite the implicit critique of church, the leaders of St Joe's recognize that at some point the young people do need to be introduced to church. However, they also admit that this is not something they are very good at despite the perceived advantage of having leaders from a number of different churches from which the young people could choose. This is a conundrum for the leaders and provides a bit of a disconnect between the self-articulated narrative of filling a niche and the ultimate aim of seeing those in the group entering adult life with a Christian faith that they have chosen and owned for themselves. The main way in which this disconnect is addressed by the leaders is through the language of sowing seeds. Even when talking about an extremely challenging period in the 11–14s group, when they were overwhelmed by over 50 young people coming along but with no intention of paying attention to the teaching that forms the first half of the evening, Richard is able to hold on to the possibility that seeds were sown that 'will hopefully bear fruit in the future'. Peter reiterates this by stating that 'something got through ... some seeds were sown'.

In one leaders' meeting Victoria encapsulated this feeling with a scriptural reference that framed the way in which the work of St Joe's could be seen as being in relationship with the conventional church in the city as well as in the manner of seeds being sown:

> What, after all, is Apollos? And what is Paul? Only servants, through whom you came to believe – as the Lord has assigned to each his task. I planted the seed, Apollos watered it, but God has been making it grow. So neither the one who plants nor the one who waters is anything, but only God, who makes things grow. The one who plants and the one who waters have one purpose, and they will each be rewarded according

to their own labour. For we are co-workers in God's service; you are God's field, God's building.[9]

The challenge from this for Victoria was that the group's leaders must play their part faithfully but realize that they need to trust God for the growth; they cannot make this happen themselves. The framing of the group as mission is also potentially misleading when referring to the seniors, as only one of the current group are from unchurched backgrounds.

The relationship between St Joe's and the church, particularly in the way that the group is deemed to meet a need that the churches are not meeting, is described as an interweaving thing, or as pieces of a jigsaw. The implication in this is that those accessing St Joe's have opportunities to connect with other aspects of Christian witness in the city, or that the group is one aspect among many different ways that particular families are engaging with Christian things. This interweaving sense of connection – and even belonging – is mirrored in the lives of the young people, each of whom have at least one church that they attend alongside Crusaders, recognizing that each is useful in their Christian development. Sally and Timothy especially spoke of at least three other places that they attend occasionally or regularly, each supplementing the other. Sally, though highly critical of her home church where her parents are involved in leadership roles – even going so far as to say she 'hates church' in reference to that particular church – still spoke of helping with the children's work there and also of two elderly ladies whose interest in her was important and whose deaths in a short space of time affected her deeply.

However, alongside this and Crusaders, she also talks of the significance of a nearby large, well-known youth church that she has started to go to, and also of the importance in her development of an annual national summer camp in which she helps with the children's work. Likewise, Timothy attends Crusaders alongside a church youth group in a neighbouring town to which a friend had invited him. He also helps with the children's work in the church where his dad serves as vicar, having previously been on the worship group in the church where his father was curate. It is indeed an interweaving thing for these young people.

The interweaving image suggests that there is not a simple one-directional movement from the groups to a more formal expression of the Church. The way in which the groups are significant for the leaders and provide a means by which their faith is enhanced through their involvement demonstrates this. This multi-directional movement was evident at St Joe's in the way that the group fulfilled a role in the lives of young people and leaders that added to their faith in ways that institutional and denominational church didn't. This interweaving nature points to contradictions and an ambiguous ecclesial identity at work in the espoused and operant ecclesiologies of the groups. This will be explored further in the next chapter.

Summary

Describing St Joe's and Newtown through the lens of modes of belonging is fascinating – they are not unusual in terms of the work going on in Christian youth groups up and down the country; however, the use of in-depth ethnographic case studies allows dynamics to be revealed that are usually hidden below the surface. By beginning to explore these dynamics it is possible to see how the groups, for both young people and leaders, provide crucial spaces that have the potential to cultivate and sustain Christian faith in community. The way the modes of belonging – social space, safe place, intergenerational work and connection with a broader tradition – operate opens up the possibility of an ecclesial dynamic at work. As the leaders and young people experience the groups and talk about these experiences the first whispers of the operant and espoused theological voices become apparent.

The significance of the groups in the faith lives of the participants – whether those already Christian or not – encourages further analysis and exploration of what the ecclesial nature of the groups might be. This is the task of the next chapter as the nature of the groups as potential ecclesial spaces that can contribute to an interweaving ecclesiology becomes clearer. This clarity emerges through further analysis of the case studies that reveals dominant and hidden discourses about the Church – within these, the hidden discourses point the way towards the constructive theological task that is central to this book.

Notes

1 Dorothy (Leader, St Joe's).

2 See Chapter 1.

3 Kathryn Tanner, 'Theological Reflection and Christian Practices', in *Practicing Theology: Beliefs and Practices in Christian Life*, ed. Miroslav Volf and Dorothy Bass (Grand Rapids, MI: William B. Eerdmans, 2002), pp. 229–30.

4 Montague R. Williams, *Church in Color: Youth Ministry, Race, and the Theology of Martin Luther King Jr.* (Waco, TX: Baylor University Press, 2020), p. 6.

5 The descriptions of practice and direct quotations from leaders and young people are drawn from 18 months of ethnographic research using both participant observations and semi-structured interviews. They will not be individually referenced so as not to disrupt the flow of the narrative.

6 Whether this is realistic or not is a moot point, but the significance is found in the experiences and expectations surrounding these friendships at the time.

7 Perhaps this is less surprising given that the group is independent of any local church.

8 This was evident almost weekly in my observation notes.

9 1 Corinthians 3.5–9.

5

An Interweaving Ecclesiology in Practice: Potential Ecclesial Life in the Groups

This has been my church for the last three years.[1]

This chapter, the second developing the thick description and consequent espoused and operant theologies from the case studies, offers further discussion of the data from the groups in order to analyse the ecclesial life that might be apparent. As evidenced by the quote above from a 16-year-old girl the groups carry the potential to be experienced as church by those who participate in them. Consequently, this chapter explores what this ecclesial life might look like and how such life in the groups relates to other, more regular forms of the church. Two forms of practice are vital in this exploration – ecclesial practices in the groups and more regular youth group practices (alluded to in the modes of belonging described in the previous chapter) that operate as interruptions, allowing participants to be drawn into the flow of ecclesial life.

What will become apparent through this exploration is that the hints of ecclesial life in the groups unveil a hidden discourse about the Church, revealing paradoxes and contradictions in a way that ultimately complexifies ecclesiological understandings. This hidden discourse reveals the interweaving ecclesial imagination at play in the groups as they can operate as a form of Christian community for the young people and leaders. The two key themes of ecclesial practices and practices of interruption provide the focus for this exploration and analysis of ecclesial life in the groups.

Ecclesial practices

Despite an insistence by the leaders that the groups are not expressions of church, three ecclesial (what could be termed 'churchy') practices are prominent in the groups. These practices are the commitment to a focus on Scripture, pastoral care and prayer. There are clear echoes in these of the early days of the praxis of Crusaders' Bible classes, demonstrating the normative value of handed-on practice.

Focus on Scripture

Both groups build their programme around a focus on learning from Scripture – St Joe's are clear on what they call the 'absolute rule' that the Bible comes first, whereas a main leader in Newtown expresses this focus in the following way:

> [Newtown is] a place to learn that something that people go through all the time, like social media for example, actually the Bible has something to say about it, God does have something to say about it … I mean, it's sort of introducing something, a problem that they all have or a question they all have or something they know about their family and relating it to the lesson in the Bible, what does the Bible have to say about this particular subject and can I learn anything from it.

Everything in the planning for St Joe's, from the timings of the group to when food is offered, is designed to create an atmosphere that is as conducive as possible to young people engaging with the Bible teaching. The leaders don't want to 'waste our time' as Christians. Richard echoed this, describing the Bible study as 'the main point', agreeing that putting the Bible study first is not simply a pragmatic decision but reflects the whole purpose of the group. Similarly, at Newtown, Andrew spoke of how each evening is based around a 'really important message'. The intention is that the subject is accessible, at least to some degree, to all those in the groups, regardless of where they consider themselves to be in relation to the Christian faith.

While the style of this focus on Scripture differs between the groups – Newtown models a relaxed approach to teaching as it builds through games, videos, discussions and short talks, whereas Bible teaching at St Joe's tends to be more formal – the desired outcome is the same. Similarly, the content varies – Newtown tends towards a thematic approach to connect the story of Scripture to the lives of young people; at St Joe's the focus is more on Bible study that starts with Scripture for its own sake. Victoria, at St Joe's, is adamant that an effort must be made to ensure that the whole of the Bible is taught, rather than sticking to popular or easy sections. The goal of St Joe's with regard to Bible study seemed to be motivated by trying to ensure that those in the group were able to make decisions for themselves about the validity of the Christian faith based on the claims of Scripture; in contrast, Newtown leans towards a philosophy of relevance – helping young people see the usefulness of Scripture in navigating contemporary life. To some extent, these differences in emphasis are neither here nor there; what is significant is that flowing through and across the modes of belonging was always the thread of Scripture and its study.

Pastoral care

In addition to teaching the Bible, the leaders of both groups see them as places in which they can offer pastoral care and support to those who come along. In Newtown, one of the leaders identifies that the value of this is in the group being neither family nor school:

> To be able to talk to them about what is going on in their lives and maybe give a response that is either not necessarily what they want to hear or what they are going to get from other people. Some of the stuff that has been going on it's been really good to be able to just get involved with that and check up every week how they're feeling about it and what's been going on ... I think you should be there for them, so I do think that's really important.

The relationships built through the groups as social space provide the context in which pastoral care is offered to those who come along. This offer of pastoral care is rarely formally articulated and yet is clearly a part of the experience of the group for many young people, demonstrating the safe places the groups offer. The quality of relationships as a basis for pastoral care is illustrated by Robin and Beth:

> With the teachers you can't really sit down and have a conversation with them ... but here, like, the leaders sort of took the time to get to know you and spend time with you and sort of built up a friendship, whereas at school it's just a teacher. And so, like, the leaders actually made an effort so I felt comfortable talking to them more than all the teachers.

> I was at Newtown on a Friday evening when I found out about my uncle. My uncle died and I wasn't my normal self and both leaders Judy and Andrew could figure it out and they were like 'you don't have to take part in stuff if you don't want to' and then they kind of prayed for me. It's more that they take a caring ... sort of parental role to us so if we have a problem we can talk about it to one of them.

The free time provides a context in which much of this pastoral care can informally take place. On one occasion, Judy had a group of about six or seven girls around her taking part in an ongoing art and craft project. The project was taking months to complete, with very little progress being made. Rather, the time was spent talking and building relationships, allowing significant conversations to go on that, at times, I needed to be careful not to disrupt.

The desire to ensure that Newtown is a place in which young people are cared for is directly related to the Christian heart of the groups – expressed as being 'like Jesus' for the young people.[2] This was discussed passionately at a leaders' meeting I attended when one of the leaders described one boy who sometimes displayed difficult behaviour as a 'twerp', in an off-the-cuff remark. This led to Andrew reminding the other leaders that 'Jesus came to the broken and this is those kids' so they must be cared for. This was reiterated when I interviewed him and he talked of how his own journey, experiencing leaders who loved him 'no matter what', had given him a 'compassion for the kids that are troubled and are having a tough time and are a bit more difficult'.

At St Joe's the pastoral care is integral to the main session, but not articulated as such. I noted on numerous occasions that even after the Bible study had begun, Victoria was very happy to interrupt the teaching if a latecomer arrived, asking how they were. Inevitably, she would know them well enough to ask after a particular aspect of their life. The young people responded to this warmly and appreciated the level of care and interest displayed.[3] This demonstrates, as in Newtown, the relational basis for this pastoral care. Sally especially talked of how she valued this. Being often late to the group, she was initially concerned about walking in when the session had begun, but Victoria's relaxed and interested nature soon helped Sally to feel valued and welcomed whenever she arrived.

The practice of pastoral care in both groups is not, however, limited to the young people themselves but can extend to the leaders who talk of the way in which they support one another and, at St Joe's in particular, the parents of those in the group. Leaders in Newtown talked lovingly of an occasional older leader who is valued as someone who is like a mum to them. She demonstrates this in very simple ways such as making cups of tea for the other leaders and inviting them to her house over the summer break when the group is not meeting. These are simple acts of care that are appreciated by the leaders to whom they are offered.

At St Joe's it becomes apparent, as Victoria moves around from room to room ensuring that everything is set up and ready to begin, that pastoral care extends to other leaders and parents as well; she finds time to notice people as they are coming in and personally welcomes as many as she can. It is remarkable how much she knows about each individual and family that comes in, asking how an ill family member is doing or whether a problem at school has been resolved, for example. Alongside this, she is quick to notice any newcomers and welcomes them enthusiastically. There is something in this behaviour that is reminiscent of the role of a parish priest or other church leader, serving to reinforce the participants' sense that their experiences in the group are in some way analogous to church.

Moreover, leaders at St Joe's are actively involved in the care of families who bring younger children to the groups. I became aware during my observations of leaders who offered to babysit from time to time to help struggling parents. Within this, though, is a critique of the church as Victoria tells me that she doesn't believe her church is capable of caring for these 'troubled families' with the help they need because they are not the conventional 'middle-class' families that the church is used to. Victoria puts it like this:

> My concern [with churches] is actually, when they have these families that need some slightly better love, care and atten-tion that is not conventional middle class, actually whether now they're capable of giving it. Certainly to the adults.

Prayer

The final regular ecclesial practice is prayer. At Newtown, for example, the pre-session run-through usually ends with a request for someone to pray for the upcoming evening. It is commonplace for the volunteer to come from a relatively small number among the group. However, on occasion others will volunteer, including younger emerging leaders who are self-described as not yet Christians. These prayers, though stumbling, are celebrated by the group especially if, as was the case for both Freddie and Robin on separate occasions, it is the first time that someone has prayed out loud. In addition, leaders offer the young people a chance to be prayed for during small groups and there would often be one or two who would ask for prayer. On one occasion, Michael reported back enthu-siastically that the prayers prayed for his family a previous week had been answered. The offer of prayer is also connected to the pastoral care, with leaders offering to pray for the pastoral situations that are talked through.

Alongside this form of prayer, from time to time a form of meditative activity is included in the session at Newtown. During one group visit I noted that an 18-year-old lad who did not call himself a Christian[4] asked one of the leaders why there hadn't been any time to 'lie down and listen to music while thinking about stuff' for a long time. A few weeks later, I experienced what he was talking about. Towards the end of the teaching in which the theme had been the resurrection of Jesus, Stuart asked those in the group to find some space around the auditorium and lie down. As they did this, some soft music replaced the usual popular music. The young people were quick to do this and were joined by the leaders. I noted with surprise how little noise or laughing and joking there was as those in the group prepared themselves for this. The relative darkness of the room and the relaxed atmosphere created by the lack of chairs and the draped curtains seemed to help. Once everyone was lying down and quiet, Stuart began to lead through some words designed to help individuals consider how the theme of the evening might affect them personally.

It is of course impossible to know the extent to which the young people were reflecting on the questions being asked and the theme of the evening; however, those who *were* reflecting would not have been disturbed by those who weren't. These reflective opportunities were described to me as possible 'God moments' – moments that hold the potential of young people becoming aware of God's presence. They can be 'preparing the ground' so that those in the group are more open to the possibility of the reality of God's existence and the Christian faith.[5]

Demonstrating a different emphasis on prayer, the leaders at St Joe's are committed to praying for the families of the children and young people who come along to the groups. One week, after the group had finished and I was helping to carry boxes of Bibles and other games back to Victoria's car with her, she filled me in on a conversation that she had been having with the parent of several of the children in the younger groups who was concerned that her son had stolen some money from her. Victoria had said that she would pray for her and for the money to be returned or found. Shortly after getting home, while we were still clearing up from the group, the parent phoned Victoria on her mobile to say that the money had been found and the son hadn't been responsible for it going missing. The parent was overjoyed and thanked Victoria for her prayers, telling her that the prayers had been answered. I noted that Victoria was really excited by this as it happened to an unchurched family.

These simple, yet limited, ecclesial practices ensure that the Christian faith remains central within the groups. Yet, despite being simple and limited, the testimony of those involved is that the practices assist in making the group a place through which Christian faith is stimulated, supported and shaped in two main ways. The first follows on from the comment above that the reflective time provides the potential for God moments in which those coming along become aware of God's presence. I would suggest that these regular practices of Bible teaching, pastoral care, prayer and meditation all contribute in this way. In addition, there is evidence that these practices serve to teach and train the young people about the things that Christians do to sustain and act out their faith. Steve talks about this in terms of noticing 'little things' that are ways in which he is growing in his faith – these include beginning to pray when he wakes up in the morning before getting ready for school. Robin echoes this by talking of the way he prays and reads his Bible 'on occasion'. Interestingly, Robin, who is not what he calls 'a full Christian', says that if he was he would pray and read the Bible more. The significance of this is in the way that Newtown has encouraged and trained him in some simple Christian practices of prayer and Bible reading and that he recognizes these as being important in building an ongoing Christian life.

These practices suggest that, in the same way as the early Crusader classes were in many ways reflective of church without naming themselves as such, there is something church-like about the regular gathering of this group around a few central, simple Christian practices. The way that young people from otherwise unchurched backgrounds pick up on these practices and begin to adopt a rhythm in their usage outside of the group suggests the group has some effect as a community that equips its members in basic Christian living. We can note echoes here of Rowan Williams's description of church happening when people encounter the risen Christ and commit to deepening that encounter together.[6]

These ecclesial practices, however, are held in such a way that the young people can access them at a level of their choosing. The non-church identity helps the groups to maintain this flexibility. While in many ways the Bible teaching at St Joe's is more formal, the overall sense that it is a vital part of the group is shared. Also, as described above, the way in which the Bible study is delivered at St Joe's tries to carry the young people along with it – as well as Victoria being happy to pause if necessary so that new arrivals can be welcomed, or questions answered. This expresses an informality and flexibility that while distinct from institutional church life helps to facilitate engagement in both groups' ecclesial practices.

To explore this flexibility further, I identify in the groups' natural praxis three 'practices of interruption' that can interrupt both these ecclesial practices and the expectations of the young people themselves. Moreover, these practices of interruption can be seen to cut across dominant discourses about church in order that an ambiguous space might be created in which the hitherto hidden discourses might be heard. This, then, begins to bring more clarity to the espoused and operant theological voices that articulate the ecclesial imagination of youth ministry and thus aid the constructive task of this book. These dominant and hidden discourses are detailed and analysed below after I have outlined the practices of interruption.

Dominant and hidden ecclesial discourses

My contention is that the case studies demonstrate how youth groups such as St Joe's and Newtown can form 'potential ecclesial spaces' that can provide part of an interweaving ecclesiology for participants.[7] It is important to note again how the inherent ecclesial imagination, a way of life together that fosters faith and emerges out of the praxis of people in particular contexts, is discernible in the historical work of Urban Saints/Crusaders, and through them has echoed into Christian youth work more generally.[8] The presentation of the case studies so far indicates it is also evident in the contemporary life of the groups. This section explores how the case studies allow a previously hidden discourse about the Church to come to the surface, as paradoxes and contradictions within and between the operant and espoused theologies of the groups force consideration of more complex understandings of the Church being embodied in this ecclesial imagination.

As cited in Chapter 1, Pete Ward has written of what he calls the 'affective gravitational pull of the church'.[9] This gravitational pull relates to the way in which people are drawn back to prior, or instinctive, ecclesiological understandings.[10] Though Ward is writing mainly of academic theologians, further analysis of the case studies demonstrates that a dominant discourse about church exists in evangelical Christianity that exerts a gravitational pull on the leaders, young people and groups. Despite the presence of core ecclesial practices and the tradition of an inherent ecclesial imagination, this dominant discourse is powerful within the groups' espoused ecclesiology. However, there are operant and previously unarticulated espoused approaches to church within the case studies that interrupt and pull against the dominant gravitational force and allow such hidden discourses to be heard and considered.

Elsewhere, Ward has described the tendency in evangelicalism, as it became a more acceptable and perhaps dominant form of Christian expression in the UK, to understand church as being most apparent in the Sunday services which all ages and generations are expected to attend.[11] The gravitational pull towards this dominant view of the Church results in an ecclesiology that can be described as minimal.[12] In the case studies these dominant approaches to the Church are articulated through boundary markers that determine the borders of church and therefore of what can be considered inside or outside of the church. On occasion these boundaries are designed to maintain a 'not church' identity for the groups in order to create distance between the groups and the congregational life of the church. Examples of these boundary markers are brought to light through contradictions in the case study analysis that open up more complex understandings of church. These contradictions suggest that the boundaries desired by the dominant discourse are not sufficient to contain the ecclesial life that is expressed through the groups and the ecclesial imagination of youth ministry. In short, the practical dynamics of the groups exhibit an interweaving in which ecclesial life moves between various expressions of communal Christian life. The youth groups have the potential to be such an expression as individuals appropriate them for this purpose.

The notion of the groups being outside the boundaries of the life of the Church was embedded within the traditional outlook of Crusaders and consequently taken on into evangelical work with young people more broadly. The echoes of this separate nature, fuelled by being able to belong to the wider network provided by the organizational affiliation, can be heard clearly in the work and self-understanding of both groups through the case study data. However, that this approach contains an ecclesial imagination outside the normal boundaries of church life suggests that this normative practice has always tended towards ecclesial contradiction.

These contradictions and boundary markers are evident, for example, when Victoria, as the main leader of St Joe's, is able to say confidently that, 'even though we're not a church we do care about families'. This short statement alone demonstrates some of the tension and ambiguity at play in the group's unarticulated understanding of church. The first part of the statement is clear on the claim that St Joe's is not a church. In this way, Victoria is clearly following the traditional self-understanding that such groups are separate from church but also not a replacement for church. The second half of the statement, however, carries within it the implicit recognition that although they are not a church there is something in what they do that reflects or replicates the things that churches do or should do. By saying that 'even though' they're not a church they do 'care for families', Victoria is suggesting that caring for families is an integral part of what churches should do, and that they are doing it despite not being a church. Consequently, the groups carry the potential for a form of ecclesial life within them. It follows, then, that it is important to discuss in detail the contradictions present in the approach of the groups to core practices and the dominant discourses of church life.

Sunday mornings and the contradiction of practice

Despite the ambiguity and contradiction within Victoria's statement above, leaders and young people in both groups articulate regularly that the groups are not to be equated with church. Robert, for example, describes St Joe's as 'a no church situation' and in his view this is an advantage, making it easier for both children and young people to come along. In addition to clearly stating that the group is not a church but instead a Christian youth group, Jonathan goes on to explain that some of the parents and young people would not even realize initially that the group is a Christian one and that this can make 'people maybe feel more comfortable'. One of those in the group, Alison, says she doesn't make the 'connection really between the churches and Crusaders'.

Similarly, in Newtown there are ways in which the leaders and those coming along seem to intentionally create a distinction in the way they talk about the group in relation to church despite the direct connection with Newtown Christian Centre. This distinction was implied at a talent show event to which the wider church congregation was invited. In an introduction to the evening, which played out like the opening credits to a film projected on to the big screen at the front of the auditorium, the talent show was described as being presented by 'Newtown in association with NCC'.

What is implied here is a separate identity between the church and the groups, that although they will work together, they are not the same. This sense of the group being a separate entity from that which is understood as the church is reinforced strongly by one of the newest leaders, Claire.

Whereas a number of the leaders had been part of the church or leading Newtown for a number of years, Claire had moved to the area a year before, quickly becoming part of the church and volunteering to help with Newtown almost straight away. When interviewed she was talking about the way in which she saw the freedom for the group to use the church building being a good thing as it helped to blur the boundaries between church and youth group for those who were not from church backgrounds or families.

However, when looking to dig deeper into this sense of where the boundaries might be, the concept of church being predominantly restricted to what happens in congregations on a Sunday morning was noticeable. I asked her to imagine the church as a circle and tell me where she would place the group – would it be in the circle, outside it or somewhere in between? Her immediate response was clear that she saw it as outside of the church:

> I think very much at the moment that it is outside and I think Sunday school is very much more integral ... And people are more happy to help out with Sunday school because that's actually within the time that they're there on a Sunday whereas youth club is always going to be outside.

In addition to the feeling that the Newtown group is separate from church, Claire points towards a different aspect of this question in highlighting how she sees what she calls 'Sunday school' as being much more integral. Sunday school here refers to the groups and activities for children and young people that take place each week while the Sunday morning service is happening.[13] This sense of those Sunday morning activities and groups for children and young people being more integral to church than the Friday night group is a clear sign of the importance of Sunday mornings as a boundary marker. It seems that for Claire certain activities are more church than others by virtue of when they take place. A Friday night youth group is not considered church.

As detailed previously, other leaders affirm such a view of

the group being outside the boundaries of church through their expressed desire to see those who come along finding their way through from the Friday night group to Sunday mornings – this is the 'flow' they really want to see. When describing this, it is clear that the direction of flow is towards Sunday mornings and that this is 'more' church, or where church is really happening. Similarly, for David the Sunday morning service is 'church proper' and this is where they really want to see the young people coming along:

> Obviously, we want to bring more of the young people into the church, quite simply, we want to see more of them there on a Sunday and exploring that side ... follow[ing] it [all] the whole way through to church proper.

This type of espoused ecclesiology is expressed distinctly in the two groups given their distinct nature – St Joe's having no formal church link, and Newtown being directly affiliated with a particular church – however, the overall sense of church being something other than the group is quite explicit. The Sunday morning service as the centre of gravity in the life of the church and thus deemed 'church proper' mirrors the phenomenon of evangelicalism's preoccupation with creating a sense of family church, whereby all ages and generations must be in attendance at one Sunday service to be said to be 'at church'.[14] This is part of the dominant discourse about church.

Leaders of both groups feel the pull towards this view of church, though it is experienced in different ways. Whereas at Newtown, as described above, they have a clear view of the flow they wish to see, at St Joe's the desire to introduce the young people to church in this central, congregational sense is there but without the leaders sharing a clear idea as to how this works. Richard sums this up well:

> One of St Joe's aims, and maybe we're not very good at doing this, in an ideal world your young person comes to, gets involved, is interested in Christian things and is encouraged to join a church. I don't think we're particularly good at doing

that. As they get older maybe that happens ... But I don't really see that process.

While these espoused positions reflect the dominant discourse and the gravitational pull towards a Sunday-centric, minimalist view of church they do not take into account the contradiction at the heart of Victoria's statement discussed above – that although these leaders of groups like to situate themselves outside of church, the practices contain something of ecclesial life within them and there is a hope to challenge or change the young people's impression of church through the groups.[15]

The evidence from the history of Crusaders/Urban Saints further demonstrates this contradiction. In part what the founders of Crusaders did through their Bible classes was to take some of the basic practices that were foundational to congregational life and put them into the drawing rooms and school classrooms in which the groups were meeting. Through a weekly programme, which was described as an order of service, including prayers, the singing of simple hymns and Bible teaching, the early Crusader groups were reminiscent of simple church services. Similarly, while no longer resembling simple church services, both Newtown and St Joe's demonstrate the simple ecclesial practices described earlier in the chapter that have an essential 'churchiness' about them.

The presence of these activities and practices, however, is not enough for the leaders to think of what they do with young people as church (indeed, the dominant discourse actively discourages this), preferring – as described above – to think of the group as outside of or separate from the Church in the same way as the pioneers of early Crusaders classes did. However, this position taken by the groups seems strange when considered in the light of a regular practice at NCC, the church to which Newtown is affiliated, and to whose Sunday service the leaders want to see a 'flow' from the Friday night group.

By visiting NCC's Sunday morning service on a few occasions during my research I noticed something that struck me as strange when considered in the light of what I had been told by the leaders, and in the context of my attempts to understand where the ecclesial boundaries were seen to be by these leaders.[16] During the morning service there was a quite large number of young people present who were also part of Newtown on a Friday night. This, I thought, is what the leaders want to see happening. However, they were only there for about 15 minutes before they left to go to their own group for the rest of the time that the service was on. This is perfectly normal, common behaviour for young people in evangelical churches up and down the country, but on this occasion the familiar stood out as strange.

This group to which these individuals went for the majority of the time that the service was going on was in essence much like the environment of Newtown on a Friday night. It comprises games, activities, Bible-based discussions and opportunities for prayer. The only thing missing is that there is no free time. These young people are, however, considered to be 'at church', whereas those on a Friday night aren't. It seems that the fact it is occurring on a Sunday morning concurrently with the congregation meeting for the service means these young people can be considered part of the church. To add to the complexity and contradictions, on a Sunday morning the young people meet in a separate building that is about 100 metres down the road. It seems that to some degree the time of the week is more important than the building in defining what is church and what isn't. The implication here is that even on a Sunday morning, church is actually constructed out of an interaction of different groups, in different places, as individuals participate in key ecclesial practices together.

Similarly, when talking to leaders from St Joe's who also serve in the youth and children's work in their churches, they find it difficult to distinguish with great detail the things they do with the young people in what is termed 'church' and the things they do with them at St Joe's. Those in the group often struggled themselves to discern what was distinct about one from the other in terms of what they did. However, despite these similarities the language of church is rarely used to describe what is happening on a Saturday evening in the school at St Joe's or on a Friday evening in the church auditorium in

Newtown. The dominant discourse of evangelical ecclesiology is evident in this prioritizing of Sunday morning congregational activity even when that activity for young people is barely distinguishable between Sundays and the times that the groups are meeting.

Indeed, to use the language of Nick Shepherd, through simple ecclesial practices the groups can become places through which participants are able to be Christian. Consequently, a form of ecclesial life might be said to be present, though this is often prevented from being made explicit as a result of the dominance of the Sunday morning discourse surrounding evangelical church life. The language of potential ecclesial spaces provides a way to frame this ecclesial life that breaks through the pull of the dominant discourse and extends into the groups as part of the whole life of the church for participants.

Church buildings and the contradiction of identity and belonging

Church buildings represent a second significant boundary marker for church in the dominant evangelical discourse. This is played out slightly differently in each case study but with a similar central theme. In St Joe's, the neutral location, which is in keeping with the historical heart of Crusaders, is seen as a great advantage. The use of a school building lends weight to what is described as the 'non-church setting' that the group provides. This non-church identity of the location is considered advantageous to the group's outreach aims. Families, it is thought, will feel less threatened by bringing young people to such a location. Similarly, the children and young adults will be more likely to invite friends to a neutral place.

In Newtown the building naturally plays a different role, given that the group uses the main auditorium of the church building. In this scenario the use of the building is seen as a great advantage to the group as it allows the leaders to effectively invite young people into 'the church' and then use the space in a way that might challenge the preconceptions about church that this age group are perceived to have. For the leaders of Newtown, then, the use of a church building is an advantage to mission as they see it, whereas for the leaders of St Joe's the use of a deliberately and distinctively 'not church' location is seen as an advantage to outreach!

There is a further nuance to the use of the building in Newtown, however, that demonstrates there are what could be termed degrees of church within the building itself. The auditorium was on occasion referred to as 'the sanctuary', with the implication that it is the room where church happens. This terminology was used on Friday nights, in interviews with leaders and also by one of the service leaders on a Sunday morning. The expectation with this kind of language is that there is something special about this room in particular. I observed the way that this expectation was built by the use of this type of language and how it influenced the way the young people approached that room. On one occasion some of them were laughing and joking with one another before the group began when one of them used bad language. Immediately one of the others corrected him in a lighthearted manner for using such language in a church – to which the first young person responded immediately that they weren't in the church, they were in the foyer! What this demonstrates is that in the dominant discourse about church-specific buildings, even rooms within buildings can be used to reinforce the boundaries of church through being synonymous with what church is or where church happens. Similarly, they can ensure something else can be identified as not church.

While potentially focusing on days of the week and buildings might seem theologically insignificant, these are the dominant viewpoints about the church that came to light in the case studies. It would be very easy to respond by saying that these are irrelevant, that ecclesiology is rather focused on who the Church is and what the Church does – its nature and purpose, or agency and activity – but a quick response such as this would ignore the strength of this dominant discourse about the Church and the subsequent ordinary theology it reveals. It is such a discourse that is in the background, for example, in Ashton and Moon's assumed understanding of the Church.[17]

Explicating this dominant discourse, though, begins to show contradictions within it. In practice, on occasion it is the building that defines whether something is church or not and at other times it is the Sunday morning time slot. The same activities with the young people can be considered as going to church on a Sunday but not on a Friday. Things happening in the 'sanctuary' are church on a Sunday but not on a Friday, though it is thought they are happening 'in' the church even on a Friday. Interestingly, little thought is given to the things that are actually being done and whether these might be what allows certain activities or groups to be considered church. In both groups, then, it is possible to discern the pull of an ecclesiology that uses in particular the boundary markers of Sunday mornings and church buildings to demarcate what is and what isn't considered church. These groups that aim to share the gospel with young people are not in themselves church as church is understood to gravitate around the centrality of the Sunday morning congregations of particular local churches. This is the dominant discourse of evangelical ecclesiology.

In contradiction to this, and building on the historical details of the Crusaders/Urban Saints story in the Introduction and Chapter 3, the strength of identity and belonging fostered within Crusaders as a movement of mission to young people through the twentieth century suggests that the ecclesial imagination of youth ministry operates with a sense of belonging that is not defined by Sunday mornings or church buildings. Indeed, the way young people and leaders identified with their Crusader group and the national organization demonstrated a stronger sense of belonging than they felt towards the particular local churches of which they were a part. This is evidenced by discussions of how local churches needed to understand that Crusader leaders would have little time for 'office holding' in the local church as a result of their commitment to the Crusader group.[18]

Similarly, leaders in both groups express sentiments of this type. Robert told me how he has often missed church events and even weddings owing to his commitment to St Joe's. Meanwhile, Victoria spoke of the frustration of feeling that what she does with St Joe's is often overlooked and undervalued in her church because her commitment to it takes her away from serving more in the life of the church. Here, then, it is the previously hidden discourse that provides a dominant thread in the interweaving of church, as it is the groups and the wider connected network that drive a greater sense of belonging, commitment and identity. It is not simply the unaffiliated nature of the St Joe's group, though, that fosters this sense of belonging. The strength of identity among leaders that was cultivated throughout the organization's history was remarkably strong. This was demonstrated especially by some of the strength of feeling around the time of the centenary celebrations for Crusaders/Urban Saints, being the occasion when the Crusader name was dropped and the organization relaunched as Urban Saints. The long-term leaders at St Joe's hold this identity strongly as well, choosing to retain the name Crusaders and maintain traditional ties to other old Crusaders groups. The presence of leaders from another traditional Crusader group some 20 miles away at a Sunday afternoon prayer tea for the group, when there was no representative from local churches other than the current leaders, demonstrates this. This is not to make an argument one way or another about whether Crusaders were right or wrong to change their historical name at the time of their centenary; rather, the strength of this point is to highlight the way that the ecclesial imagination, this way of life that fosters faith, operates outside the boundaries that the dominant discourse seeks to demarcate. As a result of this, a hidden discourse of ecclesial life is revealed.

The way in which leaders came together for the specific purpose of reaching children and young people away from the concerns of a wider congregational life allowed for a focus that strengthened the identity felt by the leaders. This is very much the case within the St Joe's group, operating as it still does in this manner. The leaders value what they see as the simplicity of focus that stepping outside or across the normal boundaries of church life fosters. Consequently, they develop a closeness of relationship borne out of that focus. It would be wrong, though, to suggest that this strong identity and belonging of the leaders only develops when the group is meeting separately from any particular church affiliation as the Newtown leaders spoke of the significance the group plays in their experience of church. The longest serving leaders in Newtown describe feeling like a house group or a family together as leaders, while also expressing frustration at the lack of recognition from the wider church of the role they play and the significance of the work they do. In addition, there is something of value attached to the role of the wider organization of Urban Saints. Young people and leaders spoke of their connection with Urban Saints and the way that they enjoyed being part of something that is 'all over the world'. The use of Urban Saints hooded jumpers to distinguish the emerging leaders and the way that groups from Newtown have regularly joined Urban Saints mission trips and holidays reinforce this. In some ways it is this parachurch affiliation that helps to create the separate identity from church. This can create a sense of a boundary marker from the Urban Saints side – the groups are separate from church as they are an Urban Saints or Crusaders group, and at times each thread can be seen to be more or less significant for participants.

Those in both groups summarize a clear sense of belonging and identity. A 17-year-old boy from Newtown told me he wouldn't know what to do on a Friday without Newtown as 'Fridays were Newtown'. Helen at St Joe's used very similar language when she spoke of 'Saturdays being St Joe's'. For both the young people and leaders, then, it seems the identity they feel with the group is important. Its importance is derived from it being 'their' place and this sense of it being their place is fostered by the way it operates outside of congregational life with its more focused purpose and objectives. This is often expressed as a stronger or closer form of belonging than felt within the local church congregation. Claire describes it this way after joining the Newtown leadership team soon after joining the church itself. The other leaders, she said, quickly became the people from church she considered friends and with whom she would enjoy spending time.

So, while church is mostly deemed to be what happens around the activity of the Sunday morning congregation, the leaders and young people derive a deeper sense of Christian belonging through their involvement in the groups. At times it is the ability to identify with the wider organization of Crusaders/Urban Saints that helps create this deeper belonging, whereas at other times it is more through the relationships that are valued through the shared experience of the groups together. Furthermore, this deeper belonging and identity is intimately connected for the participants in the experience of their Christian faith. The identity and belonging of the groups helps to develop and sustain Christian faith in ways that complement or are distinct from experiences of formal church. This hidden discourse reaffirms the groups as places to be Christian (for leaders as well as those coming along) and, as such, offers a resistance to the pull to church as defined through buildings and Sunday mornings as in the dominant discourse.

These sections have demonstrated contradictions at the heart of the interaction between the espoused and operant ecclesiologies of the Urban Saints groups. I have framed these contradictions in terms of boundary markers to define the limits of church. These form a dominant discourse in the case studies that claims the groups are not church. However, there is also a hidden discourse in which ecclesial life extends into the groups as they provide places of Christian community through which Christian faith is developed. There is evidence that this is true for both leaders and young people. Consequently, whereas boundaries of time and physical location are placed around church these boundaries are contradicted by the ecclesial practices and belonging of the groups that bring the ecclesial imagination to bear on the conversation.

The practices and belonging developed allow the groups to operate as places that create and sustain Christian faith. It follows then that, in keeping with the normative voice of the ecclesial imagination, there is something of ecclesial life that is extended into these groups. The espoused and operant theologies make clear, though, that the groups are not intended to replace traditional church life; however, they do enhance and extend ecclesial life for many of the participants.[19] The hidden discourse, then, reveals simultaneous understandings of what creates church. The way that these different threads of church come together is where what I have termed an 'interweaving ecclesiology' becomes apparent, with different threads more or less dominant for different people at different times.

This point is reinforced, despite the dominant discourse, in the way that participants in the groups do at times articulate explicitly the idea that the groups have some form of ecclesial identity. Stuart, the main leader for much of the time, is able to describe Newtown as being 'part of the church' when talking to the young people. He is not alone in this description – Andrew uses identical language in saying that the group is a 'massive part' of the church. On other occasions Newtown can be described as one of many 'avenues of the church' and 'within church'. Young people from each group at different times talked of the groups in terms of being church for them. Sally from St Joe's discussed at great length the challenges she had experienced as the daughter of prominent leaders in a local church, and how in this context the group had been her church for two years. From a different perspective, Beth in Newtown used the term 'our church', intentionally differentiating it from 'a church' to tell me what the group meant to her. For her it was their church because it felt like a family. These comments point to the hidden discourses that challenge the dominant discourse of ecclesial life that is represented by markers of time and location. The hidden discourses come to the surface in groups through certain practices that create the interruption to the dominant discourse at work.

The contradictions between the dominant and hidden discourses about church suggest a more complex ecclesial understanding emerging from the espoused and operant ecclesiologies of the case studies. It was Dorothy from St Joe's who provided the language to interpret such an approach by describing the relationship between Crusaders and the church in the city as being 'like a jigsaw' and an 'interweaving thing'. In these comments she is placing the work of the group as interconnected with and part of the overall picture of the work of the church locally. The final section of this chapter will begin to develop the way that such an interweaving approach is at play. Specifically, the section discusses practices of interruption that provide the environment through which the ecclesial practices of the groups are experienced. These interruptions mean that the groups can be understood as ambiguous spaces that have the potential of ecclesial life.

Practices of interruption

Noticeable throughout the discussion of ecclesial practices in the first section of this chapter are the threads of the modes of belonging detailed in the previous chapter – the way that belonging in the groups is inherently connected to ecclesial practices, and consequently the groups' potential to provide Christian communities. This connection allows young people to access and try out these ecclesial practices within the youth group setting. It is, however, other regular practices of the groups, though intriguingly less identifiable as ecclesial, that are key in creating space through which the groups might become part of an interweaving expression of church for the young people and leaders in the group. These other practices can be named as welcome, encouraging questions and creating fun. These are the practices of interruption and they cut across the dominant discourse about the Church in order that an ambiguous space might be created in which the hitherto hidden ecclesial discourses might be heard. Each of these can be seen embodied in one or more of the modes of belonging detailed previously.

The importance of welcome in the groups is seen as being either better than young people had received in church, or more wide-ranging than they were expecting. There were times when the practice of welcome formed a literal interruption at St Joe's. I noted on several occasions the way in which Victoria was exuberant in her welcome of young people into the group and in particular her commitment to welcome even when they arrived late, in the middle of the Bible study. Consequently, Victoria's practice of welcome interrupted even her own opinion that the Bible study is the most important aspect of the group! Sally reinforced the value of welcome interrupting other core practices when I interviewed her:

If you are late to something people kind of ignore you as if you're not there but she is interested in you and she will often ask questions later if she feels she needs to follow it up. But it's quite nice to know that you're not just sliding in on the side-lines ... No, she's like, 'hi, how are you, how's your week been, is there anything we need to know?' No 'good, this is what we've been doing and this is what we're going to do'. And she doesn't really bat an eyelid that I'm late, or if anyone is late.

As a result of the interruption of welcome, Sally is then able to participate in the more explicitly ecclesial practice of Bible study. In Newtown, on the other hand, the practice of welcome was expressed in conversation with one of the young people. Freddie, who would not term himself a Christian, recounts how people like him are welcomed into the group without judgement, despite their behaviour or lifestyles sometimes going against that which was taught in the Bible-focused sessions. This experience of the practice of welcome for Freddie had the effect of interrupting his preconceptions of Christianity and consequently helped to turn him towards consideration of the Christian faith. Welcome here interrupts an instinctive view of Christians and the Church.

Connected with the practice of welcome are two other practices that act to allow the young people to feel comfortable in the environment of the group. The practice of encouraging questions, even if these challenge the expressed beliefs of the leaders or the wider community of the group, was regularly evident in Newtown where small-group time was set aside in part to allow space for questions from the young people. I experienced this in a small group when an emerging leader who was not a Christian strongly questioned the likelihood of the resurrection having happened. In St Joe's, Victoria was always visibly excited by the occasions that the teaching aspect of the group overran as a result of individuals wanting to stay and ask questions. This practice of interruption is strongly connected to 'safe place' being a mode of belonging – by encouraging questions, the groups adopt a posture and create an environment of exploration in which participants, whether already Christian or not, regular churchgoers or not, are seen as together investigating the claims and practices of the Christian faith. This then helps to cut across an instinctive divide between those who are in or out, thus interrupting the dominant discourse about church that creates artificial boundaries to define and delineate what is and isn't considered church.

In a similar vein, the practice of creating fun helps to develop an environment in which young people are comfortable, and consequently open to the ecclesial practices on offer. The practice of creating fun is deemed essential to work with young people by Stuart, who says that 'if you're not thinking fun, you're not going to have youth work, are you?'[20] Andrew from Newtown connects the practice of fun to the desire to see those coming along being drawn into the church community and the Christian faith:

> At Newtown we are a bit crazy and we are all about having fun and enjoying God and revelling in this amazing story, and we want to do that through our young people as well and it doesn't just happen with Friday night, it happens right through from a younger age group. And we want them to be able to worship and to be able to speak openly but we don't want them to think that church is this boring thing that happens once a week, because it's not and the relationships they have and the friendships they have are something that will keep them going and going and going and they are life-changing friendships and relationships.

Similarly, in St Joe's the fun and games that are part of the free time are considered a crucial aspect of the missional endeavour and desire to reach out to young people by making it easier for new people to come along and feel comfortable in the group or for those already there to invite their friends, confident that they are going to enjoy themselves.

Taken together, creating fun, asking questions and welcome are practices designed to, in the words of Nick Shepherd,[21] create a place for young people to be Christian, through encountering the more explicitly Christian practices. Indeed, these practices are seen as ways of interrupting young people's preconceptions about church. Even though the leaders rarely connect the more ecclesial practices of prayer, Bible study and pastoral care to being an expression of church, they do make that link with these interruptive practices. Stuart, for example, wants those in the group to know that church is fun:

> Newtown is supposed to be fun and an introduction to the fact that church isn't necessarily the stereotyped image of somewhere dark and stone walls and cold and all that kind of thing ... it is running around inside the building and throwing gunge at each other and things like that; that's church. Not just sitting reading the 'Thees' and the 'Thous' and the 'Thou Shalt Nots' from a big dusty book.

The groups are able to appropriate these practices that are not specifically Christian or ecclesial and put them to use for the purposes of the group. It seems that for those who come along these types of practices help them to become open to the more clearly Christian ones. When interviewed, Robin, for example, talked through the way that friendships built with young people who were already part of the group helped him feel comfortable, and consequently more interested in and open to the explicitly Christian practices and aspects of the group. In turn he described to me how he has sporadically adopted some of these practices into his life outside of the group:

> [My first experiences of Newtown] were fun, like we were messing around with [leaders] that was really funny and all the activities were fun, they kept you like, kept you entertained ... It was a break from the normal and you got a chance to meet new people and have fun, make new friends ... I'm not a full-on Christian but I am understanding the ideas of Christianity ... I will pray to God on the odd occasion.

The way that these practices of welcome, asking questions and creating fun are means by which those in the group become open to the more explicitly Christian practices demonstrates the missional potential of them. This resonates with what Kathryn Tanner refers to as a 'slippery give and take' between Christian and non-Christian practices in which some practices of the Church are 'non-Christian practices done differently, born again to unpredictable effect'.[22] This means that ambiguity in the practices that make up Christian communities can be expected, but also be open to how such ambiguity can lead back to theological reflection and in turn can be transformative for the community.

In the case studies it is this ambiguity in the context of interaction between ecclesial practices and practices of interruption that makes it possible for something of the Church to be experienced by the young people as it extends into the space created within the groups. It is also through these practices that the Christian faith and experience of God can become possible for the young people – in this way, the interruptions are significant for those from church-going and non-church-going families, thus (to use Charles Taylor's words) helping to demonstrate the 'eligible possibility' of faith in a secular age.

Summary

This chapter has developed the presentation and analysis of the case studies by beginning to build the case for the potential of ecclesial life being apparent within the practices of the group. This drawing out of what might be termed an emergent operant ecclesiology demonstrates contradictions in the way that church is discussed and described in the dominant discourse. The groups reveal a hitherto unacknowledged hidden discourse that articulates and embodies the historical ecclesial imagination of youth ministry. The practices of interruption open up participants to the way of life in the groups that fosters faith, built around simple ecclesial practices in the context of welcome, encouraging questions and creating fun. Consequently, the groups create space in which their ecclesial identity might be understood as ambiguous but full of potential. The following chapter picks up on this, developing the idea of potential ecclesial spaces and beginning to articulate the way this expression of the ecclesial imagination of youth ministry, as detailed through these case studies, opens up the potential for new ecclesiological thinking to develop within the framework of an 'interweaving ecclesiology'.

Notes

1 Sally, a 16-year-old girl from St Joe's.

2 This echoes one of the themes explored by David Bailey in *Youth Ministry and Theological Shorthand: Living Amongst the Fragments of a Coherent Theology* (Eugene, OR: Pickwick Publications, 2019).

3 This includes chatting about exams, family situations and films the young people had seen at the cinema.

4 In his own words, he was not a 'full on Christian'.

5 This is significant in light of the move to secular three discussed in Chapter 2.

6 See Chapter 3.

7 I discuss this phrase more in the next chapter.

8 Especially within the broadly evangelical tradition.

9 Pete Ward, 'Blueprint Ecclesiology and the Lived: Normativity as Perilous Faithfulness', *Ecclesial Practices*, 2(1) (2015), p. 76.

10 Ward highlights this by the way that theologians of distinct traditions have each used the recent popular rise in Trinitarian ecclesiology to reinforce the theological basis for their own tradition's ecclesiology. See 'Blueprint Ecclesiology and the Lived', pp. 76–80.

11 Pete Ward, *Growing Up Evangelical: Youthwork and the Making of a Subculture* (Eugene, OR: Wipf and Stock, 2013).

12 Both Alister McGrath, *Evangelicalism & the Future of Christianity* (London: Hodder and Stoughton, 1994), and Bruce Hindmarsh, 'Is Evangelical Ecclesiology an Oxymoron? A Historical Perspective', in *Evangelical Ecclesiology: Reality or Illusion?*, ed. John G. Stackhouse Jnr (Grand Rapids, MI: Baker Academic, 2003), discuss 'minimalist' evangelical ecclesiology. See also Chapter 3.

13 The term 'Sunday school' is not used in any of the church literature; however, this was Claire's description of the groups that meet on a Sunday during the morning service.

14 Ward, *Growing Up*, pp. 143–4.

15 See the previous chapter.

16 Learning to see the familiar as strange is a key dynamic of ethnographic field work.

17 See Chapter 3.

18 Crusaders, 'Crusaders and the Churches' report, 1970.

19 And, for Sally, provide a replacement for a period.

20 See also the discussion of 'social space' in the previous chapter.

21 Nick Shepherd, *Faith Generation: Retaining Young People and Growing the Church* (London: SPCK, 2016), p. 68 (ebook).

22 Kathryn Tanner, 'Theological Reflection and Christian Practices', in *Practicing Theology: Beliefs and Practices in Christian Life*, ed. Miroslav Volf and Dorothy C. Bass (Grand Rapids, MI: William B. Eerdmans, 2002), p. 230.

6

An Interweaving Ecclesiology in Practice: Ambiguity and Potential

I am becoming open to the possibility of being a Christian.[1]

The previous chapter concluded that the case studies of the youth groups revealed a hidden ecclesial discourse that interrupts the dominant ways of thinking about the Church. By framing the groups as potential ecclesial spaces, this gives language to the ecclesial imagination of youth ministry and offers something distinct to ongoing ecclesiological conversations – holding forth the possibility of ecclesial life without setting out to launch and construct churches themselves. In this way, the concept of potential ecclesial spaces values the significance of the Church in mission, and mission as a vital aspect of the Church's identity, while not foregrounding the Church or delineating solid boundaries around what is and isn't church. This chapter further details an ecclesiological vision for how potential ecclesial spaces, such as those of the youth groups, can form a dynamic move in ecclesiology. It therefore continues to analyse the case studies while also beginning to bring the operant and espoused theologies of the ecclesial imagination of youth work into conversation with the ecclesiological approach of Fresh Expressions.

Using Rowan Williams's point of departure about the Church as something that happens as people 'encounter the risen Christ and commit to continuing that encounter together', this chapter argues that the Church has a fluidity built into its nature. It is dynamic, and the nature of encounter with Christ means that the Church will always be growing into new spaces within society. As a pilgrim people, the Church is moving and seeking Christ and the kingdom in itself and in the wider world. This requires porous or ambiguous boundaries where it is not clear where the Church ends. The natural consequence of this is that defining what is and isn't a mature church creates unhelpful boundaries on church life. Instead, potential ecclesial spaces seek encounter with Christ and from this encounter and ensuing Christian community recognize the ecclesial nature of the Christian faith.

This means that ecclesiology can be reversed – rather than beginning with an idea about the Church, suggesting a way that the Church looks, the interweaving approach begins with connecting individuals to Christ, and from that considers them and the community through which they connect as part of the body of Christ, the Church. It is as if ecclesial life, by the Spirit, can extend into ambiguous spaces such as the youth groups that I studied. In addition, by starting with encountering and experiencing the transcendent Christ, the prevailing secular social imaginary is interrupted in a place of safe exploration rather than a solid commitment for individuals, thus allowing for a more authentic journey of faith at the pace of the individual themselves. It also then allows for interaction with the ongoing meaning-making of young people within contemporary society to contribute to how ecclesial life might look.

The value of this as an ecclesiological framework for and from youth ministry is that it is flexible and nuanced enough to prevent a slide into unhelpful either/or debates. This chapter illustrates this through three such debates and argues for the way in which an interweaving ecclesiology can help to arbitrate these debates, and create dialogue between different understandings and expressions of work with young people in relation to the Church. The three debates investigated in this chapter are: intergenerational church versus age-segregated activities; youth congregations versus youth as part of congregations; and parachurch versus local church. The vision of an interweaving ecclesiology suggests that each of these might be a situation in which there is space and flexibility: for age-segregated and intergenerational work, for local and network ministry; and that through an interweaving approach in which connection with Christ comes before ecclesial structure a relational and openhanded vision for church can be reclaimed that is more sensitive to the rhythms of contemporary life. This also anticipates the argument in Part 3, that an interweaving ecclesiology can bring nuance to the debates – and at times polarized positions – around inherited and 'fresh' expressions of church.

Potential ecclesial spaces

The practices of interruption create an ambiguous space in the groups resulting from the way they disrupt the dominant discourse. Despite the clarity in the origins of Crusaders, that the role of the work was missionary in nature, and the similar ways in which this is expressed in the work of the current groups, both Newtown and St Joe's demonstrate a degree of ambiguity about their identity. This ambiguity is evident from both leaders and young people and refers to the ways in which the group understands itself in relation to church and the ways in which those involved access and use the groups. The ambiguity is articulated through the modes of belonging alongside the ecclesial practices and practices of interruption. As the young people attend and move between the different modes of belonging and practices, they can appropriate different identities for the group. Within the flow and movement of these different identities is the opportunity for young people to experiment with belonging in different ways. This takes place within the safety of the group which, because it has a multitude of identities each at work in an ambiguous way, is a place in between – it is not school, home or church. Neither is it simply a youth group or a Bible study group.

The space is ambiguous in part because there isn't the language to adequately define it as a result of it being space that is outside the ecclesial boundaries defined by the dominant discourse. However, it is in this ambiguous space, directly because of the practices of interruption, that young people become open to the possibility of the Christian faith. 'Possibility' is the word, drawn from one of the young people themselves, that I use to understand the experience in which those with no Christian faith or church involvement find themselves becoming open to the eligibility of Christianity. This mirrors the findings and argument of Nick Shepherd that plausibility is one of the key aspects of faith generation for young people and needs to be regularly attended to in the practices of youth groups.[2]

The creation of ambiguous space is exemplified in a description of a small-group time by one of the Newtown leaders in which he details a conversation that he allowed to take place in the group. I include the whole passage here to allow for the sense of what happened to be retained:

> One conversation, which is probably the best conversation I have ever seen there. One of the kids from the estate, real, real tough case, I had him in my small group at the end of the session and he's absolute 'God doesn't exist, you know I hate him' ... and that's kind of his view on it. And we had another guy who was 14 or so who comes from a church background and we were talking about does Jesus exist. And this lad was straightaway 'No he doesn't exist, I can't see him, I can't touch him, so how does he exist.' And the other guy was, 'Well, I believe he does exist because it says so in the Bible' and they ended up having this conversation and the rest of the group were looking at them and waiting for explosions because this lad has a real bad reputation for causing trouble ... for five minutes they just had this conversation of yes he does, no he doesn't, and it wasn't antagonizing or disrespectful or anything, it was just [an] amazing moment to watch and I thought this is why we do this. This lad would not be able to have that conversation anywhere else and he is able to do that and that was probably one of my highlights ... For him to have the conversation, to have the courage to have that conversation, in front of a group of people who do believe, was a huge moment for him ... and if those kids come to Christ or not, we're still playing a huge part in their life.

Central to this conversation is the way that the leader sat back and allowed it to continue, concluding that this is why they do what they do in the Newtown group. By allowing the conversation to run in the way that he did, without imposing himself or what he might have considered the correct answer, a certain ambiguity was cultivated. By encouraging questions and creating space in which these questions are welcomed, an ambiguous space is formed in which beliefs and practices that are considered part of church – and something of 'not church' – can come together in dialogue.

The experience of these young people is that they join the group with little or no initial interest in the Christian practices and teaching that form central aspects of Newtown. What we see instead is the ambiguous identity of the group allowing those who come along to join and find their way into the group through the social space it offers in its role as a youth group. This in turn provides an environment in which friendship can be built and cultivated. It is in this cultivation of friendship that the identity of the group moves beyond that of a youth group towards becoming the kind of safe place in which young people are able to open themselves up to the possibilities represented within the Christian heart of the group. In addition to this, though, as demonstrated previously, the experience of both leaders and church-going young people is that they find the ambiguous space of the groups helpful in providing an environment in which their faith can be developed and enhanced.

The safe place of the group is exhibited in the way that questions are welcomed, and young people feel able to be themselves. Beth exemplified these experiences in a small-group time at the end of a session when, in the context of a discussion, she stated that what she loved about Newtown was that it was a place where she could be herself and not be judged. The creation of a safe place within the group in which young people can ask questions and listen to opinions while also being presented with simple Christian teaching and practices results in their considering the Christian faith in ways they might not otherwise have done. They describe this in terms of the Christian faith 'becoming possible' or of their 'becoming open' to being Christians.

This kind of language is used regardless of whether the young people have fully accepted the Christian faith. Some describe themselves as now being Christians while others do not. Among those who do not are some who say they have considered the Christian faith and, while they are still thinking things through, they do not expect to decide to become a Christian, as well as those who use the language of journey to describe where they are in relation to the Christian faith. In this language, young people talk about moving towards becoming a Christian or taking 'baby steps'. They can also talk of not yet being a 'full-on Christian'. In these ways, while they are clear about moving towards becoming a Christian there is some hesitancy about making this definitive move. However, the group creates a community in which this in-between, ambiguous position can be held and negotiated.

These findings suggest the groups are creating places through which young people begin to consider the Christian faith. This offers an interesting counterpoint to the findings of research exploring Christian-run open youth groups that had little or no formal presentation of the Christian faith and no regular Christian practices or structured opportunity to ask questions and express belief.[3] The hope of the leaders in these groups was that through building relationships with the young people the leaders' Christian faith would be expressed and that this in turn would encourage those in the group to consider for themselves the merits of faith. However, the authors report that instead of encouraging an openness to the Christian faith among young people, the relationship with leaders who are confident in their faith serves to allow young people to be confident in the beliefs they already have rather than considering the possibility of the leaders' beliefs. As discussed in Chapter 2, this should be no surprise in the light of Taylor's understanding of the move to a secular age.

In contrast, the ambiguous space of the Urban Saints groups provides a place in which the possibility and plausibility of a Christian social imaginary might be considered. The atmosphere created by the practices of interruption is relaxed and one of exploration and experience for those who wish to investigate the claims of Christianity for themselves and their own life within the safety of a youth group community. The result of this is that young people who grew up in church-going families, those who arrive in the groups with little understanding of the Christian faith, and even a number of the leaders, find that they are able to use the groups to develop, sustain and enhance a Christian faith. In this way the ambiguous space in the groups provides freedom from expectations and facilitates the groups' role as mission-focused; this mission, however, is to all participants regardless of previous levels of Christian faith and is the heart of the groups as potential ecclesial spaces – potential meaning open to all, but space that can be utilized as ecclesial to greater or lesser degrees by different participants.

Mission has been central to the self-understanding of Crusaders/Urban Saints for the majority of its existence. The ethos of those who shaped the organization viewed it as a missionary movement seeking to reach young people with the gospel.[4] Similarly, the leaders of today clearly express the aim of reaching those who are not already part of the Church as a key aim of both groups. However, it is fair to say that the way in which this works out is more complex and the clear focus of the early days has become somewhat diffused among other understandings of what the group is for. So, for example, Newtown at its launch in 2006 was intended to be 'absolutely missional territory' by the founding leader, and was still described during my time with the group as 'primarily an outreach'. When reflecting on the role of the group in the life of the church, the leaders are also able to claim the group as the 'main mission success' in the church. Whether this is accurate or merely part of a self-sustaining narrative on the part of the leaders is to some extent irrelevant as it is the self-identity of the group that is significant in these statements and sentiments. The prominence of mission as the original intention of the group in Newtown, and among the current ways of expressing the purpose of the group, is strong enough to suggest the echoes of the earlier sole focus on mission that shaped the origins of Crusaders.

The leaders of St Joe's Crusaders also frame their purpose in terms of mission work though their preferred term to describe this is 'outreach'. In addition, for the St Joe's leaders the mission identity of the group is furthered and sharpened by the nature of the group being separate from the Church. In a comment acknowledged as being a broad generalization, but also typical of the ethos and attitude of the leaders, Dorothy expresses her view that churches are usually more interested in the children they already have, whereas the group being outside of church helps it to maintain a clearer focus on those that the Church isn't reaching. This is what they mean when they refer to the group as meeting a need the churches can't meet or filling a niche.

This analysis of the case study data reframes this mission focus by suggesting the groups offer a space in which participants can affirm the possibility and plausibility of Christian faith against both the prevailing social imaginary and the gravitational pull of the Church. As discussed in Chapter 2, the social imaginary is the underlying, often unquestioned, foundational way in which the world is understood by a particular society. Charles Taylor charts the shift in this underlying understanding and suggests that the shift is not from belief to unbelief but from one kind of belief to another. It is a shift from belief in some kind of outside force that controls the universe to a time that is driven more by a belief that derives from the internal world of the individual.[5]

The testimony from the young people, particularly in Newtown, suggests that there is something about the group that challenges this underlying social imaginary and begins to open up the possibility of transcendence and belief in God, or reinforces it for those from a faith background. Jason Lief has written on the implications of Charles Taylor's thought for youth ministry and among his suggestions is the potentially controversial idea that church must be willing to let young people go.[6] However, on a close reading what he is suggesting is actually something akin to the ambiguous spaces provided by the youth groups in my case studies. He talks of the need to give young people 'space to doubt, [and] to ask questions'[7] in the way I identified was a practice in both groups.

In addition, Lief encourages what he calls the creation of space through which young people can step out from under the expectations of the world and the Church in order to narrate their own identities.[8] This stepping out allows for a dual movement of distancing from, and drawing young people close to, the life of the Church. Both aspects of this dual movement, though, serve the purpose of developing a sense of belonging and possibility. The first of these movements, distancing, refers to the role the groups play in the lives of young people who are from families involved in the life of local churches. For these individuals, the Christian faith and involvement in church is something that they have, on the whole, grown up with. It has become the normal experience for them. In these scenarios the groups act to distance the young people from the church. This distancing allows them to consider for themselves the claims of the Christian faith. Sally from St Joe's described this process eloquently in telling me how she needed to find somewhere that wasn't the church where her parents were leaders so she could consider the Christian faith without being identified simply as a key adult's daughter. Drawing close, on the other hand, describes the way that young people begin to feel connected in some way to the church or broad Christian community through the creation of fun, welcome and encouraging questions that open up the ambiguous space of the groups.

It seems that this is what the young people experience in the groups when they talk about how they are able to be themselves and feel accepted in ways they aren't either in church or at home. Lief then moves on to endorse the importance of play and 'reclaiming a sense of playfulness'[9] for young people. In these ways Lief creates a framework whereby many of the practices outlined above that are core regular practices of these youth groups, and therefore contribute to the operant ecclesiological voice in this analysis, are vital to the task of the Church for, and on behalf of, young people in the secular age. The potential ecclesial space of these youth groups can become part of the ecclesial life of participants. They are, however, not considered or intended to be fully church for those who attend. The ecclesial life becomes apparent through practices of interruption and by interweaving with other forms of communal Christian life that help to develop and sustain Christian life and identity for individuals.

It is true, though, that these potential ecclesial spaces, characterized as they are by creating the safe spaces, still have some boundaries within which the young people are required to operate. Frustrations and challenges around the behaviour of three difficult lads at Newtown demonstrate this and there are challenges when the underlying boundaries are tested. The dynamics and overall culture of the group, however, operate to sustain and reinforce these kinds of implicit boundaries. The group is a safe place for young people to explore and to be themselves in so far as they participate as expected within the group. The example cited at length earlier in this chapter of a conversation between one believing boy and one unbelieving boy highlights this well – as long as the unbelief and questions were expressed within the accepted terms of the group they were deemed positive. This is the kind of multi-layered demarcating of boundaries in evangelical life described by Mathew Guest in his study of St Michael-Le-Belfry Church in York.[10] In this study, an innovative group on the margins of the church sought to renegotiate their evangelical identity through renewing their cultural relevance in a new form of worship that embodied a critique of the approach within the main church congregation.[11] Guest details that 'what counts as legitimate and who counts as included'[12] became key issues that the group wrestled with. In terms of the potential ecclesial spaces of these youth groups the answer suggested here would be those willing to participate, and open to the possibility of being on a journey, individually and together.

The ecclesial ambiguity of the groups is in contrast to the drive towards the ecclesial certainty of developing mature churches that is inherent in the ideas behind the Fresh Expressions movement.[13] By creating spaces that are ecclesially ambiguous yet containing ecclesial potential, the youth groups do not begin with church but might become part of the experience of the Church for participants through the interweaving ecclesiology. This reversal of thought refrains from predetermining what church might look like. Instead, the intention remains to provide a means through which individuals can connect with Christ and simple Christian practices in community. This opens up ways in which the interweaving ecclesiology of Urban Saints can contribute to the ongoing pilgrim nature of the Church. By resisting set church forms the concept of potential ecclesial spaces in an interweaving ecclesiology can provide a timely and useful contribution to ongoing conversations about church and mission in the UK. Detailing further the way that potential ecclesial spaces reverse ecclesiological thinking makes this case more explicit.

Reversing ecclesiological thinking

The dominant discourse about church discussed in the previous chapter demonstrates the way in which it is all too tempting to place hard-and-fast boundaries around what is considered church, even when these boundaries contain contradictions that make them arbitrary at best. Pete Ward, however, invites a different direction of thought. By building on the Pauline concept of being 'in Christ', and contrasting this with the commonly used evangelical terminology of being 'in church' that is so highly suggestive of the boundaries of buildings and timings, Ward suggests a reversal of the usual thinking. Individual believers are joined to one another, says Ward, because they are joined to Christ. To use another Pauline image, it is through being in Christ that individual Christians find themselves becoming part of the body of Christ and consequently the Church. The challenge here is to think the other way round from that which has become the norm, especially in evangelical church life with its congregational focus. The standard thinking suggests that it is by being in church and through participating in congregational life that one is joined to the body of Christ. Ward, however, through his imaginative reversal, is able to propose that through being joined to Christ, individuals are part of the body of Christ and therefore the Church.[14] 'We are joined to Christ and therefore joined to each other, and as we express this corporate life of Christ we are church.'[15]

Shifting the starting point from preconceived and static ideas about the Church to the notion of being in Christ means not accepting that church as it is or has been structured is the only way to express 'the corporate Christ'. This centring of congregational life in our ecclesiology comes not from academic ecclesiology but from the 'popular ecclesial imagination',[16] what I named in the previous chapter as the dominant discourse. Ward does not suggest eliminating gathering together as part of church life, but rather that this gathering does not restrict our ecclesiology. The Spirit, and therefore the love of Jesus, is not contained within meetings, but 'flows underneath, within and around'.[17] Ecclesiology, then, argues Ward, should take account of the operant ways in which people participate in this flow.[18]

Ward acknowledges that this reversal of the order of thinking around church results in less well-defined and more 'fuzzy' boundaries. As with the ambiguity within potential ecclesial spaces of the youth groups, however, this is perceived as a positive characteristic as these fuzzy edges represent the 'growing point of the church'.[19] This is similar to the sentiment stating that any attempt to plant churches should be on the 'bleeding edge' of church life.[20] Also critical in this direction of thinking is the possibility that certain activities, groups and relationships can become church for individuals in so far as they provide a means or a context through which the individual is able to experience something of what it is to be in Christ through relationships and practices, thus echoing Rowan Williams's ecclesiological starting point.

This is not to say that in each relationship, group or activity the Church is fully realized and expressed, but rather that the possibility of church is present and can become apparent as Christ is communicated and experienced. Taking this concept further then allows the spaces created by activities such as youth groups to hold within them the possibility of being church while not being defined organizationally or structurally as church. This is expressed by the young people interviewed in the various ways in which they describe the groups as allowing them to open up to Christ and the concept of Christianity in a safe environment. It also helps to articulate how the groups can form one of numerous expressions of church in their lives. While holding the possibility of church they also allow young people to participate and belong to them without the additional expectation that might come from something labelled as church.

The post-Christendom ideal in which church is understood more in terms of a movement rather than an institution is also significant here.[21] If church is a movement then it is not possible to hold on to static concepts of what constitutes church. In turn, this makes it necessary to hold loosely to any understanding of where the boundaries of church might be. Any boundaries that there are will need to be fuzzy at best. It is, however, not only those who write to defend the parish system that risk solidifying boundaries that should remain fuzzy or fluid. It has been noted in critiques of Fresh Expressions that that which begins as a fresh, innovative, grassroots movement runs the risk of institutionalizing the very things that created the movement in the first place.[22] This potentially has the effect of re-casting solid boundaries, by merely putting them in a different place than before.

Arguably, as the wealth of literature and reflection on Fresh Expressions and contemporary evangelical ecclesiology continues to grow, this solidifying of boundaries that should remain fuzzy can be discerned.[23] John Hull's concern, picked up by Martyn Percy, that there is scope for almost anything to count as church in the thinking of Fresh Expressions perhaps led to this drive to define.[24] However, the consequent reinforcing of boundaries is unhelpful. The ambiguity present within the potential ecclesial spaces of the Urban Saints groups studied is a helpful reminder of the importance of fuzzy boundaries and resistance to defining some activities as definitively church or not church. The thinking of Pete Ward aids this resistance.

The inherent freshness that comes from youth groups with the regular turnover of young people and the natural connection with the sharp end of popular culture assists these groups in resisting becoming institutionalized. This also provides an environment that is conducive to allowing questions and conversation to naturally shape the form that the communication of the gospel and the expression of the church can take. In addition, the resistance of the youth groups to be defined as churches or to be understood as inside the life of the church helps maintain a form of missional resistance while not denying the potential ecclesial space of the groups. Reversing the ecclesiological thinking serves this missional resistance while providing a theological rationale for understanding how a particular group or activity can be part of the interweaving church. An interweaving approach, then, contains the potential for endless varieties in the way that church is expressed while, in addition, developing an environment through which church can be seen to mould and change as required to maintain connection within contemporary life and culture. This means that, rather than starting with the church, the interweaving approach reverses this to begin with an individual's connection with faith in Christ and from here looks to how the Church appears.

One of the challenges when thinking about the place of the Church in the work of Urban Saints was illustrated well in the St Joe's case study. As a youth group that was non-denominational and drew its leadership from across the local churches while remaining independent of any particular church, it was clear that some from those local churches, including local clergy and other leaders, struggled to see how the group 'fitted into' the city's ecclesial scene.[25] One leader who bemoaned this lack of support or recognition expressed this succinctly by suggesting to me how easy it would be for the group to be seen as an outreach or mission activity for the parish, located as it was within the geographical boundaries of the parish, but yet the church didn't acknowledge the group's work as such. Another leader described this more generally through her sense that churches were only really interested in their own work rather than anything that took place outside of their own leadership.

At the heart of these frustrations is an issue around understanding where the church begins and ends. This is an issue regularly raised in the contemporary ecclesiological discussion. In the context of Fresh Expressions, the question of parish proves a regular sticking point. When analysed, this sticking point comes from preconceived understandings of what constitutes church in the first place. Examples of this are found within the responses to *Mission-shaped Church* that look to make the case for the traditional parish structure of Anglican church life. In these responses the authors write from the perspective of understanding the contemporary ecclesiological conversation as constituting an attack on the parish system as the moves towards network and mission-shaped churches are promoted.[26] In defending the parish system, however, what comes across is often that it *is* the Church.[27] In addition, this focus on the parish becomes centred on the building of the parish church. John Milbank in particular seems to suggest that the fullness of church can only be experienced within the walls of such a consecrated building in a designated place built for this specific purpose.[28]

Leaving aside how this understanding side-lines even other denominations and churches with long histories and tradition, what this view exposes is a preconditioned understanding of the shape that church must take that prejudices the author against other ways of thinking about church. In this view, the boundaries of church are set by the boundaries of the parish structure: geographically, structurally and philosophically. The attempts to define what counts and does not count as church within this ongoing conversation can be seen as an attempt to institutionalize experimentation and variety.[29] Two challenges are noted in particular around these definitional attempts. First, that there is a contradiction between missiological and ecclesiological imperatives. In other words, by seeking to make church mission-focused and defining the ways in which this can happen mission can all too easily become church-focused; consequently, the Church and kingdom of God can become conflated.[30] Second, by seeking to define specifically what can be counted as church in order that new forms of the Church can be seen as part of the institution, a form of control is exerted over the experimental and new ecclesial forms.[31]

Much of the ongoing ecclesiological conversation, then, has become about how to maintain some form of definition of what constitutes the boundaries of church as the Church seeks to close the gap with popular cultures. There are, though, contributions to the conversation calling for what they term a generous ecclesiology in which boundaries are perhaps more uncertain.[32] This uncertainty arises out of understanding ecclesiology as an ongoing conversation between the Church, the world and the kingdom of God. There is a sense of a necessary give and take between institutional understandings of the Church and discerning the kingdom of God in the world. In this view, the Church is deemed a pilgrim people, journeying beyond its own institution as it seeks God's activity in the world.[33] Aspects of this approach were expressed within *Mission-shaped Church*, but perhaps got lost along the way as the church-planting imperative took precedent.

Resisting solid boundaries

An interweaving ecclesiology, then, that reverses the direction of ecclesiological thought creates a framework for thinking afresh about the Church, mission and young people – it is flexible and nuanced enough to prevent a slide into unhelpful either/or debates. This final section of the chapter illustrates this through three such debates and argues for the way in which an interweaving ecclesiology can help to arbitrate these debates and creates a dialogue between different understandings and expressions of work with young people in relation to the Church. The three debates investigated will be: intergenerational church versus age-segregated activities; youth congregations versus youth as part of congregations; and parachurch versus local church.

Each of these scenarios creates unhelpful and deconstructive division in youth ministry and the wider church, imposing false and at times contradictory, paradoxical boundaries. The vision of an interweaving ecclesiology suggests that each of these might be both/and situations in which there is space and flexibility for age-segregated and intergenerational work, for local and network ministry, and that through an interweaving approach in which connection with Christ comes before ecclesial structure a relational and open-handed vision for church can be reclaimed that is more sensitive to the rhythms of contemporary life. This also anticipates the argument in Part 3 that an interweaving ecclesiology can bring nuance to the debates and challenges polarized positions around inherited and 'fresh' expressions of church.

Crucially, by drawing again on the case studies it can be seen that this open-handed approach is not a problem for young people themselves. Consequently, the way ahead for the Church in mission using an interweaving approach is modelled by youth ministry in holding together the value of separate work for young people, as well as engagement in intergenerational communities, local churches and network approaches such as that of parachurch.

As argued in Chapter 2, a key implication of the hyperconnectivity that marks a way of life for younger generations growing up as 'digital natives' is the way that previously usual boundaries are broken down or blurred at the very least. Relational and life-space divides do not exist in the same manner as for previous generations, meaning that younger people are used to living in a way that does not need or create clear lines of demarcation between, for example, school life and home life. However, oftentimes the debates within the Church about the place of young people or the way to work with them become either/or debates. These debates seek to determine the best way of structuring the Church in order to be 'successful' in mission and discipleship.

The analysis of the case studies detailed in previous chapters reveals the hidden discourse about the Church that cuts across any attempt to set hard-and-fast boundary lines to demarcate how the groups relate to, or are part of, the Church. While on the surface the dominant discourse sets the groups apart from the Church, as age-segregated youth groups that are part of a parachurch organization, the hidden discourse reveals the groups as potential ecclesial spaces, with dynamics of ecclesial life visible that complexify any attempt to form boundaries within the life of the Church. In this complexifying, each group is seen to have both age-segregated and intergenerational dynamics, be both parachurch and an expression of church life, and also a youth group and Christian community.

Reversing the direction of ecclesiological thinking ensures that space remains open for the Church to be revealed in this more complex manner. The dominant discourse works to exert its gravitational pull on our understandings of church and therefore tends towards polarized debates about the place of young people and the best form of missional church praxis. Reversing this creates a posture of ongoing discernment about where and how the Church is being revealed or disclosed. It also assists the task of not limiting the Church to a specific vision or experience. The hidden discourse revealed in the previous chapter demonstrates the way that those in the groups are able to hold the blurred lines of an ambiguous space without a problem – more than that, the way that the groups can hold various identities, among them an ecclesial one, is valued by the young people. The blurring of boundaries created in large part by the practices of interruption and the groups' externally held non-church identity allow this ecclesial life to be revealed.

Too much energy is exerted in debate between the various approaches to the Church, mission and young people when what seems to be significant from the case studies is flexibility and the ability to move between, or weave together, different dynamics of ecclesial life as the Church is seen to be revealed as individuals encounter Christ with others. Hence the debates between separate work for young people and intergenerational work, youth congregations and youth as part of congregational life, and church or parachurch.

This missionary work of Crusaders/Urban Saints can be viewed through the reflections of twentieth-century missiologist Ralph Winter as one of the forms of God's redemptive mission.[34] There are, and have been since the times of the early Church, Winter argues, both modalities and sodalities in the overall life of the Church. A modality is a 'structured fellowship where there is no distinction of sex or age'.[35] Local churches and denominations can identify with this form. Sodalities, however, are characterized by likeminded Christians banding together for specific purposes.[36] For Winter, sodalities and modalities are separate forms of communal Christian experience. In their separation they can be seen as a duality sitting at opposite ends of a spectrum. In general, and certainly within the history of Crusaders/Urban Saints, the expectation is that there will be a trajectory in which those reached through sodalities find their place within the modality of a local church.[37] The operant interweaving ecclesiology, however, despite demonstrating the need for relational connections between these two forms of Christian communal experience, shows that individuals operate within these two forms simultaneously. Victoria, the main leader of St Joe's, described how her faith as a younger woman had developed in different ways through involvement in Crusaders, Scripture Union, YWAM and other churches. Sodalities, it seems, have something to add to the ongoing communal Christian experience. They are part of the interweaving of church within the life of those in the Urban Saints groups.

While the language of modalities and sodalities is quite clumsy – they are not terms in common usage – and does not immediately make it clear what is being described, the concept is an exceptionally helpful one to reclaim since it articulates the way that the Church in different forms, in different modes, can operate together. The language of interweaving can expand and bring clarity to the concept that Winter's terms are trying to explore. The concept can be expanded as the idea of the Church operating in different modes does not necessarily need to refer to completely different entities and organizations but can help navigate the relationships between different activities within the same local church, denomination or network. It is therefore possible for both intergenerational and age-segregated activities to be affirmed; for youth churches and young people within congregations to be of value; and for the parachurch and local church to complement each other.

The key is that in an interweaving ecclesiology all the expressions of ecclesial life, all the groups and activities that cultivate and sustain faith, that work to open up participants to the ongoing eligible possibility of faith, can be seen as part of the life of the Church. In an interweaving ecclesiology solid and liquid,[38] certain and ambiguous expressions of church can all play a part in the church experience of the participants. The argument of this chapter has been to see the value of the more ambiguous potential ecclesial spaces as a vital expression of the Church in mission, one that seeks not to construct church but to create space whereby participants might be able to experience and explore connection with Christ and Christian community on their own terms and at their own pace, adopting the group as part of their ecclesial life if and as needed. Does this mean that anything goes? That anything and everything can be defined as church? Of course not, but just as the youth groups display certain characteristics that mean the hidden discourse of potential ecclesial spaces comes to light, it is also important to wrestle with ways in which the interweaving ecclesiology might be regulated without reinforcing unnecessary arbitrary or solid boundaries of church life. This is one of the questions that Part 3 tackles.

Summary

This chapter brings Part 2 to its conclusion. Overall, the chapters in this part of the book have offered a thick description and analysis of the two case study youth groups. This thick description has detailed the praxis of the groups and the understanding of that praxis by the participants. The analysis of the praxis and its understanding has allowed a fresh look at the ecclesial imagination inherent within Christian youth group ministry, handed down in norms of practice from the early days of organizations such as the exemplar, Crusaders/Urban Saints. This ecclesial imagination shows that there is indeed a way of life that fosters faith within these groups, though the ecclesial identity of the groups is ambiguous since the modes of belonging allow participants to access the groups simply as youth groups, whereas for others the groups become a vital community that helps to cultivate and sustain the possibility of Christian faith. The groups are then potential ecclesial spaces that hold both church and 'not church' identities.

Furthermore, the ambiguous identity of the groups' espoused and operant ecclesiologies demonstrates a dominant discourse about church that at times deliberately – and at times unintentionally – places the groups outside of the Church. There is also, however, a hidden discourse that reveals the ecclesial potential of the groups. Oftentimes this hidden discourse becomes apparent through the practices of interruption that can help participants navigate between the different modes of belonging and ecclesial practices within the groups.

This chapter has specifically begun to argue that potential ecclesial spaces offer a useful contribution to ongoing conversations about the shape of the Church for our times by resisting solid boundaries and definitions. Rather, they hint at the need for a reversal of ecclesiological thinking that sees the ecclesial life, and therefore the Church, flowing to spaces in which individuals are connecting with Christ. In turn this allows 'church' to be constructed from a variety of experiences, communities and groups. This is the essence of an interweaving ecclesiology. Such an ecclesiology then helps to navigate some of the unhelpful binaries that cause debate and discussion in the life of the Church – intergenerational church versus age-segregated groups; youth church versus young people as part of the Church; local church versus parachurch – through an interweaving of church in which potential ecclesial spaces are seen as part of the flow of expression in the life of the Church alongside more solid, congregational and denominational church life. Part 3 develops this further by demonstrating in particular the way that potential ecclesial spaces might help to shape the Church in mission and how an interweaving ecclesiology might be regulated.

Notes

1 One 18-year-old male, Newtown group.

2 Nick Shepherd, *Faith Generation: Retaining Young People and Growing the Church* (London: SPCK, 2016), chapter 3.

3 See Sylvia Collins-Mayo, Bob Mayo and Sally Nash, *The Faith of Generation Y* (London: Church House Publishing, 2010).

4 See Chapter 3.

5 See Chapter 2.

6 Jason Lief, *Poetic Youth Ministry: Learning to Love Young People by Letting Them Go* (Eugene, OR: Cascade Books, 2015), pp. 14–15.

7 Lief, *Poetic Youth Ministry*, p. 105.

8 Lief, *Poetic Youth Ministry*, p. 123.

9 Lief, *Poetic Youth Ministry*, p. 128.

10 Mathew Guest, *Evangelical Identity and Contemporary Culture: A Congregational Study in Innovation* (Milton Keynes: Paternoster Press, 2007).

11 Guest, *Evangelical Identity*, pp. 134–67.

12 Guest, *Evangelical Identity*, p. 135.

13 The desire for ecclesial certainty is illustrated by the ongoing discussions about how fresh expressions of church legitimately count as church. See, for example, the eight criteria set out in Archbishops' Council, *Fresh Expressions in the Mission of the Church* (London: Church House Publishing, 2012), p. 114. These are critiqued in favour of a set of ten indicators in George Lings, *The Day of Small Things: An Analysis of Fresh Expressions of Church in 21 Dioceses of the Church of England* (Church Army, 2016), p. 18. I pick this up in more detail in Part 3.

14 Pete Ward, *Liquid Church* (Milton Keynes: Paternoster Press, 2002), pp. 36–7.

15 Ward, *Liquid Church*, p. 38.

16 Pete Ward, *Liquid Ecclesiology: The Gospel and the Church* (Leiden: Brill, 2017), p. 10.

17 Ward, *Liquid Ecclesiology*, p. 11.

18 Ward, *Liquid Ecclesiology*, p. 11.

19 Ward, *Liquid Church*, pp. 47–8.

20 Cathy Ross and David Dadswell, *Church Growth Research Project: Church Planting* (Ripon College, Cuddesdon: Oxford Centre for Ecclesiology and Practical Theology, 2013), p. 28.

21 Stuart Murray, *Church after Christendom* (Milton Keynes: Authentic Media, 2005), pp. 139–40.

22 For example, Martyn Percy, 'Old Tricks for New Dogs: A Critique of Fresh Expressions', in *Evaluating Fresh Expressions: Explorations in Emerging Church*, ed. Martyn Percy and Louise Nelstrop (Norwich: Canterbury Press, 2008), pp. 35–6.

23 I am of course aware here of the irony that I am adding to the wealth of reflection in this area!

24 Percy, 'Old Tricks for New Dogs', p. 36.

25 By describing the group as 'independent', I refer to the way in which it does not come under the leadership or authority of any local church or denomination. I do not use the term to imply that the group has nothing to do with local churches as it could be said that there is a good relationship with a number of churches through the group's leadership team.

26 Archbishops' Council, *Fresh Expressions in the Mission of the Church*, pp. 26–8.

27 Andrew Davison and Alison Milbank, *For the Parish: A Critique of Fresh Expressions* (London: SCM Press, 2010), p. 95 and pp. 113–14.

28 John Milbank, 'Stale Expressions: The Management-Shaped Church', *Studies in Christian Ethics*, 21(1) (2008).

29 Pete Rollins, 'Biting the Hand that Feeds: An Apology for Encouraging Tension between the Established Church and Emerging Collectives', in *Evaluating Fresh Expressions: Explorations in Emerging Church*, ed. Martyn Percy and Louise Nelstrop (Norwich: Canterbury Press, 2008), pp. 71–2.

30 John Hull, *Mission-shaped Church: A Theological Response* (London: SCM Press, 2006), pp. 1–4.

31 Rollins, 'Biting the Hand That Feeds', p. 84.

32 Julie Gittoes, Brutus Green and James Heard, eds, *Generous Ecclesiology: Church, World and the Kingdom of God* (London: SCM Press, 2013).

33 Julie Gittoes, 'Where is the Kingdom?', in *Generous Ecclesiology: Church, World and the Kingdom of God*, ed. Julie Gittoes, Brutus Green and James Heard (London: SCM Press, 2013), pp. 112–16.

34 Ralph Winter, 'The Two Structures of God's Redemptive Mission', *Missiology*, 2(1) (1974).

35 Winter, 'Two Structures', p. 127.

36 Winter, 'Two Structures', p. 127.

37 Echoes of this can be heard in the espoused expectation of both case studies.

38 To use Pete Ward's language.

PART 3

Expanding the Scope for an Interweaving Ecclesiology

7

Beyond Fresh Expressions:
A Mandate for the Whole
Church in Mission

Do we really want to cement ecclesial boundaries?
Are these not things we should struggle with?[1]

As detailed in the previous sections of this book, the historical
and current practice of Christian work with young people, as
shown through the example of Crusaders/Urban Saints, contains practical wisdom that makes an important contribution to
current evangelical conversations about church and mission in
the UK. Through analysis of the practical normative approach
to the Church contained in the historical work of Urban Saints
and the operant ecclesiology of current groups, an interweaving approach to the Church is discovered. Young people and
leaders from Urban Saints groups make simultaneous use of a
variety of communal Christian activities in order to construct
their experience of church – this characterizes such an interweaving ecclesiology. By holding different activities, groups and
local churches in tension through simultaneous involvement,
this ecclesial approach values both sodalities and modalities.
Further, they are not seen as mutually exclusive, or different
ends of a spectrum, but rather each one is experienced as part
of a current bricolage of church. In addition, this contrasts
with the mixed economy concept of Fresh Expressions. The
interweaving approach offers flexibility and fluidity, allowing
individuals to construct a church experience out of a variety
of different communal Christian activities and relationships –

some of which might be considered mature church expressions while others, such as an Urban Saints group, are not.

Central to the theological vision detailed in Chapter 1 is the contention that theology is essentially a constructive dialogical task, and that this dialogue is necessary as a result of the participative nature of the communicative relations that are the essence of God's Triune life. It was argued therefore that ecclesiology, discerning what the Church is in the light of the person and activity of God, is also dialogical. Indeed, a key point of departure is Gerard Mannion and Lewis Mudge's claim that this can be seen through many of the key ecclesiology moves throughout history as the Church wrestled with the questions, controversies and societal shifts of its time and place.

This type of responsiveness to situations and circumstances is seen in the praxis of the case studies, especially regarding the leaders' attentiveness to specific young people and their lives. The significance of the practices of interruption is in allowing a particular posture towards young people to shape the life of the groups in order that welcome, fun and questions can disrupt the more ecclesial practices, while simultaneously opening up space for these ecclesial practices to be accessed and this aspect of the group's life encountered. This is seen in the paradox of Victoria stating that the Bible study is the most important thing, yet allowing that to be thrown off track to welcome the late-arriving Sally, thus creating space in which conversation is both metaphor for the group's praxis as well as literal experience for participants.

Similarly, conversation and dialogue are used as a metaphor for the Church within the Fresh Expressions literature. A recent example of this is found in the book *Missional Conversations*[2] which, as the name suggests, tries to model the significance of dialogical enquiry within theology by offering paired chapters on subjects that reflect on praxis, and then theology between different authors. The two chapters looking at new forms of church take this conversational structure into the subject matter itself, discussing the idea of church as conversation. As this dialogue unfolds it strikes to the heart of the issues that this chapter explores. In the first of these two chapters, Andrea

Campanale looks at the idea of church as 'God's conversation partner with the world' through her own experience of local contextual mission with a project called Sacred Space.[3] While discussing this she describes the importance of relationships not being restricted by the group having solid boundaries. Rather, the deliberately indeterminate edges of Sacred Space allow for friendship to continue in a way that suggests a similar interrupting dynamic to that which is at work within the youth groups. Just as in the groups welcome interrupted the importance of the Bible study, so here:

> Friendship and a desire to be good news in our locality are more important to us than belief ... This creates the freedom for people to question their faith and decide they no longer even want to call themselves a Christian, but they may still continue to walk with us as friends.[4]

Consequently, Campanale is able to talk about the group's 'indeterminate edges'.[5] In much the same way as the Newtown group discussed previously, the sense comes across that genuine conversation in relationship is 'why we do this' rather than a more defined outcome.

What is fascinating is that Campanale moves on to discuss the dilemma the group faces because they exist outside any official church structure. She wonders aloud whether they should apply to get a Bishop's Mission Order to formalize the group as an ecclesial community under the Church of England. The heart of the dilemma is the extent that this could change the group's identity and solidify boundaries that are meant to be porous. Essentially, she is concerned that the gravitational pull of the Church will change the nature of the group. To use the language I have developed from my case studies, 'Sacred Space' operates as a potential ecclesial space. It is able to form something of the ecclesial life for participants as they utilize it as such, whereas for others they can belong without the pressure of being part of a church community.

Overall, the group can be seen as part of an interweaving ecclesial expression for some, but not for others, while the group as a whole can see itself as being part of the overall life of the body of Christ, locally and universally. It is an ability to hold in tension exactly this kind of dilemma that the interweaving ecclesiology drawn from the inherent ecclesial imagination of youth ministry provides. The language and vision of interweaving creates the space to live in the ambiguous tension of church and not church. It is an ecclesiology that can perhaps help in what Clare Watkins describes as her 'struggle to describe the edgelessness of church [that] broke open ... expressions of church without hard edges'.[6] It is therefore an ecclesiological vision that can move beyond Fresh Expressions to further equip the Church in mission.

Similarly, in the partner theoretical chapter penned by Michael Moynagh, the topic of church as conversation is explored. In this, Moynagh, reflecting my own theological instincts, argues that 'God longs to draw the world into the eternal conversation of the Trinity', with the Church cast as facilitator.[7] What is fascinating here is that Moynagh seems to embrace the ambiguity of conversation by stating that, 'you never quite know where you will end up ... [ideas are] often taken in an unexpected direction. This requires conversations that are not controlled.'[8] I agree and, in taking this to its logical conclusion, see an intention to develop formal churches as leaning towards controlling the missional conversation, yet this is what Fresh Expressions tend towards.[9] As such, they cannot be seen as the final word for reshaping the Church for mission.

It is important to notice from the case studies the ease with which the dominant discourse, the gravitational pull of the Church, holds a powerful influence over the conversation. There are echoes here of Andrew Root's challenge to relational youth ministry that the relationship should be seen as the place of encounter with Christ rather than a means of influencing a young person in the direction of a predetermined end.[10] If the Church is to embrace conversation as a metaphor and praxis for its life and mission, then pre-judging the outcome of the conversation should be resisted. As practical theologian Terry Veling has articulated, genuine conversation means that 'you and I come to an understanding together'.[11] There is, inherent ambiguity within this.

The hidden discourse that reveals the youth groups' potential ecclesial spaces might just help to hold this ambiguity within an ecclesiological framework. If predetermining the outcome of the conversation should be resisted, so that it is not known where the conversation will end up, there must be space to fight the urge to assume that planting or forming a specific church is the outcome of missional endeavour. As with the leader from Newtown proclaiming excitedly, when witnessing a conversation about Jesus between young people who were and were not Christian, that 'this is why we do this', an interweaving ecclesiology values the space created by conversation and the ambiguous potential within that space in and of itself, rather than in order to claim that space as church. These conversations open up potential ecclesial spaces into which the Church may or may not grow as the interweaving continues. Individuals are then free to choose whether they count the community of the potential ecclesial space as part of their expression of church or not; for some it will remain simply a group to which they belong.

Consequently, this chapter begins Part 3 by exploring further how an interweaving ecclesiology based on such potential ecclesial spaces might aid a kind of missional resistance against the gravitational pull of the Church, thus moving beyond Fresh Expressions as an ecclesial vision for mission. The final two chapters of Part 3 then build on this by discussing the vital subject of regulating this kind of ambiguous ecclesiology and the role of pioneering ministry in ensuring that this creative conversation continues.

Beyond Fresh Expressions – ambiguity and flexibility

Proposing a more ambiguous ecclesiological approach for the Church in mission finds some resonance with key Fresh Expressions thinker Michael Moynagh. It is possible to trace in Moynagh's theological approach a move towards embracing more ambiguity in his language of church in relation to specific

activities that come under the Fresh
hereas in 2012's *Church for Every Con-*
nguage of 'New Contextual Churches'
on the formation of a church, his 2017
this language, preferring instead 'New
' because it leaves open the question of
vity becomes a mature church.[12] Indeed,
in Life, Moynagh argues that it is vital
not to make the question of church an in/out or yes/no binary.
This is a welcome embrace of ambiguity that tallies well with
the interweaving ecclesiology revealed in the hidden discourse
of the Urban Saints groups; however, Moynagh's ultimate
understanding is that each community, each specific group or
activity, remains on a journey towards becoming church. In
other words, his intention is that any ambiguous ecclesial identity of the groups will be resolved rather than embraced. This
reveals that, despite the shift in terminology, little has changed
in the overall ecclesiological thrust of Moynagh's thinking.

It is in this movement towards certainty that the contrast
with the way potential ecclesial spaces help to construct an
interweaving ecclesiology is most felt. While there are identifiable similarities, this fundamental distinction is key to the
argument of this chapter and the way in which the ecclesial
imagination of work with young people takes thinking
about the Church in mission beyond the mandate of Fresh
Expressions. To develop this point, and the significance of the
operant ecclesiology revealed in the hidden discourse of the
youth groups, it is instructive to look at the similarities and
dissimilarities between it and the Fresh Expressions' approach;
these become explicit when the ecclesial imagination of youth
ministry is mapped against central characteristics of what
Michael Moynagh initially called 'New Contextual Churches'.
Moynagh draws together a number of trends and characteristics shared by Fresh Expressions and other new forms of the
church; he lists these as follows:

- Missional – in the sense that, through the Spirit, they are birthed by Christians mainly among people who do not normally attend church.
- Contextual – they seek to fit the culture of the people they serve.
- Formational – they aim to form disciples.
- Ecclesial – they intend to become church for the people they reach in their contexts.[13]

The similarities with the ecclesial imagination of youth ministry, as exemplified in the story of Crusaders/Urban Saints, can be mapped against the first three of these characteristics. As we have already seen, the history of Urban Saints demonstrates the way that Crusaders began from a desire to reach boys from the upper-middle classes of British society who were not attending or being reached by the churches of the day. By inviting the boys to Bible class activities in the drawing rooms of upper-middle class households, the groups were contextually appropriate to those boys. And though this specific cultural appropriateness became diluted throughout the century the organization has been in existence, the case studies demonstrate that there remains an operant culture within Urban Saints of allowing the context of the young people to take precedence over the religiosity of the activities. This is the heart of the practices of interruption – practices that allow the lives of the young people to interrupt activity that had otherwise been described as the most important priority in the group.[14] In addition, the aim of Urban Saints has always been to develop disciples, well formed in the foundations of the Christian faith.

Where the dissimilarity is evident, however, is in the final characteristic – the intention of these groups to become church for those involved in them. This was never the expressed intention of Urban Saints. Indeed, the move towards church was always strongly resisted, with the language of missionary society preferred to understand the nature of the work. As Urban Saints and other similar youth ministry organizations proliferated through the twentieth century, the term 'parachurch' became more popular. While it is possible that the reason the early classes were not described in the manner of Moynagh's ecclesial characteristic is that the vocabulary wasn't available to do this at that time,[15] the organization and its groups have resolutely resisted any attempt to be identified as creating church. The ecclesial ambiguity of the case studies, of being outside of and yet somehow part of the Church, has been the preferred approach. It is this very ecclesial ambiguity that provides a constructive contribution to today's ecclesiological questions and conversations.

In contrast to a focus on developing mature churches, with consequential discussions as to what this looks like, the interweaving ecclesiology begins with a different focus. This allows for the reversal of the direction of ecclesiological thought discussed in Chapter 6. The starting point for the interweaving ecclesiology is the desire to create connection between individuals and the Christian community through simple ecclesial practices. The motivation for creating this connection is that individuals become open to exploring and experiencing faith in God. This is what is expressed in the case studies as those who are not yet Christian becoming open to the possibilities of Christian faith through their interactions in the groups. This implies that the Church and the form the Church takes is not the starting place, but rather the Church appears, or is created, as individuals form connections that stimulate Christian faith. Theologically this can be described as the experience of being in Christ creating the connection with the body of Christ and therefore the Church.

This reversal, by not predetermining what the Church will look like, creates an environment through which the Church can be open to its own growth and development. In addition, such a reversal, creating the space for faith to be explored and experienced, without church being foregrounded, is entirely in keeping with the challenges of the secular age as discussed in Chapter 2. In this core distinction from the ecclesial imagination of work with young people, and in their desire to form mature churches as the outworking of mission, Fresh Expressions have lost something of value – the ambiguity of identity that allows missional responsiveness to people that is still evident within an interweaving ecclesiology and practices of interruption.

Interestingly, if conversation and dialogue are central to the identity of the Church – within the underpinning theological approach to this book as well as specifically within both an interweaving approach and Fresh Expressions as discussed at the start of the present chapter – then the Church is inherently relational. Such a relational vision for the essence of church tallies with that held by Michael Moynagh. He sees the essence of each expression of church being exhibited within four interconnecting (we might say interweaving) relationships – up, in, out and of.[16] This relational view, though, is limited to these relationships being expressed within each ecclesial community. In other words, despite a relational basis each new ecclesial community is expected to move towards fulfilling all these relationships.

In contrast, by being comfortable with ambiguity about the status of its constituent potential ecclesial spaces an interweaving approach maintains a relational heart, but with greater flexibility and responsiveness as individuals develop church out of a matrix of relationships and participation in a range of groups, activities and communities. In this way an interweaving approach resists both firm boundaries in the life of the Church as a whole and any temptation to see the fullness of ecclesial life expressed in any single group, community or activity. This is helpful for Fresh Expressions in countering accusations that they are simply a re-booted version of the much critiqued 'homogenous unit principle' of mission and church growth.[17] While potential ecclesial spaces might operate for specific sub-sections of society (such as youth groups) they are not intended to be full expressions of church by themselves, needing rather to be woven together relationally. I pick up this discussion of key relational moves in the next chapter when exploring how they can serve in regulating the interweaving church, but for now suffice to say that the relationality within an interweaving approach, one that includes both individuals and groups – with no need for any to claim to be fully church – again moves the conversation beyond that of Fresh Expressions and the different forms of church it inspires.

Whereas questions about whether something is church can become the focus around which the contemporary ecclesiological conversation has revolved, the driving force behind the formation of Crusaders, and still at the heart of the current Urban Saints groups, is how to engage young people with the gospel, and through this develop Christian faith through a personal encounter with Christ. Urban Saints groups have become places of developing and nurturing Christian faith while not being formally churches – nor intending to become such. That the groups, however, can play this role in the lives of the participants suggests an ecclesial dynamic has developed from the mission-shaped imperative and actions.

This possibility of ecclesial dynamic without aiming to be fully or institutionally a church is vital. At the heart of this dynamic is the idea that 'every work done by a Christian in the name of Jesus is an expression of [the Church]',[18] without the need for 'a' church to be formed. Furthermore, this ambiguous line of thinking begins to break down the barriers between that which is considered church and that which isn't. In turn this allows the ecclesial ambiguity inherent within Urban Saints to help regulate the rush to create a form of church that dominates contemporary approaches to mission in the UK. They can do this, however, as part of the ecclesiological conversation. In this way they can assist the development of an ecclesiology that might, in the words of Bob Jackson, have 'a structure and a culture designed not to enshrine stability but to handle change'.[19]

Always learning how to be the Church

In 2002, Bob Jackson wrote of the need for such a church that might encapsulate flexibility. The only constant, he claimed, for the Church of the future should be the 'neverending need to change the way it lives and breathes and communicates the unchanging Jesus Christ'. Jackson makes it clear that although he is talking about structure and culture this is fundamentally a matter of ecclesiology – of the theology of the Church – not merely practicality. The rationale for a culture and structure that handles change is what he terms the 'giant and glorious

Trinitarian mystery ... always unpredictable, and always available to be explored afresh'.[20] While Jackson's claim that change should be never-ending for the Church is perhaps a little extreme, it does helpfully encapsulate the notion that ecclesiology should embed flexibility rather than stability within its essence. Intriguingly, and connected with this, Pete Ward has claimed that the moves towards what he terms 'solid church' – an ecclesial approach based on the stability of set ideas and meetings – flows more from a popular ecclesial imagination than from a deeper theological engagement. It is evident, he claims, that a lack of academic ecclesiology has led to the predominant evangelical understanding of the Church.[21]

The analysis of case study data in the previous chapters has shown how there is a dominant discourse about the Church which, though it contains paradoxes and contradictions, suggests that such a solid view of the Church is centred on the Sunday morning congregational gathering. This is considered 'more' church, and that even different areas of the church building reveal degrees of church within the physical structures themselves. This dominant discourse is in firm agreement with Ward's contention that 'solid church' understands the Church primarily as a meeting, something that gathers in one place, at one time, with the purpose of performing a shared ritual.[22] By drawing our attention to this popular and limiting understanding of the Church, Ward is careful not to suggest that meetings or gatherings are unimportant to the life of the Church. Rather, he claims, this solid understanding of church in which the essence and purpose of ecclesial life is contained in the one place, one time, gathered congregation has such a hold on the imagination of the Christian community that it is almost impossible to think of the Church as anything else. This is the power of the dominant discourse.

Intriguingly, though, what is revealed in the hidden discourse of Christian work with young people through my case study research is an operant and espoused ecclesiology that helps us imagine that which Ward suggests is almost impossible, and that Jackson argues is vital for the Church of the future – an ecclesiology that moves beyond the meeting or gathering as the essence of the Church, and thus helps to embed flexibility and ambiguity – and consequently the possibility of change – in the Church's theological self-understanding. It is of course important at this point to acknowledge that flexibility in form and expression of the Church is central to the vision of Fresh Expressions as well. What is distinct, however, is – as highlighted above in the discussion of Moynagh's thinking – that each fresh expression is intended to be or become a mature church in its own right, thus potentially setting in stone the form of that church – which is the fear expressed by Andrea Campanale in the discussion at the start of this chapter. In contrast, an interweaving ecclesiology refrains from bestowing a church identity on single groups or communities, thus embedding ambiguity and therefore a sense of church remaining unfinished throughout its ecclesiological vision.

Perhaps surprisingly – given Ward's disposition towards ethnographic research being able to contribute to theological notions of the Church – he creates a helpful dialogue with Karl Barth's ecclesiological point of departure, though Ward acknowledges taking a different route from Barth. This starting point recognizes the divine freedom of Jesus Christ; that in Jesus' person is both 'the electing God and the elected human being'.[23] Consequently, Ward can state succinctly, and in agreement with Barth, that the 'being of the church is Jesus Christ and it is freedom of the Spirit that brings about Christ's presence … the church exists because Christ lives; it exists because Christ exists'.[24] The direction in which Ward takes this, however, is to see in the freedom of the Spirit that the love of Jesus cannot be contained in church meetings, or institutions, as it 'flows underneath, within, and around, [it] is there in the world and in the Church'.[25] For Ward, it is this that makes the Church more than a meeting or gathering, and only within this broader understanding is the gathered church able to find its meaning.

Ward develops this thinking through interaction with Daniel Hardy's ideas around created and redeemed sociality in which the 'dynamic presence of God' might be found in society.[26] Here Hardy posits that on his missionary journeys, St Paul discovered that the world was not devoid of Christ but instead filled with his presence. Drawing on this, Ward claims that the apostle's travels involved a 'constant rediscovery of Christ'.[27] This notion is similar to the approach of Vincent Donovan explored in the classic *Christianity Rediscovered*, in which he reimagines mission in his groundbreaking work sharing the gospel with the Masai people.[28] Strikingly and memorably, Donovan, through conversation with the Masai about the gospel story, finds himself in the position of admitting that his own people, despite their Christian faith, were still searching for the one true God. Donovan's approach is akin to what Stephan Bevans calls the anthropological model for contextual theology in which the gospel can be discovered already within different cultural expressions.[29] As with the work of Donovan, the missionary's task is to water the seeds of the gospel already present. Consequently, as with the reversal of ecclesiological thinking introduced in the previous chapter, and Rowan Williams's starting point for understanding the event of church, it is encounter with Christ in the gospel – the person of Christ – that defines the essence of the Church.

This is, of course, consistent with the theological foundations for this book, and the fundamentally participative vision of God's Triune life that is at the heart of it. Paul Fiddes, in discussing such a participative vision, highlights that all of creation – not simply the Church – participates in the relational moves of the Trinity since there can be no life outside of God's own sustaining presence. Therefore, the Church is not the sole place or arbiter of sociality with God, but must be open to the possibility of discovering afresh the life of God or, we might say, be open to participation in the movements of God's life, beyond the all-too-solid boundaries of the Church. Daniel Hardy suggests the term 'pre-church' for this type of sociality with God outside of the institutional Church and sees this concept as vital to the missionary understanding of the Church.[30]

This contrasts with the way in which the *Mission-shaped Church* report, the founding and formalizing document for Fresh Expressions, ends up in a tangle with itself when talking about the place of the Church within its missional vision. In trying to background the Church, by placing the mission and the context of the mission initiative as having prior importance to the form of church that develops, a desire for uncertainty in ecclesial forms is explicit. The contention that the church planting it is advocating should not be church-centred confirms this.[31] This backgrounding of the Church is made difficult, though, given that a church is the intended outcome of what is planted. By having a clearly articulated outcome in mind, the 'conversation' in church planting becomes imbalanced. The risk within this predetermined conversation is twofold. First, that there is little genuine dialogue between the gospel and the local culture because an idea of what will be formed is already implicitly held in the minds of the church planters.[32] The second risk is that it potentially limits the missional work of God inherent within his nature when forming churches. This mirrors the critique of *Mission-shaped Church* in that this, in fact, offers a church-shaped mission.[33] There is a danger, then, that by starting with the desire and intention to start a new form of church, boundaries are placed too tightly around the potential work of God through the Holy Spirit.

In contrast, the potential ecclesial spaces within the ecclesial imagination of youth ministry, by not aiming for the Church to be the outcome, can allow the contexts of the young people to shape each group's mission. This shaping by the context happens in large part through the questions and situations that those in the groups bring with them. Conversation with these young people creates space that, through engagement with the simple ecclesial practices, has some ecclesial potential. In the Urban Saints groups conversation is more than a mere concept or framework; instead, it is a tangible ongoing practice facilitated through encouraging questions. It is also a practice that helps to create and provide the space through which the Christian faith and encounters with God become possible. The conversation is enhanced and retains the nature of a two-way dialogue. Meanwhile, the ambiguous identity of the groups is retained and something of the Church is possible amid the missional dialogue that takes place.

It is in trying to avoid this tangle of thinking and practice, and consequently to step outside the influence of the dominant discourse, that the concept of the Church's pilgrim nature is helpful, particularly when understood in light of the participative nature of God's life. As Julie Gittoes writes, the outworking of this approach to the Church can be viewed in the following way:

> The Church is called to walk in the world as Jesus walked the land ... This wandering ecclesia moves beyond the sanctuary in daily actions ... encounters occur within the boundaries of sacred places, in the context of intentional mission and engagement with the community, and in multiple contexts of human discourse and exchange.[34]

As the love of Christ in the freedom of the Spirit flows under, around and beyond the Church, the Church must become the wandering ecclesia in pursuit of Christ. Considering this in parallel with the ecclesial imagination that has become apparent through the analysis of the youth group case studies (alongside the historical influence of Crusaders/Urban Saints) suggests that there is real value in the concept of potential ecclesial spaces within an interweaving ecclesiology for moving forward the debate about new forms of the Church, and Fresh Expressions in particular. The usefulness of this is that it helps to relocate the essence of the Church as pursuit of the person of Christ rather than a meeting or gathering.

Consequently, groups such as the Urban Saints groups can play a role in thinking about the ongoing movement of the Church. It is noteworthy, though, that this contribution to the contemporary ecclesiological conversations comes from beginning by getting alongside young people in order to communicate the gospel with them, rather than starting with the Church. Ironically, by starting with the Church through frameworks such as that of church planting, those involved in Fresh Expressions might be limiting the expressions of ecclesial life available to them. In contrast, Doug Gay describes a church in which moves of renewal are inevitable. The Church, he says, is always being made and remade by the Spirit. This is a church that is 'always pilgrim, always a community of disciples, always learning how to be the church'.[35] This idea of a pilgrim, or wandering ecclesia, is echoed and developed by Julie Gittoes. Drawing on the work of Daniel Hardy, Gittoes talks of a church that needs to 'walk around embodying a presence on the actual land'. The Church should be a community that is carefully attentive both 'to God and to the world'.[36] Rather than being mutually exclusive, 'the life of the Church and the fabric of modern society are bound together relationally and with mutual influence'.[37] In this binding together it should come as no surprise that through the shifting and changing of society new spaces appear into which the Church can move.[38] The suggestion is that these fresh moves in creating Christian community among young people are significant not simply for youth ministry; they also, over time, stretch the boundaries of church life and create new ecclesial space into which the Church can move, thus echoing the reversal of ecclesiological thought described above.

Doug Gay, in borrowing a phrase from Geoffrey Wainwright, describes this kind of pilgrim church as an 'assimilative trad- ition'. This, Gay goes on to say, is inevitably a hermeneutical vision for the Church in which it is constructed by remixings of disparate and different traditions, fuelled by an ecclesial – and I would say inherently evangelical – culture of innovation and experimentation.[39] This hermeneutical vision for the Church is enhanced by a conversational image developed by Merold Westphal.[40] Westphal draws on the hermeneutical philosophy of Hans-Georg Gadamer in the service of the Church. This leads him to pose the idea of the Church as conversation in which, citing Gadamer, through dialogue we do not merely put ourselves forward 'but are transformed into a communion in which we do not remain where we are'.[41] This is the 'church in dialogue', which is Graeme Fancourt's vision for a church that addresses the postmodern condition.[42]

As a result of this line of thinking, the interweaving ecclesiol- ogy of Urban Saints groups enhances conversations around new forms of church. This means retaining the idea that the Church should not be the priority in missional moves. A reversal of thought provides a rationale for prioritizing mission without overlooking the Church, yet not allowing the Church as it is to overwhelm the aims and desire for mission. It is an ecclesial understanding that recognizes the need for fuzzy edges and, to use Clare Watkins's term, an 'edgelessness' in church life, retaining a missional resistance in so doing. Further, this line of thought leads to the suggestion that an interweaving approach that reverses ecclesiological thinking is able to serve the ongoing pilgrim life of the Church. The operant ecclesiology of Crusaders/Urban Saints is offered as an example of this.

The significance of this for the debate around Fresh Expressions and inherited or traditional forms of the Church is that the discussions can become centred on the forms of gathering that are legitimate for something to be considered church. The debate can all too easily, but unconsciously, reiterate the ecclesial imagination that Pete Ward identifies in which meetings constitute the Church. In this we return to the concerns of John Hull who feared that, while there was much to be applauded in the initiatives sparked by the *Mission-shaped Church* report, there was also a lack of theological capacity to reimagine the relationship between the Church and the kingdom of God, to such an extent that the result might simply be more café churches. The essence of this concern and critique is that the Fresh Expressions movement risks shifting one form of meeting for another as the essence of the Church. The problem for Hull lies not with some of the language used – he approves, for example, ideas such as 'start with the church and the mission will probably get lost. Start with mission and it is likely that the church will be found'[43] – but rather with the report's underlying point of departure which he identifies as the 'lineage of church planting', thus causing the ideas to become too 'church centred'[44] in their theology. When read in the light of Ward's recognition of the inherent draw towards meetings as the essence of the Church it is easy to see how the dominant discourse about church is hard to eschew. Even within the supposedly innovative and experimental (though now much less frequently discussed) emerging church movement, research has identified that many remain relatively fixed on the question of norms of congregational practice.[45] In some ways this is unsurprising given that a clear rationale for the movement, as with the related Fresh Expressions, is a dissatisfaction with traditional forms of Church – again centring the church in its theological constructions.

Ecclesiology from outside the Church

Perhaps what is needed therefore is an ecclesiology that comes from outside the usual stream of church life – from an ecclesial imagination formed with no desire to create church, but to reach young people. It is in this that the value of potential ecclesial spaces becomes more apparent – with both responsiveness and flexibility built into their operant interweaving ecclesiology. By highlighting the similarities and dissimilarities between these potential ecclesial spaces and the approach of Fresh Expressions I will conclude the argument of this chapter by showing that an interweaving ecclesiology is well equipped to handle change rather than maintain the status quo. This ensures the usefulness of this approach in ongoing conversations around church and mission in the UK.

The interweaving ecclesiology is built on the evangelical ecclesial imagination inherent within Urban Saints' history. This ecclesial imagination is in essence a further way of expressing the interweaving ecclesiological approach in which modalities and sodalities in the life of the Church are held in creative tension by mission-focused evangelicals such as those operating within Urban Saints. Characteristic of Urban Saints' ecclesial imagination is the possibility that the forms taken by the groups, relationships and networks that are part of it can be reimagined if and when necessary. This reimagining can be seen through the story of Crusaders/Urban Saints in developments of how specific groups operate and in those attending the groups. It was also seen specifically through observations within Newtown as the group reformed twice in order to connect more effectively with the young people. In this reimagining certain things are held as being of central importance.[46] This importance does not, however, prevent the groups from being responsive to the changing lives of young people.

This responsiveness is related to the evangelical character-istics of activism and innovation – innate traits that lead evangelicals to try new things in their desire to share the gospel with those around them. This leads away from set structures and forms of Christian life and community and towards the kind of relational outworking of the ecclesial imagination. There is something of this mirrored in the contention within *Mission-shaped Church* that the form of the Church and the content of the gospel need to be separated in order to com-municate appropriately within contemporary society.[47] This idea has been strongly criticized for failing to acknowledge the extent to which these things are inextricably connected, and that the form the gospel message takes is as significant to its communication as the content itself.[48]

Within the youth groups, however, the ecclesial imagination allows for responsiveness in which this relationship between form and content is negotiated. By not aiming to create mature churches but retaining some ecclesial potential the groups are able to hold lightly the form of what they do in communicat-ing the content of the Christian faith. In addition to this, the way in which young people articulate the safe place the groups provide for them indicates the form and content of the gospel are held together in a flexible, responsive manner. The con-tent of the gospel becomes the ability of the good news to be flexible, allowing the young people to approach it, as they are, confident in the safety of the group. Yet, because these groups are not becoming mature churches, this does not need to be the entire content and form of Christian life and faith.

An interweaving ecclesiology moves thinking and praxis for the missionary church beyond Fresh Expressions by requiring new missional groups to be focused neither on becoming, nor on having the potential to become, churches in their own right. Instead, the emphasis is on creating spaces in which Christ's presence can be discovered and, in this way, the ecclesial life of the group is revealed. This does not, however, make the group a church as such, but this potential ecclesial life means that for individuals the group can be part of their participation in the life of the Church. This concept is both more complex and more flexible than an ecclesiology and agenda driven by church planting.

The natural way in which an interweaving ecclesiology embraces the pilgrim nature of the Church, that the Church is always learning how to be the Church, becomes helpful not just on the fuzzy edges of church life where potential ecclesial spaces open up into which the life of the Church might flow, but also in reminding the Church in all its expressions that it is never fully the Church. This is then useful within geographical and institutional boundaries of parish life, for example, in recognizing that there is already an interweaving of activities, meetings, gatherings and relationships that make up the life of the Church in that place.

Further, it allows for members and participants to acknowledge that at times the less formal (one might say less 'churchy') activities, relationships, meetings or gatherings might be more significant than the formal congregational life of the parish. Moreover, such a vision for the Church as is contained within an interweaving ecclesiology accounts for the interactions and participation of individuals in a whole plethora of formal and informal, including digital and physical, ecclesial spaces that form their participation in church. This is therefore an ecclesiological vision that responds to and equips the Church for the disruptions that the digital age has brought to the way in which we live, move and have our being.

In practice, this then helps to navigate some of the tricky questions that can be raised about the nature of particular groups, activities or gatherings. The questions about whether something counts as *a* church can be circumvented as not everything with the potential for ecclesial life needs to be defined as such. Indeed, an interweaving ecclesiology suggests we might become more cautious when making such definitive claims about individual activities since no single thing can encompass the life of the Church. Consequently, an interweaving ecclesiology inherently embodies the Church's pilgrim nature.

Summary

This chapter has argued that an interweaving ecclesiology pushes the Church beyond ideas about Fresh Expressions when thinking about mission. This is a complex vision for church that is comfortable with blurred boundaries and no single expression of the Church. It suggests that most individuals will construct their experience of church through a variety of groups, gatherings and relationships, some of which may be part of the interweaving church for some but not for others – in the manner of St Joe's and Newtown's groups. This raises two important questions with which the next two chapters will wrestle. The first is how such a flexible, borderless vision of church is regulated. And the second is how the creative force of pioneering ministry might be released into such a vision for the Church. It is to the task of addressing these two questions that the final chapters will turn.

Notes

1 Brutus Green, 'On Popular Culture: To its Religious Despisers', in *Generous Ecclesiology: Church, World and the Kingdom of God*, ed. Julie Gittoes, Brutus Green and James Heard (London: SCM Press, 2013), p. 84.

2 Cathy Ross and Colin Smith, *Missional Conversations: A Dialogue between Theory and Praxis in World Mission* (London: SCM Press, 2018).

3 Andrea Campanale, 'Church as God's Conversation Partner with the World', in Ross and Smith, *Missional Conversations*.

4 Campanale, 'Church as God's Conversation Partner', p. 134.

5 Campanale, 'Church as God's Conversation Partner', p. 134.

6 Clare Watkins, *Disclosing Church: An Ecclesiology Learned from Conversations in Practice* (Abingdon: Routledge, 2020), p. 155.

7 Michael Moynagh, 'A Conversational Approach to New Forms of Church', in Ross and Smith, *Missional Conversations*, p. 140.

8 Moynagh, 'A Conversational Approach', p. 144.

9 And Moynagh is elsewhere a classic example of this.

10 Andrew Root, *Revisiting Relational Youth Ministry: From a Strategy of Influence to a Theology of Incarnation* (Westmost, IL: InterVarsity Press, 2007), pp. 70–1.

11 Terry Veling, *Practical Theology: On Earth as it is in Heaven* (New York: Orbis Books, 2005), p. 61.

12 Michael Moynagh, *Church in Life: Innovation, Mission and Ecclesiology* (London: SCM Press, 2017), p. 4.

13 Michael Moynagh, *Church for Every Context: An Introduction to Theology and Practice* (London: SCM Press, 2013), p. xiv; this is re-emphasized in Moynagh, *Church in Life*, p. 3. This list of characteristics is also available on the Fresh Expressions website: https://freshexpres sions.org.uk/about/what-is-a-fresh-expression/ (accessed 9.06.2021).

14 See Chapter 6.

15 Mark Scanlan, 'Youth Ministry Creating Ecclesial Space', *Journal of Youth and Theology*, 14(1) (2015).

16 Moynagh, *Church in Life*, chapter 12.

17 See Andrew Davison and Alison Milbank, *For the Parish: A Critique of Fresh Expressions* (London: SCM Press, 2013), pp. 75–81.

18 Harald Hegstad, *The Real Church: An Ecclesiology of the Visible* (Cambridge: James Clark & Co., 2013), p. 91.

19 Bob Jackson, *Hope for the Church: Contemporary Strategies for Growth* (London: Church House Publishing, 2002), p. 185.

20 Jackson, *Hope for the Church*, p. 185.

21 Pete Ward, *Liquid Ecclesiology: The Gospel and the Church* (Leiden: Brill, 2017), p. 10.

22 Ward, *Liquid Ecclesiology*, pp. 9–10.

23 Pete Ward, *Liquid Church* (Milton Keynes: Paternoster Press, 2002), p. 13.

24 Ward, *Liquid Church*, pp. 13–14.

25 Ward, *Liquid Ecclesiology*, p. 11.

26 Ward, *Liquid Ecclesiology*, p. 7.

27 Ward, *Liquid Ecclesiology*, p. 7.

28 Vincent Donovan, *Christianity Rediscovered: Twenty-Fifth Anniversary Edition* (New York: Orbis Books, 1978).

29 Stephen Bevans, *Models of Contextual Theology* (New York: Orbis Books, 1992), pp. 54–69.

30 Daniel Hardy, *Finding the Church* (London: SCM Press, 2001), p. 40.

31 Archbishops' Council, *Mission-shaped Church: Church Planting and Fresh Expressions of Church in a Changing Context* (London: Church House Publishing, 2004), p. 85.

32 Cathy Ross and David Dadswell, *Church Growth Research Project: Church Planting* (Ripon College, Cuddesdon: Oxford Centre for Ecclesiology and Practical Theology, 2013), p. 69.

33 John Hull, *Mission-shaped Church: A Theological Response* (London: SCM Press, 2006), p. 36.

34 Julie Gittoes, 'Where is the Kingdom?', in *Generous Ecclesiology:*

Church, World and the Kingdom of God, ed. Julie Gittoes, Brutus Green and James Heard (London: SCM Press, 2013), p. 100.

35 Doug Gay, *Remixing the Church: Towards an Emerging Ecclesiology* (London: SCM Press, 2011), p. 93. Ward expresses something similar in the opening words of *Liquid Church* (p. 1): 'The Church of God must not stand still. In every age, inspired by the Holy Spirit, God's people have found new ways to express their fellowship and mission.'

36 Gittoes, 'Where is the Kingdom?', p. 113.

37 Gittoes, 'Where is the Kingdom?', p. 113.

38 Specifically in the context of youth ministry, this is what Mark Senter refers to when he highlights the way that new social situations pre-empt and prompt fresh moves or 'revolutions' in youth ministry. (See the discussion in Chapter 3.)

39 Gay, *Remixing the Church*, p. 93; Gay is citing Geoffrey Wainwright, in *Worship with One Accord: Where Liturgy and Ecumenism Embrace* (New York: Oxford University Press, 1997).

40 Merold Westphal, *Whose Community? Which Interpretation?: Philosophical Hermeneutics for the Church* (Ada, MI: Baker Academic, 2009), pp. 135–46.

41 Westphal, *Whose Community? Which Interpretation?*, p. 117.

42 Graeme Fancourt, *Brand New Church: The Church and the Postmodern Condition* (London: SPCK, 2013), pp. 106–12.

43 Hull, *A Theological Response*, p. 34.

44 Hull, *A Theological Response*, p. 34.

45 Gerardo Marti and Gladys Ganiel, *The Deconstructed Church: Understanding Emerging Christianity* (Oxford: Oxford University Press, 2014), p. 111.

46 For example, Bible study, pastoral care, welcome and fun. See the modes of belonging, ecclesial practices and practices of interruptions discussed in depth in Part 2.

47 Archbishops' Council, *Mission-shaped Church*, p. 91.

48 Davison and Milbank, *For the Parish*, pp. 1–27.

8

Not Everything Goes: Regulating the Interweaving Church

An authentic Christian community is one that is connected to other Christian communities by deep bonds.[1]

This chapter will focus on the need to regulate an interweaving ecclesiology to guard against it becoming an 'anything goes' concept of the Church. Chapter 7 argued that an interweaving ecclesiology can ensure that the boundaries of the Church remain blurred, or fuzzy, in order that it does not lose the essence of its pilgrim nature and remains aware of the need to always be learning how to be the Church. The lack of solid edges, however, while being crucial to maintaining the reversal of ecclesiological thinking detailed earlier, needs some form of regulating. Such regulation nevertheless needs to maintain the value of potential ecclesial spaces. In other words, the ambiguity, the ability to hold church and non-church in conversational tension, must be maintained. Consequently, the means of regulating an interweaving ecclesiology is not reliant on conceptual boundaries, but instead is focused on practices and relationships, through an ongoing practical theological process. This is crucial for, as highlighted by Clare Watkins, there is 'great risk in recommending an ecclesiology of church on the edges and without edges itself [for it] lays itself open to the misunderstanding that it is nothing to do with the institutional church'.[2]

The Fresh Expressions literature classically discusses the legitimacy of new forms of church through a relational framework in two ways – first, through using the language of the mixed economy to describe the way that each individual fresh expression has institutional parity alongside 'inherited' churches; and second, by affirming that each fresh expression of church expresses the legitimacy of its ecclesial life through the interaction of four relationships. These two forms of relational legitimacy for Fresh Expressions result in a call for each individual expression of church to commit to both an internal and external dynamic – named in one book as *intensivity* and *connectivity*[3] – both of which seek to encourage a fresh expression towards deeper koinonia both within its own community and with the universal Church.[4]

These various relational concepts for regulating and legitimizing the ecclesial nature of fresh expressions of church are helpful in exploring the vital question of accountability within an interweaving ecclesiology, resisting an 'anything goes' attitude without reinforcing solid boundaries. In particular, the internal and external dynamic mentioned above can assist in this regulating process. The internal dynamic looks to drive individuals deeper into koinonia community with others in each expression of ecclesial life, recognizing the need for potential ecclesial spaces to provide places in which the richness of relationship demonstrates a quality that is suggestive of the life of God. In addition, these inward relational movements are built on the simple ecclesial practices identified, with these practices themselves opened up by the practices of interruption, which act as catalysts for these deeper relational moves.

However, the inward moves are not enough by themselves and, as demonstrated in the ecclesial imagination of youth groups, there must be a connection outwards in which each group, each potential ecclesial space, understands itself in relation to the wider Christian community and universal Church. This is more than understanding since it requires relationship. This outward move, however, is not one-way and necessarily needs to be reciprocal so that the wider life of the Church serves, and is served by, these potential ecclesial spaces that operate at the fuzzy edges of church life. In this way potential ecclesial spaces are blessed by, and are a blessing to, the wider life of the Church. In the life of each individual, then, the experience of the interweaving church deepens as the dynamics of intensivity and connectivity deepen and enrich the quality of relational life, both internally within particular expressions of ecclesial life and externally in relationship between these various expressions.

In discussing this question of regulating an interweaving ecclesiology in the light of the various relational dynamics discussed in the Fresh Expressions literature, the vital topic of the sacramental life of the Church must also be explored. To this point, the centrality of the sacraments in sustaining and deepening Christian community and forging ecclesial life – in particular, baptism and the Eucharist – has been noticeably absent from the ecclesial dynamics of interweaving. The final section of this chapter will then explore how the relational dynamics within an interweaving ecclesiology can facilitate a rich interaction with the sacramental life of the Church that aids the task of regulating. What becomes apparent in this exploration, though, is that the dynamics of the sacraments mean they should be seen not only as congregational practices, but also as ongoing narratives of ministry that are seen to be lived out in the potential ecclesial spaces of the case studies. Consequently, discussion of the sacraments is vital in regulating the interweaving church within its relational dynamics; but also, the way in which the potential ecclesial spaces of the youth groups embody an ongoing sacramental practice within their way of life that forms faith can draw the whole Church deeper into its own sacramental life. As such, the accountability is two-way and potential ecclesial spaces might enrich the life of the whole Church.

Interweaving ecclesiology and the mixed economy

The interweaving ecclesiology drawn from the case studies is built on numerous ways in which the groups and participants interact with other Christian activities locally and nationally. This is on both an institutional, organizational level as well as relationally, based on the choices of individuals in how they work out their communal Christian life.[5] The young people and leaders of the groups construct their experience of church through active, simultaneous involvement in more than one expression of communal Christian activity. These different expressions are interwoven to create a unique tapestry of ecclesial activity that becomes church for each individual. While there are undoubted similarities this is in fundamental contrast with the oft-described mixed economy approach of Fresh Expressions, while also being distinct from the missiological concept of the two structures of God's redemptive mission detailed in Chapter 6. It is important to outline these contrasts to set the scene further for the discussion of relational means of regulating an interweaving ecclesiology.

As was shown throughout Part 2, the manner by which leaders and young people view the youth groups to which they belong as vital to the development and experience of their Christian faith (individually and communally) strongly suggests an ecclesial dynamic is at work, despite the fact that the groups operate ambiguously in relation to the boundaries of the Church. A central theme within this experience is the quality of relationships in the groups – these are viewed as stronger than experienced elsewhere, both in other communal Christian experiences and, for the young people, other social environments. Among the leaders this strength of identity to the groups and the way in which the groups added to their individual and communal Christian experience was unexpected. What became apparent, however, was that the groups were seen as part of a simultaneous communal Christian experience and an overall part of the ecclesial life of individuals. As described in Chapter 4, within St Joe's this operant ecclesial experience was interpreted with reference to 1 Corinthians 3.5–7 – as the apostle Paul expresses here, it does not matter who performed which roles in the life of the Corinthian believers; the important thing is that God is able to grow people's faith. This interpretation of different roles being played simultaneously by different groups, churches and activities is a key relational building block within the interweaving approach to church.

Chapter 6 identified how the dynamic of specific mission work, such as that of youth groups, might be viewed through the reflections of missiologist Ralph Winter as being one of two distinct forms of ecclesial life operant within God's redemptive mission. A framework of the mixed economy in church life has similarities to this and has become a common way of under-standing and holding together a variety of different expressions of church within the Church of England. This mixed economy is defined as a mutual partnership of parochial and network churches using traditional and fresh approaches, sharing ministry in larger areas.[6] The concept of the mixed economy formalizes a core tenet for those advocating new forms of church – as society diversifies, a one-size-fits-all approach is deemed unsuitable.[7] Consequently, each fresh expression of church is envisaged as likely being for a particular interest group or network.[8] Such a mixed economy lays the foundation for choice regarding church becoming a core component of ecclesiology.[9] As a result of this thinking, the parish model for church in the Anglican context, often known as inherited church,[10] would no longer be seen as the sole model for church life.[11] The language of mixed economy was introduced to articulate an intrinsic institutional parity between the develop-ing fresh expressions of church and inherited forms.

There is not space here to delve in detail into some of the ongoing debates and controversy around the concept of the mixed economy. It is, though, important to note that there is some discrepancy between the theory and the practice – or, to use the language of the four voices of theology, the espoused and operant theology – when it comes to the mixed economy. Back in 2012, key thinker and proponent of Fresh Expressions, Michael Moynagh, was already needing to plead for what he then called new contextual churches to be birthed within the mixed economy.[12] He felt the need to make this plea for two reasons – first, the observation that many new forms of church were being birthed outside formal denominational structures; and, second, the recognition that existing church structures were not very good at accommodating the new.[13] Both in 2012 and again later in *Church in Life*, Moynagh identifies the hes-itancy of what he calls prophets, purists and pragmatists in accepting or wanting to work within a mixed economy. Proph-ets are those pioneering entrepreneurs who fear that working

within denominational structures might stifle the ⟨
their work,[14] purists are concerned that new form⟨
undermine denominational structures, and pragma
tion how it hangs together in practice.[15]

While the mixed economy is in many ways a hel̩ ⌐∪ii-
cept (as is the debate about whether it is the best terminology
– Moynagh himself mentions concepts such as 'mixed ecology' or 'blended' church being favoured by some),[16] it is not
sufficient to contain the hidden ecclesial discourse of the
youth groups that reveals ecclesial life flowing out from formal church structures into such 'non-church' activities. This
operant life of the Church spills over the concepts and terminology used to try and contain it. Similarly, this highlights that
the mixed economy is distinct from Ralph Winter's thinking,
as individuals are not required to move from fresh to inherited
forms of church. Neither, however, are Winter's two modes
of thinking sufficient for the operant ecclesial life revealed in
this study. The interweaving ecclesiology can neither be represented as a continuum between two points on a spectrum nor
as an institutional equality, but rather is a flexible and fluid
approach to church life in which individuals move between different expressions of communal Christian life and develop their
experience of church accordingly. In this way, the different
groups and expressions of church do not need to have separate
institutional equality; rather, significance is attached to each
as individuals appropriate them within an overall bricolage of
communal Christian experience that creates church for them.[17]

Consequently, the interweaving approach can be more responsive to the networks through which individuals live their lives,
as well as holding in tension both network and geographical
connections within an overall picture of the Church.[18] Whereas
the mixed economy model of Fresh Expressions limits the way
in which church can be expressed to either an inherited parish
church or a fresh expression that is aiming to become a mature
church, the interweaving approach allows for a practical ecclesiology through which a larger variety of Christian communal
experiences can be understood as part of the Church without
requiring that each aims to be a mature church expression. This

adds helpful nuance to the current ecclesiological conversation and makes sense of how many individuals practically express their church life. It is almost as if the mixed economy might be reimagined as being expressed in the lives of individuals as their ecclesial life is woven together through simultaneous involvement in multiple expressions of Christian community – some formally seen as church and others not.

The value placed on relationships in each place is what motivates and enables individuals to hold these different communal Christian experiences simultaneously. The decisions made as to which different groups or activities to interweave to create an experience of church is in large part based on the importance placed on the relationships within those places. An interweaving approach to church is then an inherently relational ecclesiology – based on relationships both individually and organizationally. While the concept of a relational ecclesiology has been suggested following research into new forms of the Church, [19] what is being proposed here is something distinct. The relational ecclesiology suggested by the interweaving approach of Urban Saints' work is one in which church becomes constructed through a variety of different activities, meetings and practices bound together in relationship. Some of these, such as congregational life, could be defined as modalities in Winter's categorization, whereas others – such as the Urban Saints groups – resemble sodalities. Some of these building blocks are simply relational and not formally organized so do not fit neatly into either category, or they operate in a way that blurs the boundaries between them. It is, then, an approach in which neither sodalities nor modalities need have priority but where these different expressions of God's work in his Church can operate together in creative tension as individuals move between, and commit to, a variety of expressions and communal activities.

What is being experienced by individuals within an interweaving ecclesiology is, then, a form of mixed economy within the Christian practice and developing Christian community of individual believers through matrices of different groups, activities and congregations that make up their ecclesial life.

This is the hidden discourse of church as expressed in the ecclesial imagination of youth groups being brought to the surface, suggesting that this is a way in which individuals relationally construct ecclesial life. Church experience is, then, adapting to the network dynamics of society but in a broader, more complex way than *Mission-shaped Church* allowed for with its proposal for single-network churches. The mixed economy of church is too narrow, failing to take account of the ways in which individual Christians live out the mission of God and express being the people of God.

Relational dynamics and regulating the interweaving

The argument so far, though, does leave the question as to how such a relational interweaving ecclesiology is regulated. To respond to this, the internal and external relational dynamics proposed from reflection within Fresh Expressions literature outlined in the opening section of this chapter are helpful. In seeking to detail how the relationships between forms of church in the mixed economy operate, the significance of various relational movements has been proposed. These movements are an inward move towards greater depth within each specific community and an outward move towards deeper relational connectivity with the wider Christian Church locally and beyond.[20] These two dynamics intend to speak of a central core that anchors a particular Christian community in the nature of the Church, locally and universally. The inward move refers to the need for a particular local expression of the Church to ensure a focus that drives the community to return often to core practices that define the way of the Christian faith.[21] The outward dynamic, sometimes termed 'connectivity', refers to movement that sees the particular community understand itself conceptually and in practice as related to the wider Christian Church. Both of these dynamics are expressions of the koinonia of genuine Christian community.

On a surface level neither of these dynamics might appear inherent in the activity of Crusaders/Urban Saints historically or in the practices of the case study groups today. Indeed, the history of evangelicals with their drive towards parachurch innovation and activism could be seen to mitigate against either of these ecclesial dynamics. This understanding would, I suggest, miss insights from the ecclesial imagination that act as a reminder of the practical normative approach to the Church within Crusaders/Urban Saints' story. Far from being satisfied with a minimal version of the koinonia of the Church, evangelicals have often sought deep community with one another, locally and more widely as they develop networks that support their work. Similarly, Fresh Expressions' literature envisages the outward dynamic being expressed through connection, and not simply to parish, diocese and denomination; by shaping churches around networks, the report acknowledges that this means they will likely be less denominationally bound and will tend to have relationship or connection with one or more resourcing networks.[22] Indeed, it has been claimed that a fresh expression of church might have more in common with churches outside of its area rather than within its deanery or diocese.[23]

The story of Crusaders/Urban Saints in particular, with its 'non-sectarian' stance from the outset but with a desire to work alongside all churches locally, demonstrates the value of connectivity within the operant ecclesiology of the organization. As exemplified by the St Joe's group, by drawing leaders together from across the churches in the town to form a team the group is able to trace lines of connection with a range of Christian communities and Christian traditions. In working together in this way there is affirmation of sharing core aspects of the Christian tradition.[24] However, the connectivity they display moves in two directions, not just through connections with the different denominations locally but by still valuing and making use of the historical Crusader/Urban Saints networks. These two directions in which the dynamic of connectivity is worked out through St Joe's demonstrate ways in which the group can be considered part of the Church. This points to the natural interweaving nature of the Church: that it comes together as a tapestry or, to draw on another image used by a leader in the case studies, like a jigsaw.

In addition, the inward ecclesial dynamic offers a reminder to those for whom groups and activities such as youth groups operate as potential ecclesial spaces within an interweaving church that they must seek deep relational connection to others in the context of core Christian practices. Within this, the sacraments of baptism and the Eucharist are highlighted as the central identifying practices of the Christian Church.[25] The absence of these from the simple ecclesial practices of the youth groups reinforces the notion that the groups alone are not sufficient to be considered churches. In order to be authentically part of the Church those who appropriate Urban Saints groups into an interweaving ecclesial expression need to ensure that they are moving inwardly within a communal Christian expression that holds the practice of the Eucharist as central; however, I also discuss below how the groups embody a form of sacramental life in their praxis that deepens and enhances this dynamic for the whole Church.

This move, then, forces the potential ecclesial spaces to avoid isolation and reasserts the value of interweaving. The need to move out from the specifics of a particular ecclesial space to move in the inward dynamic of a eucharistic community demonstrates the connectedness of both inner and outer dynamics in an interweaving ecclesiology. Helpfully, then, the Fresh Expressions conversation holds within it a means of regulating the interweaving approach, while the interweaving approach takes these dynamics and expresses them in a broader, more flexible way that is constructive for the ongoing conversations within Fresh Expressions. This flexibility provides a more dynamic response to the challenges of societal changes such as the network society described in the rationale of *Mission-shaped Church* as well as the challenges of the secular and digital ages discussed in Chapter 2. In addition, this approach allows for certain activities to maintain a mission focus in their ecclesial life, without being caught up in questions of whether they are a mature church expression or not. This in turn leads to a discussion of the relational dynamics that key Fresh Expressions thinker Michael Moynagh explores in depth.

Moynagh suggests that four relational moves are specific

enough to identify the Church within an individual fresh expression or, to use his preferred terminology, new ecclesial community. These moves are often described as up, in, out and of – seen as worship, community, mission and unity with the wider body of Christ. These four moves add detail to the dynamics discussed above that move towards inner koinonia and connectivity. Crucially within Moynagh's thinking, and within the formal ecclesiology of Fresh Expressions, these kinds of relational moves are to be developed and expressed within each ecclesial community – in other words, for a group or community to be described as *a* church it must be moving in all four of these areas. The risk here is that despite the language of relationality this four-relationship dynamic enforces a new form of boundary around the life of the Church.

Returning to Ralph Winter's concept of the two structures of God's redemptive mission, we can see that it is possible for individuals to be expressing these moves within different groups and communities, even where some are considered church, and some are not. Similarly, and as demonstrated, the ecclesial imagination of youth ministry holds this possibility to the fore; individuals' different expressions of ecclesial life, as they weave together relationally, complement one another to deepen and strengthen the relational moves of up, in, out and of. In fact, some of those relational moves are potentially much richer for being expressed in this way through the weaving of potential ecclesial spaces – to use the language of Winter again, modalities are more inclined towards the 'up' move of developing worshipping communities, whereas sodalities are more inclined towards the 'out' move of mission. And in the example of the Urban Saints groups the way the life of the Church flowed into them expands the 'of' direction by creating relationship for individuals with different parts of the wider body of Christ.

Consequently, the interweaving ecclesiology as an expression of the ecclesial imagination of youth ministry values the four relational moves that in Moynagh's thinking can provide the essence of the Church but understands them not as needing to be encompassed within a single community, activity or group, but in the dynamic interweaving of relationships formed as individuals develop their ecclesial life. Furthermore, however, the four relational moves in conjunction with the over-arching intensive and connective dynamics can ensure that potential ecclesial spaces and individuals within them are encouraged to grow their ecclesial life and relationships in each of these areas as they construct their interweaving Church. Potential ecclesial spaces within an interweaving ecclesiology, then, need not form solid boundaries and move towards taking the identity of a church, but can be held accountable to their communal relationships with the wider body of Christ and to the way they encourage their participants towards deepening their koinonia experience through the in, up, out and of relationships. Consequently, an interweaving ecclesiology can ensure that a flexible form of the Church might still be regulated without adding solid boundaries.

Moreover, by including potential ecclesial spaces such as youth groups within the relational moves of Fresh Expressions the definition of church assumed becomes broader than that of any denomination, institution or structure that might impose explicit or implicit boundaries, as revealed in the analysis of the case studies.[26] In addition, using these inward and outward dynamics to regulate the interweaving approach highlights explicitly the idea of different roles in church life being played by different activities, yet God working through each one[27] – thus in turn encouraging the ongoing pilgrim life of the Church as discussed in the previous chapter.

Sacramental relationality

A crucial aspect of the inward and outward moves in bringing some accountability to an interweaving ecclesiology – the intensivity and connectivity suggested within the Fresh Expressions literature itself – is the place and understanding of the sacraments. Just as these relational dynamics in and of themselves are crucial to regulating the interweaving Church and operate as signposts to ensure that such an ecclesiology does not fall into an 'anything goes' dynamic, it is important to explore the sacraments within these relationships.

While there is not the space here to enter into an analysis of sacramental theology, I do need to acknowledge both the centrality of the sacraments to the life of the Church and the reality that they are an aspect of the Christian life largely ignored within contemporary youth ministry practice. Indeed, it is generally not considered controversial to suggest, echoing the classic Lutheran statement, found in the Augsburg Confession, that the right administering of the sacraments is a key mark of the Church.

With this in mind it is noteworthy that neither Eucharist nor baptism – the two classic sacraments, held to be so because they are those initiated by Christ – are among the ecclesial practices identified within the youth groups. This is in keeping with a decision made by Crusaders/Urban Saints as early as 1931 to mandate that the Eucharist was not to be taken within their groups so as not to threaten good relationships with local churches and out of respect for denominational differences in approach. While this decision from the 1930s holds no particular sway in the life of the groups today, they are influenced by the tradition of praxis inherited and the ecclesial imagination received as normative. Furthermore, this absence serves to reinforce the notion that the groups alone are not sufficient to be considered churches. To be authentically part of the Church those who appropriate Urban Saints or other such potential ecclesial spaces into an interweaving ecclesiological expression need to ensure that they are also moving inwardly within a communal Christian expression that holds the practices of Eucharist and baptism as central.

An interweaving ecclesiology therefore needs to consider the place of the sacramental life of the Church as a key regulating feature, but I want to go further by suggesting that this sacramental life is enhanced by the interweaving as expressed in the existence of potential ecclesial spaces such as the youth groups studied. It is not simply that the sacraments of Eucharist and baptism are required for participants to be fully incorporated into the life of the Church but also that the kind of inward relational dynamic created within a less formal type of ecclesial life brings an added accountability to the sacramental life of the

Church itself. Two theologians operating within the discipline of youth ministry can help us here – Andrew Root and Bard Norheim.

As noted in Chapter 2, Andrew Root has written extensively on the impact of the secular age on the concept of faith, the role of the pastor and the congregational life of the Church. Core to Root's theology is an argument about the way that faith is formed in the pattern of Christ's ministry. For Root, a fundamental way of understanding the character of God is that of a minister – one who gives of oneself on behalf of others. Drawing on the biblical scholarship of Michael Gorman, and his work on Paul's expression of Christ's kenotic emptying and self-giving in the well-known Philippians 2 poem, Root argues that faith in the secular age is awakened and formed as this pattern of Christ's life and ministry is reflected in relationship of one to another in ministry.[28] The act of self-giving in ministry thus reflects Christ and, as such, Christ is revealed. Since Christ is revealed in this way these relationships can be seen to have a sacramental character to them.

Moreover, Root explores further how such ministry might be initiated. In the manner of Christ's kenotic love for the world, in which he empties himself and meets people in their experiences of loss,[29] it is in the giving of one to the other in the midst of the narrating of experiences of negation that the place of ministry, and therefore revelation of Christ, might be opened up:

> For us to help people in our churches experience faith ... is to invite them to come in and through prayer to articulate their experience of negation so that they might be ministered to ... Through the experience of ministry faith takes on a new narrative.[30]

This is precisely the pattern and process that we see being enacted in experiences described by young people in the case studies. Whether it is the self-proclaimed atheist Beth being so moved by the experience of care on the evening after a loved uncle had died, finding in the safe place of the group and the relationship with leaders the opportunity to narrate that loss and be prayed for; or perhaps it is the experience of Sally at St Joe's, who found in the consistency of the leaders giving up their Saturday evening the self-identity and value she felt was so missing from her experience of congregational church life, these young people have found something of the life and person of Christ being revealed.

By mirroring the Christlike narrative of kenosis these experiences of the young people reflect in the relational practice of the groups the pattern of the traditional sacraments of Eucharist and baptism – entering into the story and experience of Christ in order that he might be revealed afresh. It is almost as if something of the sacrament is performed in the informal ambiguity of the groups, without ever being named as such. This is an idea that reflects Bard Norheim's exploration of what he calls 'practicing baptism'.[31] In this discussion Norheim understands baptism not as a one-off event, but as a lifelong practice that is inaugurated by the event of baptism. Given that baptism is a re-enactment and participation in the death and resurrection of Christ, the practice of baptism consists of a daily practice of dying to self in the pattern of Christ. Similarly, then, we could posit the possibility of practising Eucharist in which the death-to-life narrative of Christ is both remembered and participated in through the bread and wine. Norheim's understanding of the daily practice of baptism therefore suggests that sacramental practice in relationship should be part of the life of faith. By connecting this idea with the argument for faith formation from Root, we can see how this participating in sacramental practice, which performs afresh the kenotic movements of death to life, might mean that the 'right administration of the sacraments' can move beyond the meeting of the congregation into the more ambiguous relational life of believers as we minister one to another. Potential ecclesial spaces such as Christian youth groups can exhibit just such a relational life, though often unacknowledged.

Clearly this form of relational life that creates the space through which ongoing sacramental practice can take place is not exclusive to work with young people, though the inherent ecclesial imagination seems conducive to it and brings it to light. What is vital in this discussion is the way that potential ecclesial spaces as part of an interweaving understanding of the Church interact with the sacraments as part of the inward and outward relational dynamics. This means that an interweaving ecclesiology is held accountable by interaction with the sacraments but also that such an understanding can enhance participants' sacramental life. Here the traditional intention of Crusaders/ Urban Saints is helpful – their classes were never intended to be replacements for local congregational church life.

In the same way, then, as Pete Ward's warning that the Church cannot be contained in a meeting because the Spirit of God 'passes through, moves within, and is active beyond the more solid boundaries of the Church',[32] an interweaving ecclesiology opens up the possibility that the sacramental life of the Church flows through, within and beyond the sacramental events themselves into the relational heart of potential ecclesial spaces as individuals minister one to another in the pattern of Christ. This is a vision of the sacramental life of the Church that will not conform to the paradoxes and contradictions of the Church as meeting or building, yet still values the sacramental events of Eucharist and baptism, alongside the practice of these in relationship.

This is not a radical vision for sacramental life in the Church, yet it is one that is not often reflected or expressed in practice. Stephen Pickard helpfully picks up these themes, however, in the context of various relational moves of the Church. Inspired by Daniel Hardy's language and concepts of intensity and extensity that mirror the inward and outward movements for which I have been arguing, Pickard talks about how the celebration of the sacraments – the events of baptism and Eucharist – can act as the place of release for divine energy. The sacramental life of the Church can thus be seen to flow into the 'spread-out-ness' of extensivity as baptism and Eucharist are 'constantly repeated in the ebb and flow of discipleship in the world'.[33] Pickard goes on to explore how the 'effectiveness' of the sacramental life of the Church is discerned not in the moments of inward celebration, but rather in the 'ongoing transformations of societal life, in which the body of Christ lives and moves and has its being'.[34] In other words, and to use my language, the sacramental life of the Church might discover the outflow of its energy in ambiguous potential ecclesial spaces as the Church seeks to faithfully walk in the world.

It follows, then, that while consideration of the sacraments is vital for regulating the interweaving church and providing some accountability to prevent such an ecclesiological approach from descending into a scenario in which anything goes, potential ecclesial spaces such as those of Christian youth groups can provide a context for the Church to practise a sacramental relationality that might shine a light of accountability back into more formal expressions of church in which operant sacramental understanding can find itself limited to the event or celebration. Rather, as Pickard has shown, these two sacramental dynamics operate together. Gittoes, also drawing on the imaginative theology of Daniel Hardy, argues that simple acts such as 'care for the other' draw on sacramental energy,[35] thus expressing in word what was lived out in the practice of pastoral care within the youth groups. We see in those moments, then, not simply good youth work practice but the process of the sacramental life and energy of the Church bringing transformation 'beyond the individual [who participates in the celebration of the sacrament] to others in the world ... in particular places, moments in time and face-to-face conversations'.[36]

Similarly, this understanding of the sacramental life of the Church attends to the relational moves contained in what is commonly referred to as the double listening of church planting, in which the Church is called to hear both the call of the Christian tradition and the voice of the context. The event and practice of the sacraments allow for Eucharist and baptism to connect participants to the tradition of faith through participating in that which has marked the Church since Christ's life among his apostles as well as creating space for ministering to the particular experiences of individuals and communities in context. The challenge therefore is multi-directional and in keeping with the dual movements of intensivity and connectivity. A result of this is the tantalizing possibility that pioneering ministry might be reframed as a sacramental ministry of the spread-out Church.[37]

In these movements the interweaving church is regulated and enhanced through the necessity of the sacraments as well as their performance in the ministry. Through an interweaving ecclesiological approach participants are encouraged to connect with the solid (to use Ward's terminology) congregational life of the Church alongside contexts in which relationships are central and can be deeply cultivated, as well as valuing connection with the historical community of saints alongside the particularities of cultural context.

Summary

This chapter has tackled the question of how an interweaving ecclesiology might be regulated, both for potential ecclesial spaces and in the lives of individuals. This is a tricky task given the inherent ambiguity in the operant expression of ecclesial life in youth groups and consequently in the vision for an interweaving ecclesiology. While some accountability is needed to ensure that an interweaving ecclesiology does not collapse into a situation where anything goes, it has also been important through this discussion to hold in the background the challenge, encapsulated in the Brutus Green quote at the start of Chapter 7, not to cement ecclesial boundaries in the desire for accountability. Consequently, this chapter has argued for a relational regulating of an interweaving ecclesiology and has drawn on the discussion of various relational dynamics from within the Fresh Expressions literature to do this. Within this discussion, a rethinking of the classic 'mixed economy' approach has been proposed in which the mixed economy allows different expressions of church – congregational, institutional and potential expressions of ecclesial life – to form the ecclesial experience of individual believers as they weave together to create a tapestry of church. The relational dynamics from Fresh Expressions can provide accountability to ensure that individuals do not become individualistic in their expression of church, but instead are committed to moving up, in, out and of deepening koinonia within each ecclesial expression as well as connectivity with the wider body of Christ – indeed, an interweaving ecclesiology carries this connectivity deeply within its expression.

Furthermore, this chapter has discussed the sacramental life of the Church within these relational moves, recognizing these practices as core identifying features of the Church that must be woven into the ecclesial life of individuals as they construct church through various communal expressions and experiences. Moreover, though, the chapter has argued that while the potential ecclesial spaces revealed in the youth groups do not formally practise the sacraments of Eucharist and baptism, they do embody the sacramental life of the Church in their relationships as they minister to one another in the pattern of Christ. The sacramental life of the Church then becomes enhanced as the events of the sacraments are taken into the practice of life together. Consequently, the potential ecclesial spaces might be able to shine a light back towards formal and congregational expressions of church life to prevent the sacraments being seen as events or celebrations alone, rather than as doorways into a life together that is lived within the narrative of Christ's self-giving. The accountability within the interweaving church, then, is multi-directional as both the formal congregational life of the Church and potential ecclesial spaces hold the Church true to its sacramental life and calling.

Notes

1 Anglican-Methodist Working Party, *Fresh Expressions in the Mission of the Church* (London: Church House Publishing, 2012), p. 183.

2 Clare Watkins, *Disclosing Church: An Ecclesiology Learned from Conversations in Practice* (Abingdon: Routledge, 2020), p. 155.

3 *Fresh Expressions in the Mission of the Church*, p. 154.

4 *Fresh Expressions in the Mission of the Church*, p. 155.

5 This echoes the language of Elaine Graham discussed in Chapter 1. Graham finds it more helpful to talk about intentional Christian community than church due to the nature of the term and the way it

better describes the function of such groups and their practices. See Elaine Graham, *Transforming Practice: Pastoral Theology in an Age of Uncertainty* (Eugene, OR: Wipf and Stock, 2002).

6 Archbishops' Council, *Mission-shaped Church* (London: Church House Publishing, 2010), p. 8.

7 Archbishops' Council, *Mission-shaped Church*, p. 12. See also https://freshexpressions.org.uk/find-out-more/going-deeper-3-why-do-fresh-expressions-matter/ (accessed 9.06.2021).

8 Thus reflecting something of the sodalities in Winter's approach, though with a stronger ecclesial identity.

9 As per Pete Ward, *Liquid Church* (Milton Keynes: Paternoster Press, 2002), pp. 72–7. This is strongly critiqued, albeit in a slightly caricatured form, in Andrew Davison and Alison Milbank, *For the Parish: A Critique of Fresh Expressions* (London: SCM Press, 2010), pp. 104–5.

10 I use this language as it is commonplace though I am not entirely comfortable with it.

11 Ian J. Mobsby, *Emerging and Fresh Expressions of Church: How Are They Authentically Church and Anglican?* (London: Moot Community Publishing, 2007), p. 7.

12 Michael Moynagh, *Church for Every Context: An Introduction to Theology and Practice* (London: SCM Press, 2013), p. 432.

13 Moynagh, *Church for Every Context*, p. 433.

14 Chapter 9 addresses the role of pioneers within an interweaving ecclesiology.

15 Michael Moynagh, *Church in Life: Innovation, Mission and Ecclesiology* (London: SCM Press, 2017), p. 254.

16 Moynagh, *Church in Life*, p. 117.

17 The idea of a bricolage approach to church has been suggested, with some critique before. For a description of 'ecclesial bricolage', see Nicholas Healy, *Church, World and the Christian Life: Practical-Prophetic Ecclesiology* (Cambridge: Cambridge University Press, 2000), p. 175. Bretherton offers a critique of the concept: Luke Bretherton, 'Beyond the Emerging Church', in *Remembering Our Future: Explorations in Deep Church*, ed. Andrew Walker and Luke Bretherton (Milton Keynes: Paternoster Press, 2007), p. 46.

18 Thus, responding to criticism levelled at Fresh Expressions.

19 Tony Jones, *The Church Is Flat: The Relational Ecclesiology of the Emerging Church* (Minneapolis, MN: The JoPa Group, 2011).

20 This paragraph relies on *Fresh Expressions in the Mission of the Church*, pp. 154–76.

21 The Eucharist and baptism are ascribed particular significance among these practices: 'The most intense form of Christian community is found in gathering round the proclamation of the Gospel, and in the

celebration of the sacraments of Baptism and the Lord's Supper', *Fresh Expressions in the Mission of the Church*, pp. 155–6.

22 This is happening in some situations. See Andy Weir, *Sustaining Young Churches: A Qualitative Pilot Study of Fresh Expressions of Church in the Church of England* (Church Army, 2016).

23 Archbishops' Council, *Mission-shaped Church*, p. 66.

24 In this way, St Joe's carries within it practical echoes of the concept of deep church. See Andrew Walker and Robin A. Parry, *Deep Church Rising: Rediscovering the Roots of Christian Orthodoxy* (London: SPCK, 2014); and Walker and Bretherton, *Remembering Our Future*.

25 *Fresh Expressions in the Mission of the Church*, pp. 154–6.

26 By extension, these insights might therefore be valid for other organizations usually branded as parachurch, not simply Urban Saints or other youth ministry organizations.

27 As per the St Joe's interpretation of 1 Corinthians 3.5–8.

28 Andrew Root, *Faith Formation in a Secular Age: Responding to the Church's Obsession with Youthfulness* (Ada, MI: Baker Academic, 2017), p. 136.

29 Jesus meets people in their loss of health, community, relationship or status, or he invites them into loss in order to be ministered to – for example, the rich young ruler.

30 Root, *Faith Formation in a Secular Age*, pp. 150–1.

31 Bard Norheim, *Practicing Baptism: Christian Practices and the Presence of Christ* (Eugene, OR: Pickwick Publications, 2014).

32 Pete Ward, *Liquid Ecclesiology: The Gospel and the Church* (Leiden: Brill, 2017), p. 7.

33 Stephen Pickard, *Seeking the Church: An Introduction to Ecclesiology* (London: SCM Press, 2012), p. 201.

34 Pickard, *Seeking the Church*, p. 201.

35 Julie Gittoes, 'Where is the Kingdom?', in *Generous Ecclesiology: Church, World and the Kingdom of God*, ed. Julie Gittoes, Brutus Green and James Heard (London: SCM Press, 2013), p. 104.

36 Gittoes, 'Where is the Kingdom?', p. 111.

37 I explore pioneering more in the final chapter.

9

Releasing Creativity: Interweaving and Pioneering

I don't know what it is I'm looking for, but I'll know what it is when I see it.[1]

In this final chapter, my aim is to bring the argument to some kind of conclusion; to, as it were, complete the task of theological construction that I set myself at the start. This is, however, a tricky aim for a book whose very theological foundation and perspective suggests that the task of ecclesiological construction is never complete because the Church should always be learning to be the Church, always seeking to be true to its dialogical nature and to the vision of a community participating in the communicative acts of the Triune God. In the words of Julie Gittoes, therefore, the Church and our ecclesiological claims are 'risky, fragile, attentive and incomplete'.[2] Or, to use my own language, the Church needs to embrace the ambiguity of its existence as there will always be potential new spaces into which the Church can grow. Spaces that, as with the youth groups, are not churches and do not intend or aim to be churches, but within which ecclesial life can be detected and through which those who wish can enter in order to participate in the life of the body of Christ, the Church.

Specifically, this final chapter explores the role of pioneering within the Church – and the Fresh Expressions movement in particular – in the light of the argument that a vision for an interweaving ecclesiology moves our gaze beyond new forms of church due to the risk of unintentionally reinforcing solid ecclesial boundaries. The vision of an interweaving ecclesiology, built on a tapestry of potential ecclesial spaces in the life of individuals in relationship with one another, moves the Church towards being comfortable with ambiguity and with ecclesial encounters taking place both within 'the boundaries of sacred places ... and in the multiple contexts of human discourse and exchange'.[3] The vision for pioneering that I present in this concluding chapter, then, is one that facilitates the Church in the ambiguity of its interweaving and of the potential for ecclesial life to be encountered within the multiple contexts of discourse. It is in such contexts that the dominant discourse of the Church can be interrupted as I witnessed happening within the relational space of the Urban Saints groups. These interruptions and disruptions then create the ambiguous space in which individuals can make what some of the young people described as their 'baby steps' towards the Christian life in the safety of a relational space that was both church and not church; that was outside the boundaries of the Church, yet with ecclesial life flowing in and through it by the Spirit.

Paradoxically, one of the challenges for the Fresh Expressions movement comes from the energy with which the movement has been largely welcomed within the institution of the Church. As highlighted in Chapter 7, this has led to a felt need of defining what counts as church within Fresh Expressions. Some of this need is driven by a theological urge for clarity, some of it from an institutional urge towards structure, and some of it from the practical pressure to quantify and budget accordingly. Unfortunately, this drive to define can lead to challenges for those termed 'pioneers', the ordained and lay leaders tasked with leading and developing new, mission-focused forms of ecclesial life, requiring them to answer questions that inhibit – and at times even directly obstruct – the work they need to do.

The vision of an interweaving ecclesiology in which potential ecclesial spaces play a vital part can release pioneers from needing to wrestle with definitional questions to creatively embrace the ambiguity of working missionally at the edge of the Church's pilgrim journey. Such ambiguity allows pioneering work to operate with a paradoxical combination of clarity and ambiguity – clarity that what they are doing is part of an overall ecclesiological vision, and in that way therefore has ecclesial life flowing in and through it, but holding an essential ambiguity as the particular activities and relationships in which they engage may or may not in and of themselves be understood as 'church'. Pioneers then can shape their work around the task of being creatively missional, rather than being expected to launch new churches – starting not with the task of forming church and seeking to ensure that what they develop can be clearly defined as such but, rather, seeking a connection between gospel and places in which ecclesial life may appear.

There are within this approach two benefits to the Church as a whole from pioneers being able to take this posture towards their work and ministry – first, by not needing to aim at developing churches as such there is a natural humility and interdependence within the work of pioneering. Pioneers are not those who are out doing a new thing unconnected to the wider life of the body of Christ; instead, by not beginning with such a clear aim of developing a church there is a need for relationship with the wider Church in order that ecclesial life might flow in and through the potential ecclesial spaces. This then draws on the relational accountability explored in the previous chapter. The second benefit of this approach to pioneering is that it reminds the inherited Church, the Church as it currently is, that it is not all-sufficient, that it is not complete, that it is not synonymous with the kingdom, and that it needs to be a pilgrim people seeking to move and grow into the new spaces evolving and emerging in contemporary life and culture. A vision for an interweaving ecclesiology, then, can be helpful in developing humble approaches to both pioneering and the current life of the Church. Thus this final chapter seeks to reframe pioneering as releasing creativity without the need to define too tightly what this might look like. The chapter concludes with bringing the argument of the book full circle by examining the potential role of young people (and youth ministry) as pioneering for the Church. This is important so that the Church is regularly engaged with young people embodying their natural role of cultural interpreters. In this way, they are essential to the Church's adopting a self-understanding that is open to change and a humility that recognizes the need to be always learning how to be the Church.

The challenge of defining pioneering

As this chapter is essentially about pioneering, the form of ministry specifically recognized by the Church of England and other denominations in relation to developing new forms of church, it is important to begin with a discussion about definitions. The Church of England specifically defines pioneers as:

> People called by God who are the first to see and creatively respond to the Holy Spirit's initiatives with those outside the church; gathering others around them as they seek to establish [a] new contextual Christian community.[4]

Definitions are of course useful, especially within institutions of the size and complexity of the Church of England; however, the argument this book has wrestled with throughout is the urge to define too tightly what can be counted as church, ultimately arguing for an ambiguity and flexibility in our understanding of how ecclesial life is formed in the weaving together of various strands. The paradox at the heart of the ecclesial imagination of youth ministry is a form of ecclesial life outside the flow of mainstream life in such a way that it does not fit the definitional boundaries of a dominant discourse about church. I want to suggest in this final chapter that when thinking about pioneering[5] a similar ambiguous approach is needed and that an interweaving ecclesiology can assist in developing such an approach.

The definition above encapsulates perfectly the tension faced by those involved in pioneering. On the one hand, it is to be welcomed that the institutional, established Church is embracing the uncertainty that comes with looking to release creativity. On the other hand, the risk here is that the need to define something to bring clarity within such a large institution unnecessarily predetermines the outcomes and narrows the potential of the creativity that is trying to be released. In much the same way as highlighted in previous chapters, the drive to define can put the ecclesial cart before the missional horse. As the Church of England definition above suggests, the outcome of pioneering ministry is already being determined as a 'new contextual Christian community'. It was precisely this tension between the joy that the institutional Church has embraced pioneering and new forms of church, alongside concerns that this naturally leads to a drive to define, and in defining a form of control (or to use the language of earlier chapters, a gravitational pull) might be exerted, that was expressed by Pete Rollins back in 2008:

> For while the explicit aim of labelling groups fresh expressions may be to encourage their continued development and provide space for their unique voice within the church, one could say that in the very process of doing this the radical voice of these groups is actually suppressed.[6]

He goes on to articulate the hope that those pioneering new forms of church would consider remaining a voice in the wilderness, embracing a 'less defined, more ambiguous relationship' with the Church – a place he hoped would allow such groups to speak to the whole Church.[7]

This call to remain essentially outside the formal, defined boundaries of the Church resonates with the ecclesial imagination of youth ministry, historically through the way that the founders of Crusaders developed a way of life that fostered faith among young people and leaders through to the present-day practice of the groups that sees the 'non-church' identity as an advantage in their missional outlook. Accordingly, there might be something in this ecclesial imagination, in the interweaving ecclesiology and the constituent potential ecclesial spaces, that offers a way of operating within the less defined, more ambiguous relationship with the Church for which Rollins was calling all those years ago.

There are of course definitions of pioneering that are less prescriptive of the outcome and consequently more ambiguous. The founder of Pioneer Training at CMS, Jonny Baker, for example draws on a definition from Beth Keith: 'A pioneer is someone who sees future possibilities and works to bring them into reality.'[8] Baker goes on to build on this broader definition by describing pioneers as 'dreamers who do', highlighting the necessity of this gift to the Church if it is to maintain a missional dynamic and move out of its comfort zone.[9] Elsewhere, however, pioneering appears to be framed almost as something that happens, or at least might happen, unexpectedly or accidentally. Somewhat incongruously, for example, the book *How to Pioneer*[10] opens with a number of pen portraits in which relationships built in the natural flow of life begin to raise the question of whether the Spirit of God might be birthing some kind of Christian community – or, to use my language, potential ecclesial space – from these relationships.[11] This is pioneering almost by accident rather than beginning with seeking to establish new contextual Christian communities; neither does it begin with seeing a future possibility and working to bring such possibilities to reality. It is certainly, though, pioneering as happening outside of the formal boundaries and dominant definitions of church life, but where the relationships built carry vital ecclesial potential.

There are various challenges inherent within these discussions around defining pioneering. First, as alluded to above, the institutional need to define can unintentionally lead to narrowing and limiting the potential creativity as ambiguity is squashed through predetermined ends within the definition. Second, and paradoxically at odds with the first challenge, by encouraging pioneer ministry through defining and naming, the language of pioneering becomes a kind of buzzword that leads to it being adopted so broadly across the spectrum of the Church that it loses much of its meaning.[12] Third, and implied within the first two challenges, the language of pioneering is used specifically and generally in a way that can result in some confusion. By this I mean that pioneer ministry is a specific form of ordained ministry within the Church of England, while also being recognized as a lay ministry in both formal and informal ways. As a result, pioneering is intrinsically hard to define, meaning that ambiguity is inherent in the conversation.

This chapter does not seek to enter the debate around definitions of pioneering ministry, but instead explores the way in
which the ambiguity inherent within an interweaving ecclesiology, especially in the potential ecclesial spaces that provide
space into which the life of the Church might grow, might
facilitate releasing the creativity that is central to the task of
pioneering. Given that an interweaving ecclesiology embraces
ambiguity and the tension of spaces that are simultaneously
church and not church, there are resources within this way of
understanding the Church that see the creative tension of these
spaces at the edge of the Church's existence. Pioneering, then,
can be framed as releasing creativity to enable the Church to
explore new spaces, and pioneers can be seen as those who
embody the pilgrim nature of the Church, seeking to lead a
careful walking in the world in the manner of Christ.[13]

Attentiveness and ambiguity

If we are to reframe pioneering with a less clear definition, and
focus more on releasing creativity, then the twin values of attentiveness and ambiguity will need to be embraced by the Church
in the way that they are naturally by those who themselves are
termed pioneers. In this way I frame pioneering as the ability
to live in the ambiguity of the interaction of church and not
church, in the definitional uncertainty of potential ecclesial
spaces. With similarity to the way that Chapter 7 argued that
we need to ensure a move beyond Fresh Expressions so that the
Church doesn't simply redraw where the solid boundaries of
church life lie, pioneer ministry and individual pioneer minis-
ters need to be more than church planters, aiming instead to be
those at the forefront of the Church's pilgrim wandering, those
who are constantly wrestling with what the reconstruction of
the Church looks like. Pioneers are those who embody the theological vision with which this book began so that the Church
is provoked afresh into the participative dialogue with the Spirit
and the world that defines what it is to be the Church.

The Church lives with ambiguity and needs to be reminded
of its own ambiguity and fragility, against the desire to bring

certainty through artificial boundaries. Pioneers are those who remind us of our own fragility and ambiguity, who bring to light the hidden discourses by operating in the potential ecclesial spaces that are both church and not church, in order that new threads might be woven into the tapestry of church life – this is why the ecclesiological vision in this book is 'interweaving', rather than 'interweaved' or 'interwoven'. It is in the ongoing interweaving, the potential for new threads to be added, that the ecclesial tapestry is forever unfinished. The pioneer is ultimately an ecclesial artist not a church planter. In light of the author Madeleine L'Engle claiming that 'almost every definition I find of being a Christian is also a definition of being an artist ... art is an affirmation of life, a rebuttal of death',[14] this is not perhaps as surprising as it might appear.

This imagery of the artist draws on a fascinating conversation between Jonny Baker and Ric Stott in *Missional Conversations*. Within this conversation Baker draws on research from the art world that was featured in a book called *The Creative Stance*. This work posits seven behaviours that can be seen as a type of formation for artists, with Baker seeing a resonance with these stances and those required for pioneering. The seven are: rigour, risk, imagination, provocation, agency, resilience, ambiguity.[15] Out of these, Baker specifically picks up on the challenge of ambiguity, claiming that ambiguity creates space for imagination; but he goes further by saying that for a changing world ambiguity opens the space for 'flexibility, adaptability, openness, vulnerability, resourcefulness and avoidance of monocultures'. He finishes by stating quite bluntly: 'the wider church needs the same – it really does'.[16] The ecclesial imagination of youth ministry would agree and offers an ecclesiological framework that provides a means by which pioneers can be released to operate in the ambiguous space.

As the quote at the beginning of this chapter suggests, there is always an inherent ambiguity at play in the task or art of pioneering. Ric Stott, an artist and pioneer, goes on to express this dual role as an 'attentive wandering'.[17] This use of the word 'attentive' echoes the language of Alister McGrath who discusses the importance of cultivating theological attentiveness.

In the same chapter as the one in which the quotation at the beginning of Chapter 1 can be found, McGrath suggests that a key component of cultivating the theological attentiveness for which he is arguing is taking account of the local *terroir*:

> Each is specific to its own distinct place. Each is shaped by the interaction of physical geography and human culture ... [Theological attentiveness] urges us to value the particular, identifying and appreciating its distinct characteristics, rather than rushing headlong to reduce it to another instance of a more general phenomenon or principle.[18]

This attention to the particular is part of what McGrath considers a movement towards the truth – this is no surprise in the light of the incarnation in which we see the true reality of God revealed in the particular human, Jesus of Nazareth. McGrath goes on to contrast such attention to the particular, this resistance to replicate or reduce to a general phenomenon, principle or, one might add, structure, with the pull towards universality and globalization.[19] These might be seen as helpful theological values to retain truth across time and space, yet McGrath warns against them. There can be a temptation to move towards such values as universality, given that humans are perhaps predisposed to be uncomfortable with ambiguity. The concept of the *terroir*, however, in which the interaction of elements might be constantly shifting, draws us back to the importance of remaining attentive to ambiguity and particularity.[20]

It is this same draw towards attentiveness and particularity that saw CMS-trained missionary the Revd Albert Kestin begin a conversation with a group of boys in a park on Sunday afternoon in 1900, subsequently inviting them to a Bible class that became the first Crusader class. It is this same draw to attentiveness (perhaps not of place but certainly of person) that motivates the leader at St Joe's to interrupt the self-declared most important aspect of the group (the Bible study) to offer a personal welcome to a late arriving young person. And it is the same attentiveness that resulted in Vincent Donovan declaring himself as feeling 'rather naked' as he unencumbered himself from the burden of the usual structures and expectations to travel to the Masai in his quest to explore the gospel afresh with them. It is this kind of attentiveness that points towards the creative and ambiguous role and task of pioneering.

Pioneering, the mixed ecology and the edge of chaos

Core among the challenges when discussing pioneering in this way – or indeed for those who consider themselves pioneers, or are seen by others as pioneers – is the challenge of how to frame something that leans towards ambiguity. Again, the stance of an artist is useful – at times that which is being produced will be known with some clarity from the start, whereas at other times it will emerge along the way; sometimes a piece of work will reach some form of completion, but many other times it will begin and be developed for a while before being adapted or something else being started. As per the artistic values, Jonny Baker described the process of pioneering as fragile and fraught with ambiguity.

To put it simply, there is no one thing that can be called pioneering or pioneer ministry. Since it is by its very nature breaking new ground, it is difficult to define. To try and help with this difficulty Tina Hodgett and Paul Bradbury have written about what they call the 'pioneering spectrum'.[21] In this attempt at a typology drawn from practice, they see different forms of pioneering encapsulated in concepts of adapting, innovating and activism – though they are clear in naming all pioneers as creatives in the same way as we have already identified in this chapter.

This kind of work and attempt to bring nuance to the way that pioneering is understood is really a response to what is happening in practice where there is significant variety in the way that pioneers, be they lay or ordained leaders, seek to express the mandate to develop fresh expressions of church. As entrepreneurs who embody the double listening envisaged as the starting point for developing new forms of church, in practice they operate in a variety of ways – some within traditional parish life, some outside, and others in roles that straddle both.

To echo the language of Ralph Winter, these approaches are understood as working modally, sodally or in a mixed environment. Research has shown that those who work modally and in mixed settings experience the challenge of working within a traditional church structure while trying to pioneer something new, whereas those who work sodally feel more positive about the Church and are supported by network-based organizations.[22] Among the challenges experienced by pioneers working within traditional, modal church settings is a tension between different understandings of church – they are working towards a fresh expression vision in which the new initiative intends to become a mature church for those involved, whereas the parish it is connected to struggles to see it as such or misunderstands what the pioneers are trying to achieve. In contrast, those working sodally speak positively of the relationships they have and a certain freedom is implied within the facilitative connection to the network organizations.

Recent research builds on these challenges of defining and talking about pioneering ministry by acknowledging that a significant amount of what might be described as pioneering is occurring in 'mixed ecology' contexts[23] – these being parishes in which pioneering initiatives are being developed alongside 'inherited' parish church work by ordained and lay leaders.[24] Two things are fascinating about the research into these mixed ecology parishes. First, the headlining of the creativity involved in the work that is being done; and, second, the reality that many who are 'pioneering' in these contexts are not officially labelled 'pioneers' and do not necessarily see the work they are doing as seeking to form 'new contextual Christian communities' as per the official definition of pioneering ministry.[25] Indeed, some participants in this research talked about what they were doing as simply what a church should be doing when engaged within its local context or community.

The idea of a mixed ecology in parish life is clearly being worked out in practice in a variety of contexts, but it is also a stated aim of the Church of England that this becomes the norm for parish ministry by 2030. This current praxis and future intention somewhat undercut the formal definition of pioneering that suggests forming new churches (or at least new contextual Christian communities) is the intended outcome. The mixed ecology also brings nuance to the original notion of each fresh expression of church needing to aim for the 'three-self principle' of being self-propagating, self-financing and self-governing, suggesting instead a more fluid and flexible relationship between inherited and new forms of church. One might even posit the idea of this relationship being an inter-weaving. Furthermore, given that some of the new expressions being developed within mixed ecology contexts (by those who identify as pioneers and those who do not) are not seen as developing a church as such, the ambiguous language of potential ecclesial spaces is helpful.

Consequently, the way in which the ecclesial imagination of youth groups can be seen as operating through potential eccle-sial spaces within an interweaving approach to the Church could be helpful to pioneers. In the context of the pioneers working modally, this approach could help to address the challenge they face in understanding what they are doing. This is particularly important in light of recent research into fresh expressions of church that demonstrates a significant proportion of them are not operating as independent churches, but instead have dependent relationships with host or send-ing churches. The vision of the 'three-self existence' is not working out in practice. This practical shift in the vision for Fresh Expressions itself suggests a more complex interplay of relationships in the way that church is being worked out in contemporary life. Within this, then, the potential ecclesial spaces of the interweaving approach have a helpful perspec-tive to add nuance and depth to these different ways in which church is being lived and worked out. And, furthermore, it helps to redefine the work of pioneering as releasing creativ-ity in seeking to connect with people in new dialogical spaces, rather than being about forming new churches as such.

This again points us back to the ambiguity inherent at the edges of the interweaving ecclesiology and in the concept of potential ecclesial spaces that are simultaneously church and not church, but in this way provide a space in which Christ might be encountered and faith formed. Michael Moynagh has used the phrase 'edge of chaos' to describe this uncertainty in developing new work, especially the tension between innovation and the status quo.[26] It is an ideal phrase to describe the experience of seeking to release creativity in exploring potential ecclesial spaces. Moynagh describes the state of edge of chaos as part of an innovation cycle, but specifically the crucial position of balancing 'order (continuity) and disorder (novelty)'.[27] He goes on to say that in the process there is 'shape to the process ... but this is pushed and pulled as people get to work on it'.[28] In other words, although there is a sense of what is being created there is flexibility and ambiguity, space for dialogue to interrupt and shape. The rush to define what is to be produced or predetermine the outcome for the work of the pioneers with the Church stifles this ambiguous tension between order and disorder, between church and not church.

The edge of chaos describes well the challenge for the Church in how to hold the work of pioneers – chaos and disorder is unsettling, as is ambiguity about what is being created. However, if the Church is going to keep its boundaries blurred and release the creativity of pioneers then such ambiguity and disorder is necessary, with the consequent need to resist the urge to define too tightly. It is by maintaining this ambiguous edge that the Church will be able to retain its pilgrim identity and seek to continue to walk carefully in the world, seeking faithfulness to the Spirit of Christ. Pioneers are, then, those leading the pilgrim walk of the Church and, to mix the metaphors, painting ecclesial life on to new canvases.

In this light, the interweaving ecclesiology that emerges from youth ministry, with its constituent potential ecclesial spaces, provides the framework for the Church to embrace the edge of chaos and to affirm pioneers in their creative roles. By resisting definition at the edge of its life the Church can release creativity, and pioneers are those who are not required to plant churches but to seek the emergence of ecclesial life in new spaces with the relational accountability of interweaving allowing for the Church to become apparent as various threads of ecclesial life weave together in new, fresh and perhaps ever-changing ways.

The pioneering role of young people and youth ministry

In a move that begins to take the argument of this book almost full circle, a crucial aspect of releasing creativity and reframing pioneering in light of an interweaving ecclesiology is for the Church to reposition itself in relation to young people by seeing them as potential pioneers. This is a thread that has run through the development of the concept of an interweaving ecclesiology as the Church's work with young people opens up new space into which ecclesial life might flow. This suggestion is entirely in keeping with both theological and sociological points of departure – that ecclesiology has tended to be developed out of the key questions the Church is wrestling with in particular times and places, and that young people can be seen essentially as interpreters of contemporary culture. As a result of these threads, an interweaving ecclesiology is inherently open to the lives and experiences of young people. This means that rather than being a closed expression of the Church such openness allows for the Church to be responsive in an ongoing manner to the ways of engaging in the communal life of the Christian faith. Seeing young people and youth ministry as potential pioneers can ensure that the pioneering is an ongoing process for the life of the Church.

This idea should come as no surprise for those who have developed the idea of pioneer ministry within the Fresh Expressions movement. The drive to planting fresh expressions of church is described in part as a move to close a gap between church and contemporary life in order to be more effective in the missional challenges within a society in which increasing numbers do not go to church. This move to close a gap was itself influenced by the development of alternative worship, especially among teenagers. Alternative worship sought to develop Christian worship in dialogue with the particularities of young people's cultural expressions. John Hall has argued that the rise of alternative worship was a result of a push-back against failed 'hit and run' forms of evangelism.[29] Hall goes into some detail to show how some of these leaders were key in the development of alternative worship and youth congregations, which, he goes on to say, have had a significant missiological impact. While the role of youth congregations is somewhat controversial within the youth ministry literature,[30] Hall places them in a wider context through his suggestion that they have had a transformational effect on missiological frameworks for the Church. This wider context is echoed in the thinking of Graham Cray who frames the work of youth congregations as a missiological response to changes in culture and context.[31]

This move towards developing alternative worship among, and for, the cultures of young people was a move to close the gap between the Church and contemporary life. It is this move that has been taken into Fresh Expressions and other new forms of the Church. Significantly, this move is identified both by tracing the themes but also through individuals who have moved from being pioneers in the alternative worship scene among young people in the latter decades of the twentieth century to being influential thinkers and practitioners within the Fresh Expressions movement.[32] I would argue, then, that when thinking about pioneering as releasing the creativity in the life of the Church a consideration of the place of young people – and the churches' work with them – is paramount.

I have written elsewhere of the value of drawing on the image from Scripture of the boy Samuel and his mentor, the elderly priest Eli.[33] In this wonderfully evocative story God calls out to the young boy Samuel who does not initially recognize the voice of God, imagining instead that it is Eli calling him. In this image the established Church, those versed in the dominant discourse, might find it helpful to think of ourselves as Eli, with the young Samuel running to us to find out what we want. We gradually realize that God is revealing himself to Samuel in a way that he has not to us, but Samuel does not yet have the language or experience to name what it is that he is sensing. Eli, in wisdom and humility, with open-handedness to the things of God, equips Samuel to hear from God and to bring that to the conversation, honouring and acting on what he brings even though it does not look like what Eli would have expected.

This is what it means for the Church to begin to see young people as pioneers. It begins with the assumption that young people can and will hear and discern the Spirit of God at work in their lives and the surrounding culture. Using the image of Samuel running to Eli then leads us to consider the possibility that what young people need is not so much instructing in what God is saying to them, but guidance in hearing the voice of God and wisdom in responding and reacting to that.

Returning to Vincent Donovan, I am reminded of his famous reflections that provide a similar sentiment in the preface to the 25th anniversary edition of his missionary classic *Christianity Rediscovered*. Citing the words of a student who spoke to him in response to his story he lays this challenge at the door of the Church in relation to young people:

> In working with young people do not try to call them back to where they were, and do not try and call them to where you are, as beautiful as that place might seem to you. You must have the courage to go with them to a place that neither you nor they have ever been before.[34]

Such courage is embodied by Eli as he responds to God's call on Samuel, even to the detriment of his own and his family's position of power. Donovan describes this as 'good missionary advice',[35] though I would add that this is good ecclesiological advice, stating further that to operate in this way requires bringing together the gospel and the 'sacred arena of people's lives'.[36] It is precisely this sacred arena of young people's lives to which the Church must attend if it is not to become stuck in contradictions and paradoxes of the dominant discourse, but be open to ecclesial life flowing into new spaces in order to continually learn afresh what it is to be the Church.

In a very helpful booklet, Steve Emery-Wright outlines what this might look like in practice – challenging the Church to embrace and empower young people as theologians, interpreters and liturgists.[37] Unpacking these roles, Emery-Wright explores what it looks like to enable young people to contribute to the God-talk of a community and to help curate the worshipping life. The suggestion here from Emery-Wright is that the life and language of a specific worshipping community might be shaped by empowering the young people in its midst in this way. The argument of this book, however, suggests a broader engagement with young people fulfilling these roles. This broader engagement is in essence the argument of this whole book – that the ecclesial imagination of work with young people has something to offer the whole Church in understanding its own life, its self-identity.

Fascinatingly, this ecclesiological understanding from youth ministry, termed as it is the 'interweaving ecclesiology', ensures that it is not set in stone but carries within its very essence the sense and possibility, indeed necessity, of ongoing development, ongoing weaving in of new threads to enrich the beauty of the whole tapestry. This is the gift of work with young people – that it forces the Church to pioneer and ecclesial life to move into new spaces. As I said, this brings the conversation full circle because it is pressing into new work with young people, and investing relationally in their lives, that can facilitate the Church's embracing the role of young people as cultural interpreters and therefore seeking to participate in new strands of the ongoing participative dialogue that is the theological heart of God's Triune life.

For the Church to be true to itself in the light of the theological and sociological perspectives detailed in Chapters 1 and 2 it must embrace young people as pioneers and work with them as a vital way in which the Church can be constantly learning how to be the Church. In other words, the Church must, like Eli, embrace young people as potential Samuels in our midst, providing the space and nurture in which they might hear the voice of God, and then responding with openness and humility when they do. In the Introduction I was clear that this is not a 'how to' book; however, at this moment I want to suggest that this embrace of young people in all the ambiguity of their lives is fundamentally 'how to do' church with and for them, while also acknowledging that work done with young people is for the Church as well – not in the simplistic sense of being necessary for the numerical survival of our churches, but in the more complex sense of helping the Church learn how to be the Church. Fundamentally, the Church must embrace young people in its midst and work with them to be truly itself.

Concluding thoughts

If the Church is indeed always to be learning how to be the Church it must seek a structure and self-understanding that ensures flexibility and change are inherent in its very ecclesial life. It follows therefore that the Church must be willing, and moreover actively seeking, for its life to flow into new spaces as Christ encounters people in the world. This means that ambiguity will be a constant in the life of the Church, and that there will be places where the potential of ecclesial life is simultaneously church and not church.

Though not exclusive to youth ministry, such a vision for this ambiguous, flexible essence to the Church is found in the operant ecclesial imagination of Christian work with young people; the practices of youth ministry foster a way of life that forms faith and, in addition, interrupts dominant discourses about the Church, revealing a hidden discourse in which the boundaries of ecclesial life are ambiguous and through which ecclesial life for individuals is woven together in a tapestry of activities, communities, relationships and congregations. This is the interweaving ecclesiology. And this interweaving ecclesiology offers a gift from work with young people to the whole Church.

Among the riches of this gift to the Church is the way it speaks into the conversation about mission and the Church, and Fresh Expressions especially. Specifically, an interweaving ecclesiology assists the Church in not solidifying boundaries that should be fuzzy and, in this way, provides the language and structure for ecclesial life that is not framed by a felt need to name every initiative as definitively church or not church. The ambiguity of this interweaving ecclesiology demonstrates that ecclesial life flows outside, around and through the Church and that there is potential in spaces that are not churches, nor even have the aim of developing into churches, still forming part of the experience of the Church for participants. This takes the conversation about Fresh Expressions and the life of the Church beyond a binary debate between inherited and new forms of church, while also having more integrity with regard to the way that individuals live, move and have their being as we head towards the middle of the twenty-first century.

This interweaving vision for the Church can release pioneering creativity by allowing those working on the edges of the life of the Church to be part of the ecclesial landscape while not being pressured to ensure the outcome of their creative engagement is predetermined as a church. This is to take the ecclesial imagination, as expressed in potential ecclesial spaces, of youth ministry to heart – to be willing to recognize ecclesial life without needing to name something as church, though paradoxically recognizing that for some participants at least this potential ecclesial space is part of their church life. This is inherently ambiguous – there is a risk in naming something as part of an interweaving ecclesiology while not institutionalizing it as a church, but this should be seen as merely part of the tension of the Church that is always pilgrim, always learning how to be the Church.

This is not, though, as Chapter 8 argued, an anything-goes vision for the Church. It is important to remember that the potential ecclesial spaces of the youth groups – and, as such, the ecclesial imagination of youth ministry – is built on simple ecclesial practices and a form of interrupting discourse that draws participants into an experience of the risen Christ individually and together. Consequently, the tension and ambiguity of potential ecclesial spaces and the interweaving Church can be navigated by the individuals being drawn deeper into core relationships of up, in, out and of – or, more simply, the inward and connecting dynamics that mean within the interweaving ecclesiology individuals and groups deepen both their internal koinonia community and their external koinonia community with other expressions of the ecclesial life, including its sacramental life.

Inherent to the interweaving, however, is that this sacramental life and accountability is two-way. The potential ecclesial spaces of the youth groups demonstrate that the sacramentality of the Church is not expressed solely in the event of Eucharist and baptism, but also in the ongoing sacramental practice of ministry in the pattern of Christ. Any act of ministry in this narrative pattern of self-giving is an expression of ecclesial life. It is in these sacramental moments that Christ is revealed, and faith is formed or reformed.

The interweaving ecclesiology gives the Church permission to be its true self – institutional and formal, while also ambiguous and pilgrim. It allows individuals to construct an expression of church that is made of various relationships, congregations, practices and activities. Furthermore, the interweaving ecclesiology releases those with a pioneering spirit, following in the footsteps of those such as Albert Kestin and the other early pioneers of Crusaders/Urban Saints' mission and ministry among young people, to creatively and ambiguously seek to follow the Spirit of God in interrupting the experiences of those in their contexts with the possibility of Christ, but without the burden of forming a church. In the interweaving ecclesiology this creative, ambiguous edge of church life can help the Church as a whole hold on to its own missional calling to faithfully follow the Spirit of God into the world, while preventing those pioneering from being either overpowered by the institution of the Church or isolated by being outside the life of the Church.

This vision for the Church, this gift from youth ministry, is a call for the Church to be true to its own calling to participate in the life of God, in the ongoing ministry of Christ through the Spirit in the world, and to be continually learning how to be the Church – to be continuously weaving the beautiful tapestry of ecclesial life in and for the world.

Notes

1 Jonny Baker and Ric Stott, 'I'll Meet You There: A Conversation on the Meeting Place of Mission and Imagination', in *Missional Conversations: A Dialogue Between Theory and Praxis in World Mission*, ed. Cathy Ross and Colin Smith (London: SCM Press, 2018), p. 192.

2 Julie Gittoes, 'Where is the Kingdom?', in *Generous Ecclesiol-*

ogy: *Church, World and the Kingdom of God*, ed. Julie Gittoes, Brutus Green and James Heard (London: SCM Press, 2013), p. 101.

3 Gittoes, 'Where is the Kingdom?', p. 100.

4 See 'Vocations to Pioneer Ministry', *The Church of England*, www.churchofengland.org/life-events/vocations/vocations-pioneer-ministry (accessed 9.06.2021).

5 I choose to talk more generically about 'pioneering', rather than 'pioneers' so as not to be limited to those who are specifically called, trained and perhaps ordained for pioneer ministry.

6 Pete Rollins, 'Biting the Hand that Feeds: An Apology for Encouraging Tension between the Established Church and Emerging Collectives', in *Evaluating Fresh Expressions: Explorations in Emerging Church*, ed. Martyn Percy and Louise Nelstrop (Norwich: Canterbury Press, 2008), pp. 71–2.

7 Rollins, 'Biting the Hand that Feeds', p. 83.

8 Jonny Baker, 'The Pioneer Gift', in *The Pioneer Gift: Explorations in Mission*, ed. Jonny Baker and Cathy Ross (Norwich: Canterbury Press, 2014), p. 1.

9 Baker, 'The Pioneer Gift', p. 1.

10 David Male, *How to Pioneer* (London: Church House Publishing, 2016).

11 Male, *How to Pioneer*, pp. 1–3.

12 A glance though the vacancies page of the *Church Times* can reveal how frequently the term is used across a wide spectrum of positions.

13 Pioneers as Pilgrims has been discussed in Jonny Baker and Cathy Ross, *Pioneering Spirituality* (Norwich: Canterbury Press, 2015), pp. 44–64.

14 See her interview at Tara Isabella Burton, 'Madeleine L'Engle's Christianity was vital to A Wrinkle in Time', *Vox*, 8 March 2018, www.vox.com/identities/2018/3/8/17090084/a-wrinkle-in-time-faith-christianity-movie-madeleine-lengle (accessed 9.06.2021).

15 Baker and Stott, 'I'll Meet You There', p. 199.

16 Baker and Stott, 'I'll Meet You There', p. 199.

17 Baker and Stott, 'I'll Meet You There', p. 192.

18 Alister McGrath, 'The Cultivation of Theological Vision: Theological Attentiveness and the Practice of Ministry', in *Perspectives on Ecclesiology and Ethnography*, ed. Pete Ward (Grand Rapids, MI: William B. Eerdmans, 2012), p. 120.

19 McGrath, 'Cultivation of Theological Vision', p. 119.

20 Such as in the way weather patterns and shifting climactic conditions will impact the grapes grown in the same vineyard year on year.

21 Tina Hodgett and Paul Bradbury, 'Pioneering Mission is a Spectrum', *Anvil: Journal of Theology and Mission*, 34(1) (2018).

22 Beth Keith, 'Experiences of Pioneers' (Church Army 2010), https://freshexpressions.org.uk/wp-content/uploads/2017/05/freshexpressions-pioneers.pdf (accessed 15.10.2021).

23 Some 49 per cent of Fresh Expressions leaders were not designated as pioneers and also lead inherited churches; see Ruth Perrin and Ed Olsworth-Peter, *The Mixed Ecologists: Experiences of Mixed Ecology Ministry in the Church of England* (London: National Ministry Team, 2021), p. 6.

24 Perrin and Olsworth-Peter, *The Mixed Ecologists*, p. 4.

25 Perrin and Olsworth-Peter, *The Mixed Ecologists*, p. 5.

26 Michael Moynagh, *Church in Life: Innovation, Mission and Ecclesiology* (London: SCM Press, 2017), p. 371.

27 Moynagh, *Church in Life*, p. 93.

28 Moynagh, *Church in Life*, p. 93.

29 See John Hall, 'The Rise of the Youth Congregation and its Missiological Significance', PhD thesis, Birmingham, 2003.

30 See the discussion in Chapter 3.

31 Graham Cray, *Youth Congregations and the Emerging Church* (Cambridge: Grove Books, 2002). The thinking of Cray is particularly significant given the role he has had in developing the formal thinking behind the development of the Fresh Expressions movement.

32 For example, Jonny Baker, Pete Ward, Doug Gay and Graham Cray.

33 1 Samuel 3. See Mark Scanlan, 'Interruptions and Co-construction: Towards a Theology of Equal Opportunity for Mission and Ministry with Young People', *Anvil: Journal of Theology and Mission*, 34(2) (2018).

34 Vincent Donovan, *Christianity Rediscovered: Twenty-Fifth Anniversary Edition* (New York: Orbis Books, 1978), p. xiii.

35 Donovan, *Christianity Rediscovered*, p. xiii.

36 Donovan, *Christianity Rediscovered*, p. xiii.

37 Steve Emery-Wright, *Empowering Young People in Church* (Cambridge: Grove Books, 2008).

Index